D1510883

THE EPIC OF PARADISE LOST

TWELVE ESSAYS

BY

MARIANNA WOODHULL

G. P. PUTNAM'S SONS
NEW YORK & LONDON
The Knickerbocker Press
1907

The Knickerbocker Press, New York

PREFACE

THE twelve essays that comprise this volume, *The Epic of Paradise Lost*, stand in close unity about the central idea that the epic form is indispensable for the literary treatment of the story of the origin of evil in Eden. In this emphasis upon the epic idea, the work differs from other studies of Adam's fall, and the author has therefore based her conclusions upon original research only.

The subjects discussed in these essays include the fundamental distinction of the epic theme from the tragic theme on the grounds of the scope, the method, and the kind of characterisation demanded. The evolution of the classic epic into the Christian epic is traced, and the trend of modern thought toward purer abstract ideas in spiritual conceptions is noted, with the inevitable reaction of these notions upon literary art in the epic.

The philosophical basis of every work of art is declared to be significant, and for this

iii

reason Milton's *Treatise on Christian Doctrine* is examined in detail, and its connection with *Paradise Lost* is traced. The position is taken that the battle waged by evil against good in Eden requires for its forcible presentation, on the one hand, the cause of its origin in the battle in heaven, and on the other, its issue in the scheme of salvation. No portion of this story can be presented adequately alone, and therefore the story requires the epic form. The reasonableness of this conclusion may be tested by tracing the reasons for the failure of attempts to separate the parts of this story, or to treat it as a tragedy.

In this connection, Milton's four discarded drafts for a tragedy upon Adam's loss of Paradise are peculiarly significant. The reasons for his changes and their trend from one draft to another reveal the difficulties that Milton met and what considerations led him to his decision, given later in the ninth book of *Paradise Lost*, that the theme was epic not tragic, although fraught with tragic import.

For the subject of the essays that follow, there have been chosen four typical and widely differing tragedies from the hands of other authors upon Adam's fall and Lucifer's rebellion, and an examination is made of their grounds for failure as works of literary art. They fail first of all through an attempt to throw into a tragedy, a story demanding the scope, the method, and the characterisation of an epic. The success of *Paradise Lost* lies fundamentally in those very points wherein the tragedies have failed; that is in the scope, the method, and the characterisation demanded by the theme, and it is noted that the results could not be attained without the epic form. No pains have been spared to make these reviews of the tragedies accurate and thorough, and for this reason they have been cast into the form of studies strictly.

The last essay of the volume gives in a brief form conclusions based upon two lines of research that converge to one central idea of the epic; the one is a comparative study of Milton's conception of nature with the utterances of typical poets and philosophers through the ages; the other is an examination of the grounds of Milton's influence in France and Germany in the romantic revival.

The fact is noted that there have been at moments in different stages of the world's thought, as there are to-day, two fundamentally different conceptions of nature; the one, emphasising the definite; the other, the infinite. To-day, in philosophy, these two phases are represented on the one hand by Professor Cantor and on the other by Professor Arrhenius. Milton is fundamentally in harmony with Professor Arrhenius in his conception of nature as infinite and an expression of God's infinite thought, never therefore to be completely comprehended by man. From the lifting up of his heart toward the mysterious majesty of nature arises Milton's potent influence in France and Germany in the eighteenth century. Milton's conception of nature has an epical cast, but it inspired the lyric not only abroad but at home. It is here that we find the secret of his all-pervading power over English lyrists since his day.

The introductory essay of the volume discusses at greater length the evolution of the twelve essays and their purpose.

The author has gained assistance from scientists, linguists, and critics upon details essential for the accuracy of this work. As not one could know the relation of his aid to the perfected fabric of the thought, it seems to the author fitting to make these scholars in no way responsible for the results, but it is hardly possible to omit this passing word of gratitude to them.

Thanks are also due to the librarians who have, by their kind assistance, made possible the study of rare and, without their aid, inaccessible books.

M. W.

NEW YORK, 1907.

CONTENTS

Contents

The Epic of Paradise Lost

INTRODUCTORY

WHY MILTON WROTE AN EPIC

So far as my observation goes, Milton's *Paradise Lost* has suffered from a superficial reading rather more generally than any other masterpiece of English literature, and it seems also to be true that few students entertain any very intimate personal relation with Milton, such a relation as many readers enjoy with Shelley or Browning or Wordsworth.

An examination of the works of criticism upon Milton reveals that there is a preponderance of textual criticism, of a comparative study of words and of phrases, that does not pass into a comparison of the spirit of the context; and that there is a quantity of historical criticism of Milton, with a view to biographical accuracy. There can be no question that this body of critical work is not only valuable but absolutely indispensable.   There remains however a very important phase of criticism of Milton hitherto occasionally glanced at, but otherwise neglected.   This neglected question has become the subject of this book: Why did Milton write an epic upon Adam's loss of Paradise? For many years this question has obstinately presented itself to my mind and it has impelled me to attempt a close intensive study of our greatest English epic and of the mind of the author.

We are all familiar with the statement that Milton is a great epic poet, the greatest in English literature, if not in the world's literature.   Many readers have accepted for their own Dryden's opinion, " this man cuts us all out and the ancients too," but in essays upon Milton, from Addison's to the latest writers', I have looked in vain for a solution of this fundamental problem, a problem that brings a series of questions in its train: What is an epic type of genius?   What is an epic cast of thought? What is an epic? and why did Milton write an epic upon Adam unparadised?   Did Milton write an epic because his subject demanded the epic form?

When I have heard lectures upon Vondel and

Milton, and when I have read the literature of the Lauder controversy, this question has returned with persistent force to my mind,—how can any comparison be made between an epic and a tragedy, until we first settle the fundamental principles of the epic? All lines in Milton's *Paradise Lost* radiate from the epic notion and no line in Vondel strikes out firmly from such a centre. No criticism therefore appears to be vital that ignores that essential difference; for wherein was Vondel prepared to aid Milton? Not every man who valued sleep was responsible for those lines on sleep that knit the ravelled sleeve of care; nor did every man who retold the old tale of man's fall have any important share in *Paradise Lost*. Did the lark borrow his song from the worm that he seized for breakfast? So indeed may the dust of a king stop the bunghole of a barrel, but such a pursuit of the borrowed may give a student a wild chase.

It is not that kind of a book of criticism, nor a compendium of useful facts, that I have sought to write, but a book of critical studies of Milton upon the subject, Why is Adam's fall part of an epic theme?

The question at first sight may seem needless. Some thoughtful people have at once replied, " Milton wrote an epic because he chose to write an epic." Like Raphael's advice to the inquisitive Adam,

> heaven is for thee too high
> To know what passes there ; be lowly wise :

this reply discourages conversation, but it does not still my obstinate questioning. What is more, this query, I am assured by investigation, starts the inquirer on no foolish quest; Milton had himelf, in fact, both asked my question and answered it before he wrote *Paradise Lost*. His epic did not spring Athena-like from his brain but represented the careful, deliberate labour of a lifetime, and Milton himself at first believed that his theme ought to be developed in the form of a tragedy. Nowhere in the criticism of Milton has this fact received its adequate recognition, still there is no question more vital than this for the student of Milton: How did the epic finally shape itself? out of the ruins of these discarded drafts for a tragedy upon the loss of Paradise?

Of this process, Milton has given us significant flashes of information, and if we follow these gleams, we shall learn the progress of both the thought and of the form. The unmistakable path of his quest leads through those plans of tragedy on man's fall, through his prose utterances on man's relation to the universe, particularly in *The Treatise on Christian Doctrine*, through his probable reflections upon the available literature of man's fall and the origin of evil, to his own distinct statement in the first fifty lines of the ninth book of *Paradise Lost*, that man's fall is an epic theme.

Despite all this proof to the contrary, the assertion has been made to me that Milton wrote an epic because he had an epic type of mind and when, in the maturity of his powers, he learned his own strength, he gave up the idea of writing a tragedy and cultivated his own peculiar gift in an epic. Strong as this contention may seem, it is not a satisfactory answer to my question. There is no doubt that Milton had an epic type of mind, if by that term is meant the power to write an epic, but is that power all that is required? May one at will decide to write an epic or a tragedy upon the same identical theme? Milton shows his genius not only in his power to create an epic, but also in his perception that the story of the fall of man, if it were to be elevated into the realm of literary art, must have for its adequate expression the epic form. In this, I believe that his genius bowed to what he recognised as an inevitable issue, a species of art fate.

It is then the purpose of this book to set forth the progress of this evolution of the epic idea in man's fall into *Paradise Lost* and to show the relation of this epic to the whole of Milton's thought in his prose as well as in his poetical utterances. The solution of such a problem as the one before us lies in the choice of the more, rather than the less, reasonable view of his own utterances, and in an examination of the grounds for drawing our conclusions upon the necessity of the epic form from a comparative study of other versions of the fall of man. Such an examination of proofs leads me to the opinion that to Milton's capacity to perceive that the epic form was necessary for his theme was added the greater gift of power to create a work under the guidance of his inner vision; and therein lies his claim to surpassing greatness.

There are five points that must be emphasised, then, in this book: first, the correct basis for a comparative study of Milton; second, the critical value of Milton's attempts to plan a tragedy on man's fall; third, the critical importance of Milton's *Treatise on Christian Doctrine;* fourth, the critical importance of the first fifty lines of the ninth book of *Paradise Lost*, and fifth, the significance of the lyrical strain in *Paradise Lost*.

The power to perceive the essential art form for a theme and the skill to create the form demanded combine to mark the genius of a high order and this harmony between his perception and his power to create is the essential fact about Milton. Joined to this essential fact are two important considerations.

First the *Treatise on Christian Doctrine* gives in prose Milton's trains of thought about God and the universe and man's relation to all, and a careful study of this work taken in comparison with *Paradise Lost* indicates that the epic strikes its roots deep into Milton's philosophy of life and is no less than an artistic presentation of his conception of life. In fact, this study makes reasonable the assertion that Milton has concentrated his whole nature in one supreme effort, and therefore *Paradise Lost* is at once great as a masterpiece and as a self-revelation of a genius of a high order.

Second, if this be true, then it is possible for the student to ravel back the mystic threads and to find the true Milton in *Paradise Lost* and perhaps there only. To know who was a man's tutor or first wife's father may be interesting, significant, or essential, but it is possible that it is not all three of these at once. It may be interesting and not essential, for instance, if the fact does not at all touch the central idea of a man's life. It may even be true that a man does not reveal himself in the ordinary relations of life, for it is no less strange than common that, for some reason, these relations fail to absorb the man and where his whole life centres only, does a man reveal himself completely.

There are reasons for the belief that of far more importance than biographies, however long and however valuable, is the record of a man's inner life that he gives unconsciously in his chosen work. For this reason, there is peculiar importance in the lyric strains in *Paradise Lost*, and the nature of this importance will be discussed at length in the last essay of this volume.

If the literary form for man's fall is inevitably the epic and Milton had the genius to see the inherent form in the theme, this fact best marks him as different from Vondel, on the one hand, who failed to see the unsuitableness of the form of tragedy; and from Lancetta on the other hand, who saw the need but could not create the epic of the dream.[1] The power to perceive and the power to create, together mark the man of genius. But Milton could not have perceived, in this case, the harmony between his theme and its form, if he had not the epic type of mind. Fortunately, Milton could grasp the epic background in his poetical conception just as unfortunately Vondel could not attain the epic scope.

Shakespeare, like Milton, could reach the epic scope and flash his characters upon the epic background, but his attention was focussed upon the more concrete experiences of men, and therefore, possibly from choice, he cultivated the tragic and not the epic muse. However, the indisputable traces of the epic power remain in the tendency to lift his tragedy out of the normal domain of tragedy to the epic height, where the characters move on a background that no stage can bound and where human life loses its concreteness in life's universal mystery.

This, however, brings us to the thought of

[1] See volume i., Todd's 4th edition of *Milton's Poetical Works* for quotation from preface of Lancetta.

the first essay, which busies itself with the
grounds of distinction between the epic and the
tragedy and the territory where they move
as allied not alien monarchs. We shall then
be ready to discuss in the second essay the
fundamental characteristics of the Christian
epic in general, and of *Paradise Lost* in particular, with a view to the probable destiny of the
epic form. In the third essay, it will be useful
to consider the roots of Milton's epic as they
appear in his prose utterances. In the fourth
essay we shall examine Milton's four early
drafts for a tragedy upon the fall of man and
note the undeveloped epic idea therein expressed. In the fifth essay, we shall observe
typical versions of man's fall in earlier literature, note the evolution of the theme into art
form, and trace the epical characteristics in
these works.

In the sixth, seventh, eighth, and ninth
essays we shall examine four tragedies on man's
fall that were known in the seventeenth century,
and note the defects that arise from their authors' lack of clear comprehension of the epical
demand of the theme: the first of these four
studies will be of *Adamus Exsul* by Grotius;
the second will be of *Adam in Ballingschap* by

Vondel; the third, of *L'Adamo* by Andreini; the
fourth, of *Lucifer* by Vondel.

In the tenth essay, some attention will be
given to passages that were epical in attempt
in the literature of the sixteenth and seventeenth centuries upon the same theme or
allied themes to that of *Paradise Lost*, and the
fact will be noted that these passages, because
they had the epic method and the epic elevation, were of more direct aid to Milton than
were the attempts at a tragedy upon the origin
of evil.

In the eleventh essay, we then shall be ready
to note, in brief, Milton's treatment of the epic
background with the epic method, and to examine his skill in the epical characterisation of
God, of Satan, of Adam, and of Eve, characterisations that had fared so ill at the hands of
the workers in a tragedy upon man's fall.

In the twelfth essay, we shall examine the
personal touches of emotion in *Paradise Lost*
and note their dependence upon the epic scope
of the poem, and we shall point out Milton's
position among the lyric poets and the reason
for his influence to be found in his epical conception of Eden.

I

WHAT IS AN EPIC?

THE purpose of this essay and of the next is to show that a comparative study of the great epics and of the great tragedies makes reasonable the conclusion that the ancient theme of Adam's loss of Paradise must find its inevitable consummation in art in an epic and not in a tragedy.

Our thought upon this subject must follow after Milton and eventually strike the path of his quest. Gleams of the way he went may be seen in his four discarded drafts for a tragedy, clearer marks are traceable in that long neglected work, the *Treatise on Christian Doctrine,* and in *Paradise Lost.* Nor is this all that is to be held in mind at the outset of our study.

With the theories of the epic and the tragedy laid down by the critics of the past and of the contemporary periods Milton was thoroughly conversant but, like all great artists, he cared

less for Aristotle or Bossú than for Homer
and Virgil, less for the man who preached dog-
mas than for him who created a masterpiece.
Independent as Milton was in his cast of mind,
he developed his own theories and thought his
own thoughts, but he mined so deep and broad
a vein of thought that he struck beneath the
superficial peculiarities of a century, or of a
nation, into the more universal thought of man.

Upon this deeper train of thought rather
than upon the foibles of seventeenth century
England, the reader should centre his attention, if he is to advance far in the appreciation
of *Paradise Lost*. Indeed there is little reason
for discussing a fact so obvious as that Milton
has some defects common to his century, for
these faults, indeed, may be picked off easily
from the surface of *Paradise Lost*. And if
they were ever worth an argument, all that is
to be said was chronicled long ago. Beneath
all this exterior criticism, lies the epic's enduring strength and beauty, and that is found in
the harmony of the most important of all
themes elaborated in its essential art form.

A comparative study of the great masterpieces in the epic and in the tragedy, and of
the typical versions of man's fall produced

from the fourth to the eighteenth centuries, leads one to the conclusion that for aid in treating his difficult theme of man's fall, Milton was not indebted, in a very vital way, to any writer who had not himself grasped the essential epical idea in the subject. It is true enough that Milton culled from a wide field of sources numerous fragments which he fused with his work, but for an appreciation of his genius, it is not so essential to attain a knowledge of the source of the fragments as it is to grasp the fundamental conception of his art. Without such a comprehension, the student may sail indeed without a rudder or a pilot and thus unguided he may find himself at the mercy of every modern Lauder—and the danger is not past—who proclaims his discovery of a man of small genius from whose well-nigh forgotten works Milton has filched his fame. It is only by a comprehension of the inevitableness of the theme's expression in art form that the clearer vision is gained of the sense in which Milton bettered the borrowed and proved himself a giant indeed, but no plagiarist of pigmies.

For the conclusion, that the episode of man's fall must find its inevitable expression not in a

tragedy but in an epic, there are three fundamental reasons. In the first place the material
required for a portrayal of Adam's fall is too
extensive for a tragedy, and requires the whole
background of the infinite. Indeed, the episode of Adam's disobedience must be shown in
its sequence in the longer narrative of Lucifer's
struggle to avert the decree of God, that unto
His Son every knee should bow. For Milton
views Adam's fall as an incident in the long
war between Satan and the Messiah, and it
cannot be told apart from its setting in the
larger story of the contest of evil with good.
Not only the presence of the mystical background, but the unavoidable length of the
story; the demand for the deliberate analysis of
character; and the need of many marvellous
and illusive details require the elaboration of
the epic rather than that of the briefer, more
concrete method of a tragedy. All of the
scenes in this spiritual conflict of Adam fall
naturally under the double related episodes that
are characteristic of every epic. The two interdependent plots in this case are the fall of
Lucifer and the fall of man.

The second reason for holding the epic
method as inevitable is found in the fact that

the theme of man's fall requires for its successful treatment such surprising and marvellous
details as are impossible for portrayal in a
tragedy, but such as are fitting in an epic.
The ideal beauty of the garden of Eden, of
Adam and Eve in their state of innocence appeals more accurately to the inner vision than
to the outward eye. Moreover the guardian
angels flashing their celestial beauty among the
trees of the garden, the lurking fiend with his
countless transformations, his amazing voyages
into chaos, and his flights through the solar
system are all details unsuited to a tragedy, but
if attempted at all are dependent for success
upon the devices peculiarly fitted to the epic.

There remains to be mentioned the third and
the greatest reason for holding the epic form
as inevitable for man's fall, and that is found in
the fact that throughout the story Milton's belief compelled him to make prominent the domination of Christ over Satan. For this reason
man's fall issues necessarily, not in a tragedy,
but in a Christian epic in which Christ is the
hero who triumphs over Satan; and man becomes a victorious hero only when, through
faith and hope, he partakes of the Messiah's
triumph.

Whether this view is accepted as a dogma or not, the hopeful view of man's regeneration is necessary in this story, not only for the sound philosophy of life but for the strength and dignity of the art. Without this underlying optimism the theme would lack vitality, for whatever one may assert about the necessity of pessimism, he must concede that no great art was ever yet produced that had for its theme the final triumph of the evil over the good, but all great art is based upon the ideal that somehow and somewhere the evil is purged away and the good triumphs. If this be true, the theme of man's fall requires for its culmination such an expression of the triumph of the good as is afforded in Christ's victory over Satan.

A final calm after the battle is essential in both the tragedy and the epic, and is a subtle revelation of an element of hope common to humanity; but in an epic the emphasis is thrown upon the triumph of a cause, in a tragedy the stress is upon the suffering of the hero. The light of hope breaks from afar upon a black horizon in the tragedy; in an epic this light irradiates the end. But the fundamental difference between the epic and the tragedy lies

2

in the extent and in the method of presentation of the background of life's mystery.

The reason for the difference in the scope is allied to the difference in the method of the epic and of the tragedy. The normal tragedy is a direct dramatic appeal to the sympathies made by a worthy hero who by conscious or unconscious act sets loose the conflicting forces of evil and of good that bring about his suffering or his death in a sad and important crisis. In the Renaissance it became common for scholars to write tragedies as academic exercises in the style of the classic authors of Greece or of Rome. As the performance of these productions upon the stage was an entirely secondary consideration, and they might therefore overlook the direct artistic appeal of a tragedy, these plays were digressions from the normal evolution of tragedy from Æschylus to Shakespeare, or from Marlowe to the present time. With this literary type in mind, it is possible to divide tragedies into three groups: those written to be acted and performed successfully; those written to be acted and performed unsuccessfully; those written without the slightest regard to presentation.

This last class, of tragedies to be read only,

has multiplied and differentiated into several types. Whatever their success, the first two classes have the aim of normal tragedy in the nature of their artistic appeal to the audience; the third, apart as it is from the logical development of the tragedy, is a distinct subject for research in itself and throws no new light upon the consideration of the basis of difference and of likeness in the epic and the tragedy.

We shall, therefore, in these essays, confine our attention to the normal tragedy. An epic, like a tragedy, does not fail to present a hero of strength and of force of character, who seems never unworthy of attention nor incapable of bearing the theme to its logical conclusion, but the story of the epic differs from the tragedy both in its method and in its scope. The epic takes for its theme no less than a problem of importance to a nation or to the human race. A hero renowned in history, or in the popular belief, strives and is impeded, or is attacked and resists, and the end of the epic is usually the triumph of the hero; at all events, the issue heralds the success of the principles for which he has striven. There may be within the confines of the epic, themes for a score of tragedies, but such a tragedy does not take for its subject the whole epic theme, for the scope of the epic is too vast for a tragedy.

Upon this point it is necessary to dwell at some length; scores of writers had attempted to write a tragedy upon the subject of Adam's fall; why had they failed? I have been told that it was because they were men of small power and that if Shakespeare had attempted to write a tragedy on man's fall he would have succeeded. When this statement is analysed into its component parts, it is not, I believe, impregnable. Why may it not be more reasonable to hold that Shakespeare had too much literary insight to attempt the theme, Adam unparadised, in a tragedy?

Indeed such an attempt is foreign to his whole art method. No subject was better known in pre-Shakespearean drama than Adam's fall: a subject so prominent could hardly have failed to take his attention, if its possibilities in a tragedy were great. It is more reasonable to infer that he was too wise to attempt such an impossible theme. An examination of the underlying notions leads one to infer that the authors under observation did not fail to construct an impressive tragedy upon man's fall because they were men of small power so much as that they proved that they were men of small endowment by persisting in an impossible attempt. Milton on the other hand did try the task of creating a tragedy upon the origin of evil and he gave up the undertaking; in that fact I believe that he showed his artistic insight. Nor are we at the mercy of vague hypotheses if we can solve the fundamental difference between the epic and the tragedy; and that difference, I believe, is to be found first of all in the extent of the background upon which the master artist causes his figures to move.

By the epic background, we mean the realm whence issues life's unsolvable mystery.

An examination of the great epics from the *Odyssey* to *Paradise Lost* and of the tragedies from Æschylus to Shakespeare and his successors reveals in all a tendency to picture man as moving in a world too vast for him to comprehend, and yet there is an obligation resting upon the hero to face the mystery and valiantly to play the man. Meanwhile the gods wrought their mysterious will and " so fell this marvellous thing." There is a difference in interpretation but the same strength of appreciation of life's mystery is in the *Odyssey* and in *Job*, in *King Lear* and in *Paradise Lost*, as also in *Medea* and in *Alcestis*. Our present interest must be this ungrasped element in life that both the tragedy and the epic present in varying degrees of prominence.

This element of the unknown, this mystery however named is not to be ignored in the life of the most practical man; no matter how much he looks into the seeds of time to see which grain will grow and which will not, he knows not the events of his future years, nor its calamities, nor its successes. He knows not the hour of his death, nor has he a clear picture of the after life. This element of uncertainty we usually declare to be so fundamental that it is too self-evident to be mentioned, or in our scientific longings for definiteness, it is frowned upon, as too vague to be dwelt upon; but neither the tragedy nor the epic will consent to ignore the mystery that baffles our intellects and forces mysticism upon the most common-sensible of men.

Indeed if this element of mystery in life is so vitally blended with all human experiences, it can by no possibility be eliminated from art. Out of this mysterious past and future of the race emerge two notions, the one of a power of evil and the other of a power of good, and they are at perpetual war. Either from the influence of the past evil choices of men, or from a power of evil pressing upon man, there has evolved a conception of a total force of evil that rushes in like the flood tide at the slightest weakening of the defence. But if one has not separated one's self from the forces of good, there is nothing that can intercept the flight of good angels to the rescue, not even tribulations nor distress, peril nor sword.

The background of the mystery of life, whence the two warring forces of good and of evil emerge to fight out a portion of a desperate battle, is treated in both the epic and in the tragedy, but with a difference.

The duration of the conflict of good and of evil in the tragedy is brief, for the problem must be presented by a series of startlingly clear pictures. The emphasis must nowhere be doubtful; therefore the appeal to the imagination should be definite, the sympathies enlisted from the outset, and carried with increasing emotion to the tragic end. Othello is duped by Iago, but the most ignorant man in the pit understands well enough this son of darkness; for subtleties of criticism nowhere are needed for the observers' direct comprehension of what forces are at work; that is the tragic method. Concreteness is its supreme need and definiteness of appeal its artistic goal. After the play, the student may reason and welcome, and there is legitimate ground unquestionably for his thought, but the philosophy is not the drama any more than the root is the flower.

Since concrete vividness is the life of the tragedy, the attention cannot be distracted by too large a field, therefore the mystery of life should not be presented entire. That human suffering is not meted out in payment for sin, is too common a mystery to be foreign to the tragedy.   Why do the righteous suffer? is an older problem than the book of Job, but a display of the whole background of life's mystery is suited only to the epic, and there alone can find the means for its presentation, which is by the epic method, and by the suggestive devices peculiar to the epic.

But what is the epic method?

The scope of the tragedy should be relatively intense rather than broad and should preserve its vividness by concrete pictures from human life.   The epic has no limit in its scope, indeed

it may aim at nothing less than the flashing
forth of the whole background of life's mystery, for it moves upon the stage of the universe and by no means confines itself to the
actualities known to the senses; Olympus,
Earth, and Hades have been its scene of action,
or Heaven, Earth, and Hell, and all that lies
between. Vividness it must have, but its
method is extended and deliberate and therefore it may have leisure for developing, by a
wealth of devices, suggestive pictures that attain its art purposes.

The epic's scope extends so far outside the
visible life of man that it must build for itself
a magic bridge of philosophical and poetical
thought upon which man may penetrate into
the infinite mystery. The success of an epic
must depend upon the author's subtle power
to span this gap. The modern man is peculiarly sceptical of the safety of such a bridge
and therein lies the chief difficulty in writing
an epic to-day. In an epic, we cross and re-
cross the bridge of thought and imagination;
in the tragedy, I believe that we stand always
at the visible end and strain our eyes across the
gap for a moment. In an epic, we see not
alone the gods on the battlefield, but we are

present at their council in Olympus; we witness
not alone the strivings of the hero on the field
of the world, but we follow him to that bourne
whence no traveller can return. In the tragedy, our attention is centred upon the concrete
effects of these mysterious forces rather than
upon the forces themselves; that is the capital
difference between the epic and the tragedy.
It is, for instance, the suffering of Everyman
in his last hour,—in his consciousness that he
has misspent his life—that rivets our attention, not the abstract forces that surround him.
Indeed the tragedy that holds our eyes is very
concrete in *Everyman*.

This restriction of a tragedy has been questioned, but setting aside the hybrid offshoots
of the tragedy, there seems to me among the
great masterpieces of literature either a tacit
or a pronounced admission of this principle.
Goethe's *Faust*, Marlowe's *Dr. Faustus*, Shakespeare's *Macbeth* and *Hamlet,* and Hauptmann's
Versunkene Glocke, are among the works that
have been cited and doubtless will be urged in
disproof of such a limitation of tragedy; but
is this objection well founded?

Surely Shakespeare in his most truly dramatic tragedies shows a subtle and skilful

method of limiting the mystic background to that which is presentable in concrete pictures from human life. In so far as the mystery of our actual life is intensified by glimpses of the unseen world, it may be urged that *Hamlet* moves against a background vaster than I have indicated and that it involves a field of epic scope. In a limited sense this seems at first thought to be true, but the method in *Hamlet* is not the epic method, nor is the epic method required, for the epic background is not really presented.

It must be remembered that the important fact in *Hamlet* is not at all the appearance of the ghost, but Hamlet's emotions and reflections upon the advent of the ghost. The ghost himself does not take us in imagination to the epic background, he does not invite us to journey with him to that mysterious bourne. He reveals no mysteries of his prison house, but he confines his confidences strictly to matters of this earth, to his own family affairs, and even to the grounds of Hamlet's own suspicions. This ghost, indeed, startles us far less than he arouses our sympathies; we think of him as kind, noble, and likeable, but we cannot conceive of his being very wise in the affairs of the unknown world. There is no trace of his having power to lead us into the infinite, but he stands at the human end of the bridge. Neither the witches in *Macbeth* nor the ghost in *Hamlet* are half so mysteriously horrible as Goneril and Regan or Iago; they indeed would more potently present the mystery of incalculable evil.

In *Macbeth*, the witches are emissaries of evil, but they do not sweep us in imagination to the realm of Chaos and old Night; we do not feel the awesome horror of hell, but the grewsome fancy of black art whose feet rest on the earth. Indeed the witches are earth-born,—tricksy, malign spirits, bubbles, Banquo calls them,—but they are of folk-lore descent and therefore they are adapted to concrete present-ation, for they are nearer to humanity than to Erebus. This degree of concreteness, which might be a defect in an epic, is artistically bet-ter in a tragedy, for as the witches are only on the border-land of the world of abstractions, the backward plunge into the actualities of the stage is more easily made.

All through Hauptmann's *Versunkene Glocke*, the same border-land of actualities is skirted, and folk-lore, which is never a great mental tax nor an imaginative tax, so that we

be simple in heart, is the basis of this tragedy,—
and folk-lore does not illuminate the epic background. The author of this play, *The Sunken
Bell*, after long research in folk-lore, produced
this combination of ancient belief in demonology
and of modern psychology. Reduced to its
simplest outline, it is a story of a man who is
led aside from the simple path of duty into a
selfish Faustlike quest of the unattainable and
intangible. He seeks he knows not what; lost
in unhuman passion, he is oblivious to his bond
to the village community and even to his obligations to his wife and to his child—until the
tolling of the bell of the memory of his former
aspirations to serve mankind awakens him too
late to a realisation of his failure.

In the development of this plot, with a machinery of superstition, lies its claim to origin-
ality; it nowhere ventures into the vastness
of the epic background, but skirts the shore
of the material world in its emphasis upon folk-
lore. This preponderance of the folk-lore
superstition in the *Versunkene Glocke* must
cause the tragedy to be placed among productions that at this age of the world are exceptional and somewhat artificial, no matter how
interesting.

The success in the presentation of the *Versunkene Glocke* lies in the romantic interest that the novelty of folk-lore may arouse in the audience, for a sympathetic attitude is demanded toward a belief in demonology, which makes its appeal through the material world of our sensuous impressions, like the lubber fiend who with his shadowy flail hath threshed the corn and drunk the cream bowl duly set. The real power of the play is in the thought that underneath the folk-lore lies a general psychological truth, in a very human struggle with a very human temptation, but it is not fought in the field of the epic background—the earth is the scene.

As to *Faust*, no student could substantiate a claim for that as formal tragedy in the artistic sense of the word. It is indeed in many respects epical. The Marguerite episode is a tragedy in which Marguerite is the heroine. The Helen of Troy episode is not a tragedy; and in the final choice of Faust to serve his fellow-men, he " cheats the devil " and reaches the chastened triumph of the Christian epic hero. In the marvels of this work of Goethe, it is noticeable that the preternatural is of two contrasting sources; either as a concrete expression for an abstract philosophical thought, or as the simple homely folk-lore of demonology.

Students of Goethe do not claim that he has perfected his art form in the *Faust*. The work is not successful in its entirety upon the stage, and even in the opera, with the advantage of a wealth of device, despite Boïto's attempt, the three parts have not been successfully presented. The full art evolution of *Faust* as philosophically conceived by Goethe would, I believe, form an epic, but in the work, as it now stands, there is a certain emphasis thrown upon the method of a tragedy in the clearer presentation of the human end of the bridge into the infinite, and in the earth-born horrors of the Walpurgis night.[1]

In Marlowe's *Dr. Faustus* the full presentation of the prince of darkness is not given, nor of the forces of evil, but our attention is centred upon the human hero and his visions of evil. The tragedy has indeed epical characteristics still it does not move upon the epic background but remains in the field of tragedy.

But there are tragedies that do flash forth,

[1] Ibsen's *Peer Gynt*, "the Norwegian Faust," with its machinery of folk-lore and satirical comedy elements, ends in an epic strain, but the author leaves his work wisely unclassified as "a dramatic poem."

at moments, the full background of mystery, to the distraction of our minds from the concrete picture before us. What shall be said of these tragedies? My opinion is that they are in this regard epical and that they may, by this widening of scope, rise in grandeur, but that this gain in elevation results in a corresponding loss in tragic definiteness. This rise into epic height is conspicuous in *King Lear*, when we are led into the heart of life's mystery and the rumblings of the deep and the shock of unchained forces startle our ears; while we strain our eyes for rays of hope and find peace in the triumph of the spirit. Although I believe that the epic background is present in *King Lear* to the disturbance of the clearness of the dramatic scenes, the method is not the epic method. We still stand at the human end of the bridge and look aghast and wonderstruck into the infinite; and while *King Lear* has epical characteristics, it remains, in method and development, a tragedy, but a tragedy that is burdened with the "mystery of all this unintelligible world," a tragedy with an epical trend.

It is evident that the theme—the origin of evil in Eden—moves upon the whole epic background, in relation to that realm its scenes are alone intelligible, and that it requires the epic method of presentation; for the characters and the entire story are unfitted for the degree of brevity and of concreteness demanded for a successful tragedy.

The first essential reason for the epic method in the treatment of this theme is found in the need of a narrator. Milton had tried the services of a chorus in his drafts for a tragedy on man's fall, but he had decided that no chorus however communicative could convey what the epic story-teller has the privilege of relating and the subject required the aid of the epic narrator.

Nor is it possible for the writer on the theme of Adam's fall, if he is to give probability and convincing power to his story, to dispense with a variety of other epic devices, concrete enough for an appeal to our imaginations, but not so realistic as to lose the hold upon the shadowy vastness of its background, nor to make it the story merely of a man and of a woman rather than of universal humanity. In this particular, the artistic gain by the epic treatment in *Paradise Lost*, over the tragic method in *Lucifer* and in *Adam in Ballingschap* of Vondel, is a conspicuous proof of Milton's genius and of

3

his growth in wisdom in abandoning his early schemes for a tragedy upon the fall of man.

With the services of an omnipresent and omniscient narrator the epic writer may, as in *Paradise Lost* or in the *Æneid*, by a skilful use of metaphor and allusion, present a striking picture to the reader's imagination of what could not be presented in any way upon the stage. The remarkable artistic achievement of Virgil in book sixth of the *Æneid* is dependent upon the epic method.

Nor must it be forgotten that in *Paradise Lost* Milton's problem like Virgil's was made doubly difficult by the fact that he was attempting to express in poetry notions familiar in religion, philosophy, and art. The tendency of religious thought is to seek expression through imagination in spiritual conceptions relatively concrete; philosophy on the other hand aims at purest abstract terms; and art strives to embody spiritual conceptions of religion and abstractions of philosophy in a form that must be concrete, if it be art at all. With this difficulty in mind, we view the author's skill by the nature of the concrete appeal to the imagination that is chosen by his art. What shall be the basis of the concreteness? The easiest method is materialistic but it is not the most efficient. The folk-lore of demonology and of the miracle and of the morality play indeed presents spiritual conceptions in the terms of the material world. But modern ideas show the progressive tendency of the nautilus and discard the past sensuous portrayal of spiritual conceptions as incomplete or absurd and demand a new picture that more adequately depicts the product of advancing abstract thought. Living as he did in the midst of the seventeenth-century dogmatism about spiritual conceptions, Milton was not however either totally iconoclastic nor wholly conservative, but he did earnestly seek to reconcile his own notions of philosophy, of religion, and of art in the relatively concrete imaginative product of *Paradise Lost*. A study of his epic in the light of his *Treatise on Christian Doctrine* reveals that he is constantly aware of the demand of philosophical abstraction on the one hand and of religious spiritual conceptions on the other. It is therefore frequently necessary in the examination of *Paradise Lost* to refer to the realm of the philosophically abstract. For however opposed the method of philosophy may seem in its expression to art, it is, after all, the fundamental basis of art, if that art has advanced far in the evolution of its mission. How to portray the world of the spirit in the imaginative terms of art and in the language sanctioned by his notions of abstract truth was the most difficult problem in *Paradise Lost*. Milton's solution of the problem may be discovered by an examination of his epical devices.

In the description of Satan, Milton calls to his aid the close alliance of metaphor and of allusion; and both are essential for establishing the elevation of tone and the reasonableness of character and of action in the epic. Allusions also aid Milton frequently to create an atmosphere, without which the details would seem more improbable than interesting.

For instance the battle of the good and bad angels is inconceivable and is perilously near to the grotesque, indeed in *L'Adamo* the combat becomes ridiculous; but in *Paradise Lost*, the attention is withdrawn from the difficulty of forming the picture of Satan as a general, by a comparison with the struggle of Charlemagne and his twelve peers and the tragic battle at Fontarabia, or the romance of Uther's son, begirt with British and Amoric knights—

> And all who since, baptised or infidel
> Jousted in Aspramont, or Montalban,
> Damasco, or Morocco, or Trebisond.

By means of these allusions the reader forgets to be literal and enters into the imaginative world of romance, where all seems reasonable and clear, but there is no loss of philosophical accuracy. Nor are the spirits made to seem of material substance. Even in the battle in heaven, the mystery of chemical explosions and of thunderbolts redeems the scenes from the charge of ordinary realism.

Another instance of the aid of allusion is found in the calling of the council at Pandemonium and the report of the speeches, for we unconsciously compare Moloch, Belial, Mammon, and Beelzebub, with the Grecian heroes in consultation. By means of this use of allusion, Milton gains clearer-cut individualities that are seized by our imaginations as vivid, although philosophically considered the speakers at the council are all expressions of the great all-embracing spirit of evil, Satan himself, and they can say only what he wills them to say. From an artistic point of view, however, this complete subordination should not be prominent; if it were, there would result only the barrenness of allegory, fatal to the epic. Still the failure to show the proper degree of subordination would render the portrayal untrue.[1]

Another skilful use of allusion is noteworthy; in *Paradise Lost* the rank and file of Satan's followers is made reasonable by a catalogue of forces, that, although it leaves them in the spirit world, makes them seem more concrete by allusion to familiar names from the Bible and classic lore:

Say, muse their names then known, who first, who last,
Roused from the slumber on that fiery couch
At their great emp'ror's call, as next in worth,
Came singly, where he stood on the bare strand,

Then follow the names and exploits of the fallen angels[2] when they wandered abroad among the sons of men, enticed the sons of

[1] This failure appears in Vondel's Lucifer in his relation to Beelzebub and Belial.

[2] The idea of the fallen angels entering into idols and misleading the sons of Adam is found in the works of St. Jerome, *Lucifer the Schismatic*, Lactantius, *Divinarum Institutionum*, Libri VII., 307–310 A.D.: *De falsa religione*, Liber I.; *De origine erroris*, Liber II.; *De vita beata*, Liber VII., and St. Augustine, *City of God*.

Israel to idolatry on their march from the Nile,
and reared their pagan temple high in **Azotus,**
dreaded through the coast,

> Of Palestine, in Gath and Ascalon
> And Accaron, and Gaza's frontier bounds. . . .
>
>   .   .   .   .   .   .
>
> The rest were long to tell, though far renowned ;
> Th' Ionian gods.
>
>   .   .   .   .   .   .
>
>   These first in Crete
> And Ida known ; thence on the snowy top
> Of cold Olympus rul'd the middle air,
> Their highest heaven ; or on the Delphian cliff
> Or in Dodona, and through all the bounds
> Of Doric land ; or who with Saturn old
> Fled over Adria to th' Hesperian fields,
> And o'er the Celtic roam'd the utmost isles.
>   All these and more came flocking ;

The forces of Satan in this way become more
clearly defined through the association of
ideas that have already taken an imaginative
form.   These very complex devices available
in an epic are impossible in a tragedy, and the
representation of the fallen angels brings always the peril of laughter, which defeats the
author's purpose in a tragedy.   In order to
avoid the danger of a grotesque picture, the
writer of a tragedy may make the fallen angels
simply bad men.   This solution of the difficulty

is adopted in *Adam in Ballingschap* with a definite loss to the theme.

By the epic method Milton overcomes another important difficulty. These fallen angels are liable to seem only airy nothings, but by the aid of the use of metaphor they make a more lasting impression upon our minds. We are told that they are " thick as autumnal leaves that strew the brooks in Vallombrosa " (302-303, Book I.). They are like

> a pitchy cloud
> Of locusts, warping, on the eastern wind,
> That o'er the realm of impious Pharaoh hung
> Like night, and darken'd all the land of Nile.

They resemble forest oaks, or mountain pines, with singed top, on the blasted heath, or

> As bees
> In springtime, when the sun with Taurus rides.

Thus by a variety of metaphor, writers of an epic may convey an imaginative portrayal of what cannot be accurately described. These comparisons create an illusion for our minds, so that we may grasp a picture intellectually reasonable and possessed of relative concreteness, a picture, however, that could not bear the test of visual presentation before a modern audience critical of the accuracy of abstract ideas, and therefore it cannot be given in a tragedy. For that reason, the figure of Satan may be given in the epic, but is unfitted for a tragedy.

Milton had indeed a very difficult problem to solve in the presentation of the figure of Satan to our imagination, now gigantic enough to seem a reasonable antagonist with God and his angels, now small enough to perchance elude detection as he disseminates himself in a mist and enters into a lion, a leopard, a toad, or a serpent. All this the poet must do and his art must never impress us as grotesque. If Milton failed of a touch of sublimity, the price was absurdity and loss of all dignity. And this issue greatly to be feared is exactly what must happen if one attempts to depict the Satan of the story of the fall of Lucifer and of the fall of man in a tragedy.

Nowhere has Milton shown subtler art than in his extending of his description of Satan over five hundred lines of the first book of *Paradise Lost*. This description is frequently interrupted by details that lead us by degrees that look reasonable to our imagination to a progressive portrayal, carried forward chiefly by metaphor, aided by allusion, and by Satan's own bombastic speeches that make the reader feel that the fallen archangel must be a great power, indeed, lifting his defiant head against high heaven and unconquered by his fall; thus we are led to the most finished part of the description, in these lines:

> He scarce had ceas'd, when the superior fiend
> Was moving towards the shore ; his ponderous shield,
> Ethereal temper, massy, large and round,
> Behind him cast ; the broad circumference
> Hung on his shoulders like the moon, whose orb
> Through optic glass the Tuscan artist views
> At ev'ning, from the top of Fesole
> Or in Valdarno, to descry new lands,
> Rivers or mountains in her spotty globe.
> His spear, to equal which the tallest pine,
> Hewn on Norwegian hills to be the mast
> Of some great ammiral, were but a wand,
> He walk'd with to support uneasy steps
> Over the burning marle, not like those steps
> On heaven's azure, and the torrid clime
> Smote on him sore besides, vaulted with fire.
> Nathless he so indur'd, till on the beach
> Of that inflamed sea he stood, and call'd
>
> . . . . (283–300.)
>
> He call'd so loud, that all the hollow deep
> Of hell resounded.   (314–315.)

This effect of power could not be given in a tragedy; nor what follows from line 587 when the description is resumed:

> Thus for these beyond
> Compare of mortal prowess, yet observ'd
> Their dread commander : he, above the rest

In shape and gesture proudly eminent,
Stood like a tower ; his form had yet not lost
All her original brightness, nor appear'd
Less than archangel ruin'd, and th' excess
Of glory obscur'd : as when the sun new-ris'n
Looks through the horizontal misty air,
Shorn of his beams ; or from behind the moon,
In dim eclipse, disastrous twilight sheds
On half the nations, and with fear of change
Perplexes monarchs : darken'd so, yet shone
Above them all th' archangel : but his face
Deep scars of thunder had intrench'd, and care
Sat on his faded cheek, but under brows
Of dauntless courage, and considerate pride
Waiting revenge : cruel his eye, but cast
Signs of remorse and passion to behold
The fellows of his crime,   (587–606.)

Satan's action is dramatic and his speeches
are spirited but they are unsuited to a tragedy
in every way because they require the epic
scope.   Even when it is possible for the tragedy
to borrow from the epic, the purpose of what
is borrowed is changed in the process, from
the fact that it is no longer subordinated to
the development of such important problems
as the saving of a nation, the founding of an
empire, or the origin of sin in a world otherwise
perfect.   The sorrow of Satan, or the sadness
of Adam is not the theme of *Paradise Lost*.

In a tragedy there is not time for the wealth
of episode that is useful in the deliberate method

of the epic. Mrs. Fiske's rendering of Becky Sharp is an example of the loss of opportunity for deliberate character development effected by the stage. The brilliant characterisation that has made Thackeray so justly renowned pales into comparative insignificance in the brevity of the portrayal. Mrs. Fiske may be very interesting as Becky Sharp, but she is not more than one phase of Thackeray's wonderful creation.

Mrs. Edith Wharton confesses that she has met an insurmountable difficulty in presenting the Lily Bart of *The House of Mirth* upon the stage. For her character, the deliberate method of the novel is indispensable. It is too great a demand upon any actress to comprehend the subtleties of Lily's complex motives of action and after that to compel them to be understood by a varied and indolent audience. Like the novel, the epic has opportunity to explain changes of slow growth, of hidden tendencies that suddenly leap into control of the impulses.

In an epic like *Paradise Lost* the main purpose is promoted by a great variety of episode, which, by an appeal to the imagination of the reader, promotes the establishment of neces-

sary harmonious illusion and likeness of truth.
There is, for instance, the minor episode of
Satan caught by the angelic guard, at the ear
of Eve. The episode, in itself, is not necessary for the plot; other stories of the temptation have no such scene, but it has great value
in making vivid the perils of Satan's undertaking in entering the garden of Eden, this
stronghold of God and of his angels.

By means of this scene we first realise the
hollowness of the arch-fiend's boasts; we see him
cringe at the awful beauty of Ithuriel, before
whose spear he shrinks as a guilty thing surprised, and he drops perforce all subterfuge.
Unconscious though the dwellers in Eden are,
while this martial display of heavenly power
against Satanic blazes forth beside their bower,
the scene furthers the human plot by adding
impetus to our thoughts upon the origin and
growth of sin; Eve's fall afterwards comes to
our mind with a less abrupt shock. From the
standpoint of God and the heavenly hosts, the
scene is significant; Satan quails before God's
representatives and loses his false glitter of
heroism. The power of beauty and of goodness stands supreme.

Of less importance but not less skilful are

a score of minor episodes in *Paradise Lost*. Satan's second entrance of Eden, cautious yet poetical as he plunges into the stream, percolates under the cliff, and rises in the mist, whence he makes his fearsome way to the serpent, is skilfully depicted. The dramatic scene of Eve's waywardness and coquetry on the morning of the day of the temptation, the momentous visit of Raphael to the dwellers in Eden, the marvellous bridge made by sin and death to facilitate the transference from earth of their prey, the mysterious beauty of Pandemonium rising like an exhalation, and the vivid portrayal of the council that therein assembled, are typical manifestations of Milton's art in the use of the devices of the epic.

There still remains the most important of all the considerations for preferring the epic to the dramatic treatment for the fall of Lucifer and the fall of man, and this is found in the fact that, unlike the usual epic story, where to promote the elevation and the importance of the theme, the machinery of the gods may be introduced at will, in this case the very plot itself involves divine characters.

Without the account of the part played by the gods in the *Iliad*, the return of Achilles

to the battlefield after his reconciliation with his
commander-in-chief might be related. Although it is true that Athena took an active
part in the death of Hector, her interference
from the standpoint of the theme might be
reduced to the statement that " Hector became
confused and fumbled over his arrows, thus giving Achilles a moment's advantage, and the
fatal dart sped to its goal." The situation is
very different in the interdependent plots of
Paradise Lost.

In the story of the fall of Lucifer, all of the
characters are parts of the divine machinery;
God, the Son, Michael, Raphael, Gabriel, and
Uriel marshal the force of goodness against
Lucifer, Beëlzebub, Belial, Moloch, Mammon,
and the force of evil. So complete is the influence here of Milton's belief in an omnipotent
God that he does not speak of the Son as devising any action of Himself, but all of His
movements are inspired by the supreme source
of all goodness, God himself; so also are Michael, Raphael, Gabriel, Uriel, and Ithuriel varying minor manifestations of God. On the side
of evil, Milton is consistent. Lucifer is the
arch plotter, all action, all words of his followers take their source in him, he becomes the

omnipresent force of evil, in all hearts that are open to receive him. The plot of the fall of Lucifer is formed of spiritual notions more or less defined. Lucifer is more clearly individualised than God. But these conceptions are more remote from human life than the gods which, for instance, in the *Iliad*, are not deeply imbedded in the plot but they are there the machinery of the epic. This difference between *Paradise Lost* and the *Iliad* must affect the epic pitch throughout. In its remoteness from actual life, the fall of Lucifer is complete and the details of his rebellion can be made reasonable only through the skilful illusion of the epic; it loses all possibility of visual representation in tragedy except in a most uncritical age, and the epic is the only literary form that it can reasonably take.

Not only are the devices of the epic necessary for presenting the commanding figure of Satan in his relation to the mysterious warfare of evil with good, but the deliberation of the epic method is necessary for presenting a reasonable and dignified story of his rebellion against God and his machinations against the dwellers in Eden.

The protagonists in the first great battle

meet again and for a second and more desperate conflict in Paradise; therefore the spiritual characters are not like the machinery of the gods in the *Iliad*, in the *Odyssey*, and in the *Æneid*, but are the chief actors, for Adam and Eve, the concrete human personalities, are more acted upon than acting. Moreover they are not so much individuals, in the very nature of the theme and the plot, as they are universal man and woman.   As in the first great episode, Lucifer is more individualised than God, so in the second, Eve is more clearly sketched in personality than is Adam, but we have not the definiteness of an Achilles, nor of a Helen—such is not the poet's intention. Milton's theme is exceptionally universal and requires at every point an aloofness from realism, to preserve the needed elevation and the harmony of the tone. In a plot representing universal human experience this artistic harmony could be attained only with generalised characters, and only with epic treatment.

Moreover since the interwoven plots form a single transaction they should not be separated, and if the plots are united the action is too long and requires too many scenes for a tragedy. The method of the complete subordina-

4

tion of the one plot to the other has been adopted in *Adamus Exsul* by Grotius; in *Adam in Ballingschap*, by Vondel; and in *L'Adamo*, by Andreini. In these tragedies the fall of Lucifer is given briefly in an opening soliloquy of the arch-protagonist. In *Lucifer*, by Vondel, the fall of man is subordinated to a brief report, of a messenger in heaven, where his tidings fall discordant upon the song of victory of Michael over Lucifer. In all these tragedies, there is loss in the characters and in the action of the principal plot, as well as in the subordinate episode in these points,—Lucifer's fall is not complete until he seduces Eve; Adam and Eve's fall is not treated adequately without a full knowledge of the foe with whom they have to deal; in a soliloquy it is impossible to portray Satan, the Prince of Darkness, in his full proportion, and, therefore, the action of the whole plot loses in importance and reasonableness from compressing the struggle in heaven, of Lucifer against God, into a monologue preceding a tragedy, whose scene is laid in the garden of Eden and whose subject is man's fall.

The whole problem resolves itself again into an attempt to treat the epic background and a story requiring also epic deliberation and epic

methods in a tragedy. The best achievements
of masters of literary art indicate that, in practice, they recognised the suitable field for their
art, just as the artist separates his picture
from the broad expanse of nature, and my contention is that in the case of man's fall the
whole story moved with the epic scope or
dropped out of art realms altogether.

II

THE CHRISTIAN EPIC

THE plots of the fall of Lucifer and of the fall of man either separate or combined are epic in character, for they require the full epic background and the epic method. Indeed the scope of these episodes includes the background of life's mystery and is no less than an attempt to present a picture to our imagination of the very origin of that deathless struggle of the evil and the good. No attempt in literature demands more courage or needs more literary devices marshalled to its aid. The heavenly muse, the well-nigh omniscient narrator, the variety of minor episode, of metaphor, and of allusion of the epic type, are indispensable. But the greatest difficulty of all in these plots is found in the fact that upon the epic background there move not ordinary human beings; although two of the characters must typify human life. Indeed all of the characters except Adam and Eve are marvellous creations and play the part of the divine machinery of the classic epics. Moreover in this case the supernatural characters are not accessories to the plot, but they are the chief actors in the story; for these characters and for this story the epic form is essential.

Upon this question of the marvellous in the epic and in the tragedy much has been written but more must be said. A comparative study of tragedies indicates that a tragedy composed of spiritual conceptions is at variance with the underlying principle of tragedy, with usage, and with public approval of what is suited to a tragedy. In the first place it may be well to notice what has been written by some typical critics of the past.

Bossu, speaking for a large faction in the seventeenth century, has said: "Allegorical presentations that would be obscure, improbable, and absurd upon the stage seem clear and reasonable in the narration of the epic poet." Aristotle, whose name has been one to conjure with for many centuries and whose penetrating common-sense gives peculiar force to his utterances, has expressed it as his judgment that "It is necessary in tragedies to produce the wonderful, but that which is contrary to reason is better fitted to the epopea. . . . Hence the sense of the wonderful is excited in the highest degree from the agent's not being seen." Horace agrees with Aristotle upon the danger of the loss of power through the use of marvellous details in a tragedy but he is more explicit, for he declares that in his opinion, " The soul is less affected with what it hears than with what it sees."

Tasso, who has written at length upon the proper domain of the epic and of the tragedy, states that it is his belief that transformations are not suitable to a tragedy. The marvellous seems inappropriate when bodily represented, therefore the intervention of the gods is not suitable in tragedy, but in the epic this device is frequent and desirable; for it arouses wonder and admiration and aids the elevation of the tone of the epic.

Boileau accepts the theory that the epic has superior ability to clothe the marvellous, for he says: " The epic is loftier than tragedy; as the treatment is longer, it must be vivid, spirited, . . . every virtue is a divinity, a storm is the anger of Neptune or of Jupiter."

Dryden writes upon this subject:

"I might also add that many things, which not only please, but are real beauties in the reading, would appear absurd upon the stage ; and these not only the *speciosa miracula*, as Horace calls them, of transformations of Scylla, Antiphales, and the Listrygons, which cannot be represented even in operas, but the prowess of Achilles, or Æneas, would appear ridiculous in our dwarf heroes of the theatre. We can believe that they routed armies in Homer, or in Virgil, but ' *Ne Hercules contra duos* ' in the drama."

These utterances from these dictators of criticism have no value except as they bear the test of a comparison with the practice of the great masters in the epic and the tragedy in the past, and with the verdict of modern analytical thought. The epic and the tragedy are alike in treating important characters, involved in a contest with powers beyond man's completed knowledge, and both the epic and the tragedy present forcibly universal truth; the one at deliberate length, the other with the intensity of a crisis. The difference in their method is more than superficial; for it proceeds from an inherent difference, not obvious at the starting point, but capable of a development into the extreme of the corresponding opposite.

There are tracts where the epic and the tragedy flow together, there are numerous episodes that aid the epic and that are at the same time not only tragic, but are fitting themes for formal tragedy. As for instance, the fall of Turnus in the *Æneid*, and the episode of Dido are themes for a tragedy; as are also the death of Patroclus in the *Iliad*, and the episode of Clorinda and Tancred in the *Jerusalem Delivered*. In this way the epic frequently partakes of the nature of the tragedy; and the tragedy also joins with the epic in so far as it presents a small portion of the epic background, and at moments of great elevation where its spirit reaches the epic height; but the plot of the epic could not be thrown into a series of tragedies nor could a tragedy be transformed into an epic. For instance, in *Paradise Lost* there are tragic episodes; but no one of them is fitted to form an independent tragedy and it should remain as a tragic scene in the epic for its own integrity as an incident; for it is not clear in itself apart from the train of thought elaborated in the epic entire.

Not from points of resemblance but of difference can the distinction be safely traced between the epic and the tragedy. From the fact that the tragedy presents a hero in a brief intense struggle with the great forces of good as in *Macbeth*, or with evil as in *Hamlet*, and in

Lear; and an epic relates the exploits of a hero
in a contest more general in interest, more
comprehensive in its range, affecting a race, or
a nation, or a cause, it may be seen that tragedy
is based upon concreteness, while the epic moves
from the individual interest toward a common
interest for the nation, or the race, and therefore is an artistic rendering of a relatively abstract conception. From the fact that the
tragedy is realistic in its intensity, its danger
is the narrowness of sensationalism, of a provincial or exceptional realism that interferes
with its universality; the corresponding danger
of the epic is too great breadth for vividness.
In its graphic realism or intensity of emotional
passages, then, an epic swings toward the tragedy; and in all great tragedies there is an upward sweep toward the epic where the intensity
of the passion appears no longer the emotion
of the single man, who faces his foe, but the
passion of all right-minded men in like situation; the hero then stands not for the individual, but for the race.[1] This is an intensity of
passion that escapes the bounds of the concrete example into a universal conception and

[1] But there is here a difference of degree, the hero of
tragedy is not so universal as Adam for instance; the
distinction is that of any man and of every man.

this is an epic movement. This upward sweep of the tragedy is not to be found where every man is represented in his humour or out of his humour; but where both the characters and the situation have universal significance. Tamburlaine may be a human Lucifer; but he is unresisted and the spectator is unconvinced that he is not shown simply a *lusus naturæ*. *Hamlet, Lear, Othello*, rise to epic moments; not at the crisis of the death of the hero, but in the intensity of the struggle of good and evil that to the eye of the observer is as clear a contest as though abstract spiritual forces fought out the battle, and no longer is the sympathy for Hamlet, Othello, Lear, as individuals, but for universal man who may be thus beset.

Beyond this degree of the epic development, the tragedy cannot safely venture from the realm of the concrete. Upon this opinion there is an approach to agreement; but Dryden was not perfectly consistent. He had a lingering desire for lesser marvels like magic and spirits on the stage, and Voltaire and Lessing were frank in their avowal of their belief that such marvels were both permissible and desirable in dramatic art. Voltaire, impressed by his study of Shakespeare, has discussed the ques-

tion, at great length, and has not only declared
the ghost in Hamlet a striking device, but has
sought to imitate it in his ghost in *Semiramis*.

Lessing, in his *Dramaturgie*, discusses the
ghosts and asserts that

"a disbelief in ghosts cannot hinder the dramatic poet
from making use of them, for the seeds of a possible
belief in apparitions are sown in us all. It depends upon
the degree of the author's art, whether he can force these
seeds to germinate ; whether he possesses certain dextrous means to summon up rapidly and forcibly arguments in favour of the existence of such ghosts. If he
has these in his power, no matter what he may believe
in ordinary life, in the theatre we must believe as the
poet wills."

This skill to marshal arguments in favour of
his ghosts, Voltaire lacks, in the opinion of
Lessing; for "In *Semiramis*, Voltaire's ghost
breaks over the tradition of spirits and visits
a large assembly, seeking neither shadows nor
seclusion." Moreover, Lessing declares that
this ghost of Voltaire's creation has no personality and arouses no interest in his fate.

Lessing lived in the century that had believed
in the efficiency of the struggle of Cotton
Mather to suppress black art, and in the exploits of the Cock Lane ghost. His opinion
may be therefore not other than an interesting
step in the evolution of human thought. But

there are grounds for believing that there is far-reaching truth in his statement that if the author possesses " dextrous means," " no matter what we believe in ordinary life, in the theatre we must believe as the poet wills." There is no doubt however that the demand is increasingly exacting about these same dextrous means and as a consequence the modern poet more sharply defines the scope of his dramatic art within which limits he is to play the necromancer.

The survey of the theory and of the practice of the past and of the present literary ideals makes reasonable the statement that although tragedies have been written in which supernatural forces play an important part, still from the days of Aristotle the question has been raised whether this use of marvels is in accordance with the fundamental nature of tragedy, which, by imitation of human life, is to convince the spectator of the reality of what his eyes behold, so that he shall be purified, through pity and fear, from such like passions. If any question of probability arises, force is lost. A very great master of his art may, as Dryden and Lessing declare, so skilfully introduce the marvellous that the observer may be convinced of its reasonableness, despite the testimony of his eyes. However, through the necessary brevity of the tragedy and on account of its visual presentation, reasonableness is exceedingly difficult to establish when marvels are introduced on the stage, particularly as playing their part among normal human personages. With the evolution of critical thought, the difficulty increases and the attempt must become exceptional. In the larger development of the epic, with the privilege of the narrator to explain what the dramatist cannot put into the mouth of the actors, the likeness of truth may be not only more readily attained and kept but the epic problem may be vastly aided by the use of marvels and of the divine machinery.

The anthropomorphic conception of the gods of Greece and Rome made their presentation more possible in a tragedy. Æschylus introduced the Eumenides to struggle with Apollo, for the supremacy over Orestes, in one play; in another, Hephæstus binds Prometheus, for his rebellion against Zeus; Io appears as his fellow-sufferer from the tyranny of Zeus, and Hermes as a divine messenger; but Æschylus did not have the approval of public sentiment in his own day in these presentations of the divine in a tragedy.

From the anthropomorphic conception of the gods, however, arises in Greece a second type of tragedy wherein are presented characters that were of divine as well as of human parentage. These demigods were sometimes held as divine, sometimes as human but endowed with certain supernatural powers. Herakles, son of Zeus and Alcmene, was worshipped as a god, but he had human as well as superhuman characteristics. This conception of the gods as both divine and human gives freedom to the writer of a tragedy to present marvels, not out of harmony with the theory of the tragedy to those who accept such a view of Herakles. Euripides introduces this god and hero in the *Madness of Herakles*, where he appeals most strongly as a mortal at the mercy of an angry god; but in *Alcestis* it is not with mortal but divine strength that he triumphs over death and the grave. With less divinity and more of the preternatural than of divine power, appear two other characters in the work of Euripides: Medea, the daughter of the Sun, who is a witch rather than a goddess, and Helen, the daughter of Zeus, whose wraith only

officiated at Troy, while she, for the preservation of her dignity, was borne to Egypt. The
human side of the demigod in all of these
last mentioned plays made possible their presentation in a tragedy before a Greek
audience.

It is true that at an early stage both of
modern dramatic art and of modern thought, as
an outgrowth of the Christian Church services,
and of the activities of the clergy, arose the miracle plays and later the moralities and the
masks, wherein God and the angels, Satan, the
even deadly sins, and the cardinal virtues appeared as sensuous realities and played important parts. But the purpose of these plays
was too didactic, the conceptions of the vices
and virtues either too concrete both for good
taste and for clear thought, or too attenuated
and too allegorical to be artistic according to
the law of imitation in tragedy; and not even
the attractive presentation of *Everyman* convinces one that the form should be permanent
in dramatic art. Whatever was of permanent
value in this form of art evolved into the epic
or into the tragedy.

In *Everyman*, as in *Peer Gynt*, we have not
all men but some men. The epic background

in *Everyman* is approached from the tragic not from the epic standpoint, and for visual presentation the abstract forces that the man meets in his last hour of life might be far more effectively presented on the stage by concrete pictures from human life. Indeed in so far as they are dramatically effective, they are too far individualised for philosophical truth. To have raised the individual toward the universal conception would have been the more effective method.

It is not a little difficult to remember that our problem, of the trend of the evolution of art ideals, should not be confused with a variety of other problems allied only by an association of ideas. The appeal, for instance, to a sympathetic imagination that links us pleasurably with men of other centuries and other climes is an experience to be prized but not to be confused with the problem of the evolution of art standards. The pleasure afforded to a sympathetic observer of a performance of *Everyman* is complex. The scene is unusual, there is attractiveness in the quaintness of the life presented, there is a stirring of reverence for ideas relatively universal, there is a sense of respect for the simple sincerity of the author, and there

is a prevailing charm in a phase of art that is
like mural decoration; but all of these forms of
pleasure are aloof from the problem before us.
Everyman is surely a transitional, not a finished art type, however interesting and however beautiful it may appear.

Our conception of God is not anthropomorphic and there is a corresponding tendency to-
day toward purer abstractions in spiritual
matters; but we hesitate to apply our theories
in art.   Abstractions, we are told, are at variance with art.   What then shall we do?   Must
there be hostility between the trend of modern
thought and the best development of art?   As
this question surely cannot be escaped it must
be faced with courage.

Although the visual presentation of the gods
and of other spiritual conceptions is more in
keeping with the ancient world than with modern thought, we have noticed that even Aristotle
and the contemporaries of Æschylus demurred
at the introduction of the gods in a tragedy.
We may then form a reasonable hypothesis,
that there is, in the universal judgment of man,
a recognition of a principle of good taste that
tends to restrict the visual presentation of
spiritual conceptions; and that the difference

5

between the modern and the ancient art ideal is the growth of a more sharply defined theory of the possibility of the presentation of these spiritual ideas in a concrete form.

Voices from the tomb, ghosts, talking statues, apparitions, persisted upon the stage, for the same reason that anthropomorphic ideas of God appeared in Grecian tragedy, because the people believed in these manifestations and therefore the verisimilitude, necessary for a tragedy, was not disturbed; and the heightening of the interest from the novelty of the scene was a gain in force. While the belief in these marvels was spontaneous either in the mind of the writer, or embodied by the author, as a common notion of his audience, the preternatural was no defect. In the hands of so skilful a necromancer as Shakespeare, these marvels may have given a wider importance to his work than contemporary superstition or folk-lore could conceive; these marvels may indeed have lent an epic dignity to his work. When, however, the marvels ceased to be real, either to the artist or to his audience, would Shakespeare have found further use for such devices? Would he indeed venture to present ghosts and witches on the stage, before an

audience that were too sophisticated to find
reality in such marvels?

We may safely infer from a study of Shakespeare's local colour, from his grasp upon contemporary thought, that he would not dream
of presenting marvels in tragedy that his audience held as incredible; nor would Shakespeare
sanction the tribute paid him by Lessing, in
advocating the continuance of a practice made
attractive by the amazingly successful devices
of *Hamlet*. Indeed it may be urged that,
deeper than the appeal to contemporary be-
lievers in ghosts and witches, in *Macbeth* and in
Hamlet there lies an epical significance in the
widening of the field of action into the realm of
the unseen, whence preternatural machinery is
about to issue and take part in the contest.
On this score, students find in these scenes rich
mines for thought; but shrink from their visual presentation upon the stage. We may delight to listen to ghost stories, but we do not
so willingly see them acted and the ghost in
Hamlet is a severe test of the courage of a
modern actor; nor is the device usually impressive to those who have not entered into sympathy with the play by long study. The chances
are that such students give it an epical inter-

pretation and do not view the ghost simply as a marvel, surviving from a naïve and uncritical age. For this reason *Hamlet* at its best is not actable.[1]

Since the superhuman is unsuited to a tragedy the theme of the fall of Lucifer is unfitted for the stage; for it is entirely composed of spiritual conceptions, and it demands elaboration in the epic form. The fall of man is nearer to the concrete domain of tragedy but can be treated with loss only in that form; for a difficulty arises in the emphasis that should be thrown upon the abstract ideas. Adam and Eve should not be so much individualised that they do not reasonably represent all men; the contest of spiritual forces must be fierce and strong, and that strength can be presented with dignity in the epic only, for it requires the full epic background.

But the objection will be urged that there is an essential element of tragedy in each of these plots, the fall of Lucifer and the fall of man, and that they combine to form a sad conclusion to *Paradise Lost*. Is the sad ending peculiar to the tragedy and excluded by theory and practice from the epic?

[1] See Charles Lamb, vol. vi., Lucas Edition.

Not even do the masters, often quoted as dictators of form, lay down a hard and fast rule here. Aristotle says that "The nature of the epic does not exclude a sad ending." Bossu writes,

We cannot, then, from any of these principles determine anything concerning the fortunate or unfortunate end of an epic action. Practice is, no doubt, in favour of a happy ending. It is, however, involved in the very subject, the fable, and the action of the *Iliad* that the end should be fortunate for the Greeks. So also in the *Odyssey*, the fable demands success for Ulysses, but in the *Thebaid*, unity of action is marred by the happy conclusion. In the *Æneid*, the fable demanded a happy ending.

Bossu concludes,—"Let the case be how it will, yet, I fancy, there needs a great deal of skill to give the hero of the epopea a sad and mournful end, which might be received with general applause." [1]

Dryden, misunderstanding the scheme of *Paradise Lost*, thus comments upon Milton: "That his subject is not that of an heroick poem, properly so called; it being the losing of our happiness, where the event is not prosperous like that of other epick works." [2]

---

[1] Monsieur René Le Bossu's *Treatise on the Epick Poem*, made English by W. J., Book I, 17.

[2] Dryden. Dedication to Translation of Juvenal.

The principles of the epic require one no more than the other, but precedent is in favour of a happy ending; for in the epic there are chronicled the exploits of a dignified and powerful hero and unless there appears to be exceptional cause for defeat, it seems more reasonable that he should triumph, but what is the nature of his victory? The points first to be considered are these:

First—that it is possible to have a perfectly correct epic with a sad ending.

Second—that usage is not in favour of a sad ending.

Third—that it is harder to write a successful epic with a hero not prosperous and not successful at the conclusion.

In regard to the usage—which is in favour of a happy ending—it may be said that in the *Iliad*, the *Odyssey*, and the *Æneid* the fable required a happy ending. It is possible to conceive of a perfect epic fable in which a happy ending is not required. Indeed, in the *Iliad*, the fable required success of the troops of the combined Grecian forces, but the fable did not demand the survival of Achilles. Had he been fatally wounded on the battlefield, the convincing power of the treatment of the theme would have been unaffected, provided his death caused no disruption of the forces. It is only necessary that he should slay Hector and that the Greeks should be victorious, but it is more pleasing that he should live.

It is unnecessary for the essential idea of the epic that the action should emanate from the hero. It is possible for the action to emanate from the resistance of the hero to a foe who has himself originated the action, as in *Paradise Lost;* all that is required is that the theme should be substantiated in the epic. The happy or sad ending is only incidental, but the struggle of the hero should not be futile and a hero may conquer even by his death. Indeed, it must be conceded that although the convention of a sad ending is usual in the tragedy it is not a necessary conclusion; perfect purification of the emotions is possible in *Alcestis* [1] and yet the ending is happy, as likewise it is in the *Cid;* it is necessary that the struggle should be fierce and strong, that the hero should be tried to the uttermost, but the question of the ending is a convention rather than a principle, so that the theme be clear and established by the

[1] "For now to happier days than those o'er past
Have we attained."
(A. S. Way's translation.)

dénouement. As to the convention of success in
the epic, it may be well to inquire what considerations influenced its adoption.

The Greeks in life, in philosophy, and in art
laid a stress upon fame, success, and victory,
that is not in accordance with the trend of
modern thought. With this emphasis in their
thought, they naturally and fitly conformed
their art to their ideal, otherwise they could
not have attained the degree of sincerity and
of spontaneous enthusiasm that is necessary for
art. For the same reason modern art must
preserve its sincerity and spontaneity by the
same means;—if the Greek and Roman idea of
success is not dominant in our philosophy,
neither can it be in our art. It is true that art
is imitation—imitation not however of other
people's ideas but of truth as we conceive it.

The Christian ideal of the sacrifice of the
individual to a cause is a universal ideal older
than the days of Marcus Curtius; and the belief that a hero may succeed " in that he seems
to fail "; that " fame is no plant that grows
on mortal soil, but in Jove's court," alone, the
victory can be judged; that the final judgment
and final reward are hereafter,[1] are not ideas

[1] See *Lycidas; Passing of Arthur*.

devoid of universal truth recognised by some
thinkers in different ages of the world, but, to-
day, emphasised and accepted as conventional
forms of belief, by many who avoid them in
practice. However, so long as these notions
are prominent in our thought, not opposed to
the fundamental ideals of the epic, and capable
of arousing enthusiasm and of carrying conviction, they are not unworthy of epic treatment, and they must appear in the epic written
in modern times, if such a production is written
at all. Contemporary literary forms must embody modern ideas; a conventional epic, con-
sciously avoiding all that is not classical, must
result therefore in failure; frigidity, insipidity,
and insincerity will be its doom. Doubtless in
so far as modern thought differs from that of
the classical world, the effort to exclude modern
thought must be conscious. There is no more
dreary reading than the self-conscious eighteenth-century attempts in the classic epic.
As a contrast to these, stand the *Davidëis* of
Cowley and *Paradise Lost* of Milton.

The question of a comparison of the ancient
and the modern epic resolves itself into the
problem of a change of the ideas clothed in art
form, not in the art form itself. Is there not,

however, a fundamental difficulty that does affect the art form—a difficulty apart from the sad ending, but indicative of a similar fundamental difference between ancient and modern thought? It would be indeed significant, if an examination of the train of thought involved would reveal that not only is the fable to explain the presence of evil in the world unfitted to tragedy, but also unsuited to the epic form. To such a conclusion are we tending?

The difficulty in presenting modern abstract ideas in the epic is independent of the sad ending, or of the postponement to the hereafter of the judgment of the issue. The very real difficulty that may confront any modern writer of the epic emanates from a different cause. Are modern thinking, modern sentiment, and modern taste, modern philosophy, modern religion, and modern art, at variance with the portrayal of spiritual conceptions in any form of art because they fall short of the ideal and thus are liable to the defect of absurdity or of irreverence?

We have seen that through the anthropomorphic conception of the gods, the classic divinities were available in dramatic art and the exploits of such demigods as Hercules were not opposed to the classical ideas of taste in a tragedy; although from a sense of reverence the Greeks objected to the presentation of Apollo upon the stage.

In the classic epic no difficulty appeared in the introduction of the divinities as characters in the story because the gods of the *Iliad*, the *Odyssey*, and the *Æneid* came from no farther away than Olympus. In Homer, the fable is conveyed by a plot that deals with individuals, who, in so far as they are true to life, possess universal human characteristics—and by a machinery of the gods, who are on the border-land of concrete personalities and are certainly more individual than universal, more material than spiritual. There is not here therefore the difficulty that confronts us in modern thought.

The epic based upon the two plots, the fall of Lucifer and the fall of man, chronicles a struggle of spiritual forces. In such an epic, dominated by spiritual conceptions that are given imaginative reality to preserve them from the barrenness of allegory, the nature of the spiritual becomes an important consideration. The divine in *Paradise Lost*, for instance, differs from the *Iliad*, as the God of Milton differs from the gods of Homer;—not sipping nectar, half in jest, half in earnest did the Almighty sit at ease, adjudging, in material things, victory to the heroes, but the song of triumph rang from the angels in heaven over one soul that repented, who came up out of great tribulation, who received the palm of spiritual victory and entered into his birthright of ideal beauty on earth or in heaven.

The farther away from the material life we place the world of spiritual conceptions, the more difficult it is to grasp; divinity is not so easily imagined, nor so effectively pictured today as it was in the classic world of Homer or of Virgil. For this reason mankind is no longer delighted with attempts to express in art the idea of God. With the introduction of Christian notions arose a serious difficulty, so that no longer is it a question of eliminating the supernatural from tragedy only, but from art forms altogether.

We may then conclude that the classic freedom in portraying divinity is not in accordance with the modern Christian idea of reverence. If the epic demands the high seriousness promoted by the divine machinery, what can be done? This question was discussed long ago by Tasso and by Boileau among others. It was thought that if the reader no longer believed in the gods of the classic world, it was a violation of truth and at variance with the high seriousness of the epic to introduce the ancient divinities. But if the writer of an epic banished the classic gods, what would be substituted for the divine machinery? The portrayal of God and of the angels was declared irreverent and in bad taste. Magic and allegorical presentations of virtues and vices were attempted, but it was later thought that the epic suffered in dignity, and that these devices were in time open to the censure of insincerity. Should there on this ground be an end of all writing of epics?

Boileau shows himself loath to declare that the epic must become a dead form, no longer possible to be produced, nor does he sympathise with the exiling of classical divinities from the figures of speech and from literary ornament, and he believes also that the epic should celebrate classical heroes.[1]

[1] To quote in brief his utterance upon the subject of the Christian Epic:

"It is in vain that recent authors attempt to lay them [classical divinities] aside with the idea that saints, prophets, and God might play the part, startling the reader with thoughts of hell, of Astaroth, Beëlzebub, and Luci-

No one to-day seriously questions the use of classical imagery and allusion for the beauty of poetry and surely any one who should gravely censure such a practice would be considered petty and narrow in criticism; but the future of the epic is not so easily settled. The difficulty that arises from the loss of the anthropomorphic conception of God, whether Christian or otherwise, emanates from the development of thought into purer abstractions and this evolution is attended by a scepticism about imaginative, concrete expressions for the unknowable and indefinable.

The attempt to present what the author believes is unknowable is fatal to that degree of concreteness that is essential for art; for even the epic must give abstractions a degree of concreteness, or they otherwise become rational

---

fer. . . . What pleasure is there in hearing the devil always hurling against the skies his determination to overcome the hero, and often with God balancing the victory?" Boileau continues, "Some say that Tasso has succeeded, but we should not read of his hero, always in prayer against Satan, if there were not Rinaldo, Argantes, Tancred, and Clorinda to interest us." . . . "It is not," Boileau declares, "that Christian poems should be filled with idolatry—but in a common subject to banish Tritons, Pan, and Fates is to banish poetical description from poetry."—*Art of Poetry*, CANTO. III.

speculation only and no longer are in the domain of imaginative art.

Arising from this phase of modern scepticism, a species of scepticism inseparable from analytical thinking, is a lack of reverence for dogma, but the presence of an intellectual reverence for the infinite, from which attitude of mind proceeds a sentiment that is at the basis of our modern taste. All three of these forces—modern thinking, modern sentiment, and modern taste—are opposed to naïve, concrete pictures of abstractions because they fall short of the intellectual claim and therefore are open to the defect of absurdity.

If, on the other hand, the concrete of Charybdis is avoided there is peril to art in the hollowness of Scylla,—for abstractions pure and simple become allegory, which is opposed to the deeper reality of art. Indeed it may be questioned whether allegorical art does not ever lastingly attract for the something that it contains which is not allegory. Is not Bunyan great because his characterisations, which are in harmony with his allegory, appeal to the reader as real, like characterisations of Cervantes, or of Shakespeare? No one claims that the perfecting of Spenser's deficient allegory would have improved the *Faerie Queene*. The work is successful in spite of the allegory.

Upon this train of thought Milton appears to have pondered and he faced these difficulties in *Paradise Lost*. He avoided the barrenness of allegory, on one side, and the seduction of anthropomorphic art on the other. His early drafts for a tragedy on the classic model contain also traits of the miracle, of the morality, and of the mask, and indicate a necessity for allegory if the theme is to be elaborated. By the comparison of these plans with the later work of *Paradise Lost*, we discover that Sin and Death are the only survivors of his allegory unless it be the seven deadly sins of Andreini that he has metamorphosed into a vision [1] of the concrete life of the world in the tenth and eleventh books of *Paradise Lost*. Milton did not favour allegory in art.

In the progress of religious thought away from the anthropomorphic conceptions, toward purer ideals, one must pass through the colder period of philosophical abstract analysis into the realm of higher spiritual conceptions, that in turn present themselves to the poet for scrutiny to discern whether he can clothe them

[1] See also Bk. X *Lusiad;* vision shown by Thetis.

in the concrete form of art. The problem at best is difficult and may be without solution. The wonder is not because Milton failed in presenting spiritual conceptions to a certain degree, but because he achieved in his superhuman effort so great a measure of success.

It is not probable that the attempt will be made again by a great poet or artist to present the personality of God. Never again can a poet attempt such a task in an epic. But the future of the epic may even so be secure. The time is not ripe perhaps for the elevation of the novel into a pæan of triumph of a worthy hero in the spiritual warfare common to nations and to humanity. Toward the ideal of such an epic we may be moving, but such an epic exacts from the writer powers never yet attained by any author.

The study of *Paradise Lost* brings proofs that Milton made his way through seas of perplexity, for any minor artist, to the inevitable decision that *Paradise Lost* must be an epic with the double plot of the fall of Lucifer and the fall of man, an epic essentially of abstractions which should be both philosophically clear and religiously and artistically concrete, through the use of imaginative devices; neither

6

naïve on the one hand, nor allegorical on the other.   I am not unaware of the objection that will at once be raised, " Have you not fallen into the error of making Milton a modern man and not an interpreter of the seventeenth-century dogmatism upon spiritual conceptions? "   If this be an error, into such I have in part fallen. I believe that Milton's genius took a tinge from the seventeenth-century foibles, but that he was too great an intellectual force to be dominated by the peculiarity of any century and I rest my belief upon his own utterances.   Did any man indeed whom we recognise as a genius ever fail to connect the stream of thought of his period with the universal thought of man? That fact is the source of the chief interest in the comparative study of literature.   To Milton's *Treatise on Christian Doctrine*, we must first turn for Milton's utterances upon his theory of evil and note their relation to his epic of *Paradise Lost*.

III

THE train of thought that lies at the basis of *Paradise Lost* may be found in the *Treatise on Christian Doctrine* by John Milton. This has been the most abused of books, a posthumous child of its father, frowned upon by Lord High Chancellor and other dignitaries in the hour of its birth; wrested from the hands of the printers and of its timorous guardian and tossed aside to gather the dust among neglected state papers at Whitehall, and forgotten for over a century. Surely the evil star of its birth has not ceased to cast a malign influence over its fortunes; for in the years since its rescue from oblivion, it has found no voice to advocate its supreme importance for the student of *Paradise Lost*. More than one reputable critic indeed has, to my mind, misquoted its utterances and apparently misunderstood its connection with *Paradise Lost*. In the prose of the *Treatise on Christian Doctrine* we have the root, in the poem the flower; if the treatise is not identical with the epic, neither does the root resemble the flower.

When Milton wrote his four drafts for a tragedy on Paradise Lost, he had not solved the problem of the relation of his story to the epic background. There could be no reasonable conception of this epic scope without long and careful trains of analytical thought which had grown so familiar to his mind that they became stuff that dreams are made of; and they were ready for the spontaneous action of his imagination and emotion, then and only then might these rational trains of thought pass into the domain of art. The process of thought in a field so vast as *Paradise Lost*, and so incomprehensible in any perfected sense, must necessarily be slow and cautious and years must pass before that magic bridge could be trusted, whereon benign or evil angels might pass to and fro, from the storm-swept background of mystery.

But the question is asked, why talk of dreams and mystic backgrounds; why not confine ourselves to facts? All men admit that the problem of life is unsolvable, why not enchain one's thought to what can be proved? The answer is, because this suggestion is impossible and ignores the inalienable freedom of the human mind. The mind of man cannot be confined to one routine; one son takes his spade and digs his ancestral acres, another sails the seas to penetrate unknown lands, one man grasps his hammer and asks the solid rock to give up its secret, another casts off all moorings and tempts the dark unbottomed infinite abyss, satisfied with nothing less than the hidden roots of things. To ask why one chips the rock and another skirts the impalpable obscure, argues a lack of breadth of human tolerance; both are honourable manifestations of the free mind of man; all that we can demand is that the treasure trove should bear the light of reason, however it transcend our actual knowledge. Here and here only has the questioner the just right of playing the examiner.

Some eyes are skilful with the microscope and others with the telescope; Milton's course demands the long look and the far sight. Before Milton took his daring flight, he paused and pondered long his way.

Between the period of the construction of the schemes for a tragedy on man's fall and of the completion of the epic of *Paradise Lost*, Milton elaborated a theory of evil and of its relation to God's plan for the government of the universe. This theory of evil, inseparable in its explanation from his theory of good, was written out at length in the *Treatise on Christian Doctrine* which was left in the hands of Daniel Skinner and not published in Milton's lifetime. We have no proof that the composition of this prose work antedated the great epic. It would indeed be probable from both external and internal evidence that he had not planned to publish this treatise at the time when he completed his epic, *Paradise Lost*. There are good reasons for believing that the idea of giving to the world these dryer bones of his theories arose from his discussions with such immature young students as Skinner, who might be easily confused in the arabesques of fancy of the great poem and needed to have the epic resolved into its original trains of thought. Out of these discussions arose very probably many other bold interpretations of Bible texts, and explanations of ideas rooted in the personal bias of experience or of individuality. With these side excursions we have nothing to do, but we are to confine ourselves to the central idea of the epic, as it is explained by the *Treatise on Christian Doctrine.*

The question before us is this, if there must be somewhere discoverable the philosophical basis for every work of art, shall we be justified in concluding that we have found the scheme underlying *Paradise Lost* in this *Treatise on Christian Doctrine ?* And another question follows in its train? Did Milton's philosophical explanation of the origin and of the persistence of evil predispose him to an epic conception of man's fall? A study of the *Treatise on Christian Doctrine* reveals that only an epic could interpret in art the theme of *Paradise Lost,* and Adam's fall must be regarded as unsuited to the form of tragedy but it reasonably stands as an essential episode of a Christian epic. While it is true that tragic episodes, like the story of Dido, of Turnus, of Clorinda and Tancred, are common in great epics and frequently lend themselves to successful treatment in an independent tragedy, according to Milton's belief this disposal is not possible of the tragic theme of man's fall. Not Adam's fall but Christ's triumph is the underlying motive in Milton's work; for this reason, man's fall cannot be presented apart from the complete train of thought which may resolve itself into the two epic episodes of the contest of good and evil in heaven, and on earth. Our line of investigation in the *Treatise on Christian Doctrine* leads us to nothing less than the whole epic background, a field where no man can dogmatise; but by examination of his thought and by a comparison with other men's thought, he may say only " this appears to me to be reasonable."

In Milton's thoughts upon this epic background of mystery, in the relation of the forces of good and of evil, there are indications that he turned over the writings of the early Christian Church fathers, particularly of St. Augustine; that he culled from the Bible phrases that he set together with more than a touch of the rational freedom of the higher criticism, and he welded all together with the spirit of Plato.

In extracting from the *Treatise on Christian*

---

[1] *Treatise on Christian Doctrine*, Book I., volume IV., Milton's Prose Works, Chas. R. Summer; *Treatise on Christian Doctrine* discovered among state papers in Middle Treasury Gallery, Whitehall, 1823. MS. delivered to Sir Joseph Williamson about 1676. Summary of all points touched upon in *Paradise Lost* is given in this essay.

Doctrine a brief summary of the thought that touches the problem of *Paradise Lost*, it will be valuable to cite other prose utterances of Milton that throw light upon the same problem of the existence of evil. Such quotations may be made from the *Areopagitica*, from the preface to the second part of *The Reason of Church Government urged against Prelaty*, and from his epistles.

In the *Treatise on Christian Doctrine* there cannot be other than deep interest for us in the picture that Milton has constructed of the universe; of its relation to God, and of the Creator to his handiwork; and of an all-wise and all-powerful God's part in the origin of evil and in its continuance in a world that was created perfect.

Milton conceived of God as infinite, therefore unknowable and incomprehensible, who created all things. First, by divine decree, he created His Son, who was, therefore, neither coeval nor coequal with God, but as vicegerent had divine power delegated to Him by God.

Nor did God separate himself from his creation; but remained supreme above all to govern the world; we may quote Milton's own words upon God's attitude in this matter:

" He upholds and preserves the immutable order of
causes appointed by him in the beginning. This is commonly and indeed too frequently described by the name
of nature ; for nature cannot possibly mean anything but
the mysterious power and efficacy of that divine voice
which went forth in the beginning and to which as
to a perpetual command all things have since paid
obedience."

How then did sin enter into this perfect
world? The answer is found by Milton, in the
freedom of the will. To the angels in heaven
was given freedom to choose their own relation
toward God; in a right decision lay their bliss
and their true liberty, in a wrong choice was
entailed their downfall and their separation
from God. Lucifer rebelled in heaven against
God's decree that all the angels should welcome the Messiah as God's vicegerent. After
this, he was no longer the angel of the morning star, but Satan, an adversary. He sinned
" from the beginning " [of sin] and became
the father of all evil, and God spared not the
angels that were led astray by the rebel angel
but cast them out of heaven into the bottomless pit, whence they later emerged to mislead
the dwellers in the earthly Paradise and to
become the omnipresent force of evil in the

world. But the world was not given over to
evil.

Hosts of good angels stand as ministering
spirits near the throne of God for

> his state
> Is kingly ; thousands at his bidding speed,
> And post o'er land and ocean without rest ;

to become the guardian angels of man and
check the machinations of Satan and his hosts.
One among the angels stood supreme, Michael,
captain of the hosts of heaven. Absolutely
obedient from choice, the loyal angels were not
all-seeing nor all-wise; God only could not err
in insight and in wisdom.

Man created in the image of God was the
crown of creation. Made a little lower than
the angels, he might rise to a place beyond
their destiny through the latent divinity of the
godhead. After man had been tempted by
the foe of God, the prince of darkness called
Satan, and had through a neglected tendency
in his nature become vulnerable to Satan's
shafts, he fell, but he was not given over to
the forces of evil. God had not appointed
man to wrath but to gain salvation, and the
Messiah was to find his enduring glory in the
overcoming of Satan and in the redeeming of

man.   Hence it was that man's dignity reached its highest possibility in this tinge of reflected glory; for he was counted worth the sacrifice of God's self in His Son.

Through this exaltation man might attain heavenly dignity, and emphasis is thus thrown upon man's power, through the divine aid, to triumph over evil.   The whole question of triumph or defeat lies then in the choice of man's free will.

But the question is very old and still very new, why was evil permitted to enter into the heart of man?   In the *Treatise on Christian Doctrine*, Milton reasons thus, that God was concerned in the creation of evil, in one of two ways:

1.   God permits the existence of evil by throwing no impediment in the way of natural causes and of free agents.

2.   God tempts the righteous, for the purpose of proving them.   God is not responsible for the existence of sin in the heart, which is the cause of evil.

But why did God permit man to be liable to sin?   Upon this problem, Milton in his *Areopagitica* wrote words that are of peculiar interest as an aid to the comprehension of the structure of *Paradise Lost:*

Many complain of Divine Providence, for suffering Adam to transgress. Foolish tongues ! When God gave him reason, he gave him freedom to choose : for reason is but choosing, he had been else a mere artificial Adam. We ourselves esteem not of that obedience, or love, or gift which is of force. God therefore left him free, set before his eyes an enticing object ; herein consisted his possibility of merit,—herein the right of his reward, the praise due to his abstinence.

As interesting as these words of Milton must be to one who wishes to penetrate the fundamental mystery of his epic background, they do not dissolve the mists that obscure the seeker's vision. The question arises at once in our minds how could sin find any entrance into the springs of action of a perfectly good man? Milton had evidently pondered long upon this problem and from comparison of his thought with an utterance of St. Augustine's in the *City of God*, the answer adopted by Milton can be made clear. St. Augustine says:

For if the will remained firm, in the love of that higher and stronger Good, which gave it light to see it, and zeal to love it ; it would not have turned from that to take delight in itself, and therefore have become so blind of sight, and so cold of zeal, that either Eve should have believed the serpent's words as true, or Adam should have dared prefer his wife's will before God's command and to think that he offended but venially, if he bear the partner of his life company in her offence.

The evil, therefore, that is this transgression was not done
but by such as were evil before.[1]

The reasoning of St. Augustine is like that
of Milton. In *Paradise Lost* Milton presents,
with the deliberate method of the epic episode,
the unmistakable impression of Adam's gradual drifting into danger, rather than that of a
sudden plunge of a perfectly sinless man into
evil. There was peril for Adam in the freedom
of his will, if he did not keep his spiritual perception undimmed; for from the defect of his
inner vision must result a loss of unity of purpose in his life; and from these two allied defects might arise the possibility of his fall.
An unworthy element in his love of Eve did in
fact dim Adam's vision and did destroy the
unity of purpose of his life.

But Milton's theme in *Paradise Lost* was not
strictly the fall of man; for the first fifty lines
of Book I. reveal that his purpose was rather
a fundamental conception of the struggle of
good and evil and of man's relation to Satan's
warfare with God. In the consequences of the
fall, appears triumphant God's dominion over

[1] St. Augustine, *Civitas Dei*, 413–426, A. D., Part II.,
Creation: fall of Lucifer and angels, fallen angels became
demons, formed fundamental principle of paganism.
Book 13, Chapter 14, recounts the fall of Adam and Eve.

the universe, and this leads us to note at length Milton's conception of Christ as a manifestation of God's power. In the *Treatise on Christian Doctrine*, Milton thus reasons:

If man fell through his own free will, he also may be redeemed through the choice of his own free will to accept the salvation offered in Christ. Beneath the religious tenets that Milton next discusses, there lies a careful psychological analysis of the human soul. What is the process of salvation? Christ as the epic hero comes to free man from his captivity to the malign forces of evil. The contest is a spiritual battle. Man's foe is now within him, how can the evil spirit be cast out? It is evident that man must first desire for himself alliance with the forces of good and put himself in communication with the leader of the hosts of heaven. Nothing then can prevent his immediate rescue; although he cannot be spared the unpleasant consequences of his former failure to be armed against the foes of heaven. Like the Red Cross Knight freed from the dungeon of Orgoglio, he may have lost for a time his pristine courage and beauty; but in the house of holiness his spiritual power will come again.

Milton reasons that Christ's salvation has two phases, which he names, humiliation and exaltation. Christ as a manifestation of God stooped from high heaven to rescue man and to perfect the spiritual victory and He hesitated not to meet the humiliation of death upon the cross, but His death released Him from the need of further humiliation and He ascended to God's right hand amid the triumphant chants of the angels. But brighter than the glory of the welcome in heaven, was the consciousness that man had learned through Christ, once for all, how to defeat Satan and his emissaries, and how to free himself when temporarily made captive. This achievement constitutes Christ's exaltation and this kind of triumph is the basis of the difference between the Christian and the classic epic. The death of the hero may look like failure, but it may be his highest guerdon of success.

Milton states that there are not only thus the two steps in Christ's saving of man, but man must likewise traverse these two steps of humiliation and of exaltation in accepting the offer of salvation. There must be humiliation; for erring man must humble himself before the higher power and acknowledge his need of help.

By this surrender of his pride may come his exaltation through being made participant in Christ's triumph over death and sin and a sharer in Christ's glorious entrance into life eternal, amid the rejoicing of all the heavenly hosts. In this sense, Adam becomes a hero and triumphs over Satan.

But there remains the question of how man may make this alliance with Chirst's his rescuing hero. The humbling of himself to beg for help divine requires from him repentance and faith. Through these experiences, his vision is purified and he regains spiritual perception of good and of evil. By his fall Adam lost innocence; but by repentance he is led through the strength of his hero Christ to a knowledge of righteousness, and he is still heir to a place higher than the angels.

Nor is there any respect of persons in the democracy of the armies of the Lord. Salvation is offered to all men, Milton asserts boldly, and therefore rejection of divine grace is of voluntary choice. Satan is thus defeated in his plan of corrupting all men in Adam; for every man may fall of his own free will, and every man may accept salvation of his own free will. To the strong in faith and heart the spiritual victory is secure; but there is no promise of material success; Christ died on the cross; other heroes in his army may die in the battle that they win.

Even without the names of Christ or of Adam the underlying truths here involved remain reasonable to the general evolution of human thought. They lie deeper than the boundaries of nations, of religions, or of creeds, deep in the general heart of man. These are the theories that lie at the basis of *Paradise Lost*. The train of thought of the *Treatise on Christian Doctrine* thus brings us to the full epic background of life's mystery, and the poetical conceptions, created by Milton's imagination to present the background, are dependent upon the epic method. On the *Treatise on Christian Doctrine* alone may be based the explanation of the fact that the fall of man could find its permanent art expression only in the form of the Christian epic of *Paradise Lost*.

Nor is this all—from a wider examination of Milton's literary work there is discoverable a strong epic bent in Milton's type of mind which reinforced his choice of the epic form for *Paradise Lost*. Indeed closely allied with Milton's conception of evil was his theory of beauty; for Milton was a Platonist in his conception of beauty as divine.

Milton loved beauty as divine and his own words show how he sought the vision of its loveliness, as Arthur's knights pursued the quest of the Holy Grail. Milton says, " Never did Ceres seek with half so much labour Proserpina, as I pursue this same idea of beauty, as some most admirable object, through all the forms and forces of things, for the gods have many forms."[1]

Ideal beauty, like Proserpina, is lost and has become a quest. What is the explanation of its loss? The answer that Milton, the poet, brings, is that evil is the cause and that originated in the world from a bad choice of a free will. In the first episode in *Paradise Lost*, Lucifer, the angel of light, the most beautiful spirit in heaven, by an evil choice, became the prince of darkness, hideous to look upon, the father of sin and death. In the second episode is depicted the idyll of Adam and Eve, happy in their garden of wondrous beauty, until an evil choice destroys all beauty, and expels them from the garden, as Lucifer was banished from heaven.

[1] Milton, *Epistle VII.* (1637); written to Diodati.

The defect in Adam was a gradual dimming of his perception of God and therefore of celestial beauty. To him Eve looked more desirable than God and her request became more imperative than the Almighty's command; and so Adam fell. After his fall he was near-sighted, and could not see the approach of the flashing wings of the angels from afar. Adam had been dimly conscious of his danger and he had confided his doubts to Raphael. He confessed to the angel that he realised that he might not think clearly, where Eve was involved; and since reason is free will, as Milton affirms in the passage quoted from the *Areopagitica*, there was a defect in Adam's will, and he might fail in the worship of the highest beauty. These are Adam's words of explanation to the angel:

> " . . . yet when I approach
> Her loveliness, so absolute she seems
> And in herself complete, so well to know
> Her own, that what she wills to do or say
> Seems wisest, virtuousest, discreetest, best ;
> All higher Knowledge in her presence falls
> Degraded, Wisdom in discourse with her
> Loses, discountenanc'd, and like Folly shows :
> Authority and Reason on her wait,
> As one intended first, not after made
> Occasionally ; and, to consummate all,
> Greatness of mind and nobleness their seat

> Build in her loveliest, and create an awe
> About her, as a guard angelic plac'd."

Raphael replies:

> " In loving thou dost well; in passion not,
> Wherein true Love consists not : Love refines
> The thoughts, and heart enlarges ; hath his seat
> In Reason and is judicious ; is the scale
> By which to Heavenly Love thou may'st ascend."
> .   .   .   .
> " Be strong, live happy, and love ! but first of all
> Him whom to love is to obey, and keep
> His great command ; take heed lest passion sway
> Thy judgment to do aught, which else free will
> Would not admit ; thine and of all thy sons
> The weal or woe in thee is plac'd ; beware !
> I in thy persevering shall rejoice,
> And all the blest : stand fast ; to stand or fall
> Free in thine own arbitrament it lies ;
> Perfect within, no outward aid require,
> And all temptation to transgress repel."

But Adam does not take the warning of the
angel. Eve is near, God seems afar; and her
loveliness for the time overshadows the radiance of God rather than appears as an expression of celestial beauty. Thus Adam falls.
Still, after the fall, the force of good in Adam
is stronger than the power of evil. He does
not continue to choose evil. He finds no joy
in sin; he mourns his lost perception of divine
beauty, and longs for forgiveness and peace
with God, not so much from fear of punish-

ment, as from a sense of anguish in the loss of righteousness, which means a corresponding loss of perception of spiritual beauty. Ever after the fall, there is a sharp struggle between the forces of evil and of good within him. By painful effort, only, can he return to that happy state,—

> Where love is an unerring light
> And joy its own security.[1]

Beauty is lost by choice, but if one chooses may one regain the priceless boon? and the answer of Milton as philosopher and poet is, "Yes." But the upward path is toilsome. A series of choices marks the upward, as the downward way.

Lucifer, fallen, bereft of his beauty and of his heavenly name, continues to make evil choices. He will never submit to the will of God, through which alone, Milton says, is perfect freedom. The curse upon evil is continuance in evil and, after a time, the loss of power to choose anything but evil.[2] When Satan hurls his defiance at the beams of the sun, hates God's goodness and mercy, and falls into contortions of dark passions on seeing Paradise,

[1] Wordsworth, *Ode to Duty.*
[2] See Shelley, *Prometheus Unbound,* Act I.

we are prepared to hear that his form has lost "all her original brightness": to see him a poor skulking spirit of darkness squatting at the ear of Eve, or starting up at the touch of Ithuriel's spear, with an empty vaunt of his past dignity; for he is no longer recognisable to his former heavenly associates. Nor is Satan unmindful of his degradation, for

> abashed the devil stood,
> And felt how awful goodness is, and saw
> Virtue in her shape how lovely, saw and pined
> His loss.[1]

But the most complete humiliation of Satan came in his hour of seeming triumph over man and God, a triumph that, in Milton's conception of the plot, could be only the darkest defeat; that the curse of evil is continuance in evil is again emphasised. Satan goes back to his assembled followers in hell to receive the applause for his victory, when he discovers that there is no glory for him that does not entail greater ugliness and greater degradation, and he falls headlong, a dragon among his hissing followers.

In this second episode that completes the fable of the epic of *Paradise Lost*, there is

[1] *Paradise Lost*, (Book IV., 846-849.)

hope: Adam is not given over to Satan any more than was Job after his contest, nor Faust after his ordeal. Satan, the spirit of negation, in *Paradise Lost*, could not satisfy the human heart; this is as much the conclusion of Milton as of Goethe. The possibility of triumph offered to Adam through Christ casts in the east a glow of beauty, as Adam and Eve leave their ruined Paradise.

Some natural tears they dropp'd, but wip'd them soon ;
The world was all before them, where to choose
Their place of rest, and Providence their guide.
They, hand in hand, with wandering steps and slow,
Through Eden took their solitary way.[1]

With Michael's report of the promise of the incarnation of Christ as a Son of man and the complete vanquishing of Satan, the epic ends. Evil, loss of beauty came into the world by Satan through successfully tempting the free will of man; Satan was not triumphant, but condemned by his own wickedness to deep degradation. Evil may be driven out by Christ, whose grace restores the beauty; but Christ's passion is another plot, just as Æneas's peaceful reign in Latium is another episode and a sequel to the *Æneid;* but we have been led at

[1] *Paradise Lost*, (Book XII., end.)

the end of *Paradise Lost* to the promise of the return of man to his ideal, and nothing stands able to defeat the prosperous issue.

Upon these fundamental principles, Milton reared his thoughts shaped by emotion and imagination into literary beauty. Adam could not appeal to the imagination of Milton as an individual man, hated and entrapped by Satan, but as the human race loved and favoured by God: thus falling through evil, but lifted by divine strength.

The trend of the changes from plot to plot in the four drafts reveals the nature of the difficulties that beset Milton, at the outset, in his attempt to cast this theme into the mould of a tragedy. The vastness of the background, all heaven and earth and hell, demands the epic grandeur; the characters of God, of the Messiah and of the good angels resisting the attacks of Satan and his hordes of fallen angels, of Adam and Eve as types of the human race; all this requires the devices of the epic and can be presented by fragments only in a tragedy. The whole train of thought is interdependent, no part can be adequately presented without the whole, and the whole is essentially a Christian epic. While there may be sub-plots in tragedies there could not be unity brought out of two such important interrelated plots without the deliberation of the method of a novel or of an epic. As in the *Odyssey*, the triumphs of Odysseus over obstacles before he reaches Ithaca, and the trials that he victoriously meets at home, form the two great divisions of the unified epic theme; as also in the *Æneid* the obstacles successfully met by Æneas before he reaches Latium and the difficulties that he overcomes in Italy until he stands the triumphant man of destiny, who by the will of the gods shall found the Roman Empire; so in *Paradise Lost*, the two plots, the fall of Lucifer and the fall of man, complete the epic unity. The origin of evil in Lucifer and in Adam, and the nature of Christ's triumph over evil in the fields of heaven and on earth is the epic theme; beyond the tenets of any one religion reigns the ideal of God conquering evil.

Milton has shown us his experiments in the form of tragedy, he has shown us clearly his underlying train of reasoning that must be clothed in *Paradise Lost*, and he has given, in no doubtful words, his own conclusion that man's fall was a part of an epic whole " not less but more heroic than the effects of Achilles' wrath."[1] To the mind following closely Milton's train of thought the conclusion must seem not only reasonable but inevitable, and *Paradise Lost* again illustrates the dictum of Coleridge, "No art permanently pleases that does not bear in itself the reason for its own form." We must next examine in detail those often hitherto quoted drafts of a tragedy upon Adam's loss of Paradise.

[1] *Paradise Lost*, Book IX., 1-50.

IV

MILTON'S DRAFTS FOR A TRAGEDY

IN the preceding essays, there have been frequent references to Milton's own drafts for
a tragedy upon Adam's fall and we must now
no longer delay the examination of these very
significant early plans for his life work.
What were Milton's reasons for his change of
plan? We shall note the indications that his
maturer thought convinced him that the theme
demanded epic treatment.

During the years of deliberate and stately
preparation for writing *Paradise Lost*, Milton's
aspirations for his great life work several
times found expression. There are two of his
early utterances that are particularly interesting and predict the donning of " higher
buskins " than could be assumed by most
poets. His great poem was to be

a work not to be raised from the heat of youth, . . .
nor to be obtained from convocation of Dame Memory
and her siren daughters, but by devout prayer to that
eternal spirit who can enrich with all utterance and

knowledge, and sends out his seraphin with the hallowed fire of his altar, to touch and to purify the lips of whom he pleases.[1]

There is here a suggestion of the bourgeoning of forces that he did not yet himself fully comprehend.

As early as his thirty-first year, there are proofs that he had considered fitting themes for his great work, but his plans were not yet clear. In *Epitaphium Damonis*, that, after his return from Italy, about 1639, he wrote upon the death of his friend, Charles Diodati, there occurs this passage,—Milton had been in the habit of confiding in this friend and he falls very naturally into his accustomed confidential strain,—

. . . but I, too—'t is eleven nights and a day now since I—ah, I know what large strain my pipe was trying to sound—I was accustoming my lips to new reeds perhaps: suddenly the fastening burst; the reeds flew asunder, unable to endure longer the grave sounds to which I racked them. I know not—perhaps I am over bold; still, I will tell about it. Give way my pastoral song, to a sterner theme.

Go to your folds unfed, my lambs; your master is troubled. I am about to sing of the Trojan ships that passed along our Kentish coast, and the old realm of Imogene, Brut's wife, and the ancient chiefs Brennus

---

[1] Preface to second part of *The Reason of Church Government urged against Prelaty* (1641).

and Arviragus and Belinus, and the colonists who settled in Armorica under British laws.   Then I shall tell of
Igraine, pregnant with Arthur through the fatal wiz-
ardry of Merlin, who gave to Uther Pendragon the face
and the armor of her husband Gorlois.   Oh then, if life
is granted me, thou, my shepherd-pipe, shalt hang neglected on the gnarled pine, or be changed to shrill forth
the strains of my native land, and the cry of Britons in
battle.   Native strains do I say?   Yea, one man cannot
hope to accomplish all things.   It will be sufficient reward and honour for me, even though I remain for ever
unknown and inglorious among the other nations of the
world, if only blond-haired Ouse shall read me and he
who drinks of Alan Water, and the whirling Humber,
and the woods of Trent; above all, if my Thames shall
sing my songs, and Tamur mineral-stained and the far-
off wave-beaten Orkneys.[1]

The themes of the Trojans cruising around
the southern headlands of Britain, the early le-
gends of England, of Arthur, Uther's son, were
abandoned and were not even mentioned by
Milton in the list of one hundred subjects, written as early as 1641 probably, preserved in
Poemata Miltoni Manuscripta, in the library
of Trinity College, Cambridge.   Indeed the
thirty-three subjects for " British Tragedies,"
in this manuscript, do not touch upon a period
so early as that of Arthur, but range from
the early fifth to the eleventh century.

The sixty-one themes from the Bible selected

[1] W. V. Moody's translation.

for a tragedy reveal Milton's agreement with the ideals of Famianus Strada. In his fifth *Prolusion*, which Milton undoubtedly knew, this celebrated Jesuit professor presents his eloquent plea for pure and noble poetry upon subjects of universal interest, from the Bible, the won-ders of creation, and the spiritual life of man. Milton has chosen eight topics from the New Testament centring about Christ and John the Baptist; and fifty-three from the Old Testa-ment. In early Jewish history, Abram and Isaac receive more or less extended mention; but the plans in the entire list of one hundred subjects that reveal the most care and interest are the four upon the subject of the fall of man or of the loss of Paradise.

Do these drafts indicate any latent tendency in Milton, as early as this, to write an epic rather than a tragedy upon man's fall? The first draft for a tragedy upon Adam consists simply of a list of characters, as follows:

The Persons: Michael; Heavenly Love; Chorus of Angels; Lucifer; Adam, Eve, with the Serpent; Con-science; Death; Labour, Sickness, Discontent, Ignor-ance, with others, Mutes; Faith, Hope, Charity.

But Milton was discontented with this plan,

for the draft was erased and written parallel
with it was the second as follows:

The Persons: Michael or Moses (Moses held as prefer-
able): Justice; Mercy, Wisdom; Heavenly Love; The
Evening Star, Hesperus; Chorus of Angels; Lucifer,
Adam; Eve; Conscience; Labour, Sickness, Discontent,
Ignorance, Fear, Death; Mutes; Faith; Hope; Charity.

The second plan was also erased, but the third
is left standing in the manuscript, as follows:

Paradise Lost, The Persons:—Moses προλογίζει re-
counting how he assumed his true body, that it corrupts
not, because of his [being] with God in the Mount;
declares the like of Enoch and Eliah, besides the purity
of the place that certain pure winds, dews, and clouds
preserve it from corruption ; whence exhorts to the sight
of God; tells they cannot see Adam in the state of innocence, by reason of their sin.—Act I: Justice, Mercy,
Wisdom, debating what should become of man if he fell;
Chorus of Angels sing a hymn of the Creation.—Act II :
Heavenly Love ; Evening Star ; Chorus sing the Marriage
Song, and describe Paradise.—Act III : Lucifer, contriv-
ing Adam's ruin ; Chorus fears for Adam and relates
Lucifer's rebellion and fall.—Act IV: Adam, Eve, fallen;
Conscience cites them to God's examination ; Chorus
bewails and tells them the good Adam hath lost.—Act V :
Adam and Eve, driven out of Paradise, presented by an
angel with Labour, Grief, Hatred, Envy, War, Famine,
Pestilence, Sickness, Discontent, Ignorance, Fear,
Mutes, to whom he gives their names ; likewise Winter,
Heat, Tempest, etc. : Death entered into the World ;
Faith, Hope, Charity comfort him and instruct him ;
Chorus briefly concludes.

The fourth draft bears the title, *Adam Un-*

paradised. Although the scheme is not divided the plan naturally falls into five acts, as may be seen:

Adam Unparadised: The Angel Gabriel, either descending or entering,—showing, since this globe was created, his frequency as much on Earth as in Heaven—describes Paradise, next the Chorus, showing the reason of his coming—to keep watch, after Lucifer's rebellion, by command from God ; and withal expressing his desire to see and know more concerning this excellent new creature, Man. The Angel Gabriel, as by his name signifying a Prince of Power, tracing Paradise with a more free office, passes by the station of the Chorus, and, desired by them, relates what he knew of Man, as the creation of Eve, with their love and marriage.—After this, Lucifer appears after his overthrow, bemoans himself, seeks revenge on Man. The Chorus prepare resistance at his first approach. At last, after discourse of enmity on either side, he departs ; whereat the Chorus sings of the battle and victory in Heaven against him and his accomplices, as before, after the first Act was sung a hymn of the Creation.—Here again may appear Lucifer, relating and insulting in what he had done to the destruction of Man. Man next and Eve, having by this time been seduced by the Serpent, appear confusedly, covered with leaves, Conscience, in a shape, accuses him, Justice cites him to the place whither Jehovah called for him. In the meanwhile, the Chorus entertains the stage, and is informed by some Angel the manner of his Fall.—Here the Chorus bewails Adam's fall. Adam then, and Eve, return and accuse one another ; but especially Adam lays the blame to his wife—is stubborn in his offence. Justice appears, reasons with him, convinces him. The Chorus admonisheth Adam, and bids him beware by Lucifer's example of impenitence.—The Angel is sent to banish them out of Paradise ; but, before, causes to pass before his eyes, in shapes, a masque of all the evils of this life and world. He is humbled, relents, despairs. At last appears Mercy, comforts him, promises the Messiah ; then calls in Faith, Hope, and Charity ; instructs him. He repents, gives God the glory, submits to his penalty. The Chorus briefly concludes. Compare this with the former Draft.

In a little space below on the same page with the first three drafts of *Paradise Lost*, is jotted under the heading, " Other tragedies," simply the words "Adam in Banishment." Whatever may have been Milton's intention, the fifth scheme did not find fuller expression than the noting of a title used later by Vondel, for his tragedy, *Adam in Ballingschap*.

The examination of these four drafts for a tragedy written some fifteen years before the epic, *Paradise Lost*, sanctions certain conclusions.   It is apparent that Milton was not satisfied with his plans for a tragedy, upon a theme that he afterwards stated thus,—

> Of man's first disobedience and the fruit
> Of that forbidden tree, whose mortal taste
> Brought death into the world and all our woe,
> With loss of Eden, till one greater Man
> Restore us and regain the blissful seat,
> Sing heavenly Muse.[1]

But toward what goal does the poet seem to

[1] *Paradise Lost* , Book I, 1–6.

be striving, as he discards one draft after another and, at length, reaches a balance of
doubt between the last two schemes? He seeks
a better portrayal of the two plots,—warfare
against God in heaven and against God on
earth. He is perplexed by the need of an imaginative presentation of truths that are involved in doctrines, creeds, and philosophy.
There is apparent a latent realisation of the
difficulties entailed by an attempt to cast his
theme into the form of tragedy. With his
fine taste, he avoids the presenting of the state
of innocence, and the sudden lapse into evil of
a hitherto sinless hero; at the same time, he
throws away the dramatic opportunity of the
scene of the temptation. He is conscious of
the need of a clearer portrayal of the motive,
of the characters, of the dramatic situation
and action. The variations are toward the
epic rather than to perfect a tragedy, and it
was inevitable that these changes should continue until the double plot, of the fall of Lucifer and the fall of man, should emerge as the
twofold episode of a well constructed epic;
until the philosophical doctrines should be
clothed in the imaginative dress of the episode
and the metaphor; until the colourless stud-

ies of Satan and of Eve should stand forth strongly drawn personalities through the deliberation of the epic method; and the temptation scene should become the vivid centre of the dramatic action in the epic of *Paradise Lost*.

The characters are indeed few in Milton's first attempt to clothe artistically his difficult theme in a tragedy. Adam and Eve are the only persons of any degree of concreteness. Michael and the chorus of angels represent the forces of heaven, and Lucifer and the Serpent, the forces of hell. Besides these opposing forces, there are ten purely allegorical conceptions, seven of whom are mutes to appear in a tableau, or in a pantomime. This vague scheme, with its preponderance of allegory, must have been a foundation for a morality play with some characteristics of the mask. But Milton's imagination was not eventually attracted by allegory, as the epic, *Paradise Lost* strikingly shows. There is an effort in this first plan, to attain two, at first sight, conflicting ideals, the imaginative concreteness of a tragedy, and the dignified aloofness to be sought in portraying the spiritual conceptions common in an epic. The reconciliation he

later decided could be made successfully in the
epic, but as yet Milton was to struggle further
with this philosophical and artistic problem.

Milton's reflection upon his difficulties found
expression in the type of changes in the second draft. His subject is too intangible: he
feels the need of an authorised narrator: this
is an epic tendency. To this end, as a substi-
tute for Michael, he suggests Moses and holds
this change as preferable. No reason for this
idea can be asserted from the reading of the
second draft alone, but the foreshadowings here
find clearer outline in the third plan for a
tragedy. Erring man cannot see Adam and
Eve in their state of innocence, therefore Moses,
who has been translated, is introduced as an
interpreter between sinful man and the purified world of the spirit, that he may relate what
cannot be shown visually upon the stage, nor
be chanted by the already overburdened chorus.
It is very reasonable to suppose that Milton had seen the obscure seventeenth-century
prose Morality of Lancetta and that his attention had been arrested by the opening
words,—" One night, I dreamt that Moses explained to me the mystery almost in these
words." The step from Moses as interpreter

is not far to " Sing Heavenly Muse," and we then recognise a device of the epic.[1]

In the second draft, the grotesque figure of the Serpent is dropped from the cast of characters, and more machinery is added to the heavenly forces. To the abstractions are joined the divine attributes, Justice, Mercy, and Wisdom, and the poetical conception of the Evening Star, or Hesperus. The allegorical elements remain unfused but the growth is away from the morality toward the oratorio, and an epical tendency is here unmistakable, a tendency hampered by the concreteness and the brevity of a tragedy.

The trend of the rejected second draft is more fully explained in the third plan. The prologue prepares the reader for the revelation that Adam and Eve shall appear only after their fall, therefore the main action of the tragedy is reported rather than presented on the stage by the chief agents in the transaction. Milton's artistic insight later grew clearer and it led him to conclude that he lost the deeply dramatic possibilities of his theme, through an attempt to cast into the form of

[1] See in *Poetical Works of John Milton*, J. H. Todd, 4th Edition, Volume 1, Introduction.

tragedy what were really the dramatic scenes
of a larger epic plan.

A varied difficulty arose from remanding the
important scene of the temptation to the report of a messenger or an interpreter. How
were the personalities of Adam and Eve to be
portrayed? What was the motive for their
fall? How did Lucifer gain influence over
them? Why does not the issue prove that the
prize was to the stronger? What proof is there,
from the standpoint of the story, that Satan
was properly resisted? Was he stronger
than God? If not, has the theme been adequately developed?

There are proofs that while he was writing
the second and third drafts these problems were
in the mind of Milton, but as yet not altogether
solved. Act I of the third draft, which is
purely allegorical, is of importance in explaining man's free will, his ability to stand or fall,
and his relation to God's justice and mercy.
This act contains premonitions of a tragic import and the concluding song of creation con-
veys news that Adam now exists; the forces of
good and evil are ready for action.

In the second act, the art promises to be
purely lyrical with the freshness of the bird

notes in *Siegfried* or the song of the shepherd in *Tannhäuser*. Innocence, beauty, joy are here the predominating notes. The Evening Star and Heavenly Love sing and the chorus takes up the theme of the marriage of Adam and Eve and of the joys of Eden. All heaven is interested and we must couple hell, as the third act reveals, when Lucifer enters, " contriving Adam's ruin." The scope is epical; it is too vast a canvas for a tragedy.

In the fourth act and throughout the draft, Adam lacks motive and clear-cut characterisation; Eve suffers even more, for she is simply a lay figure. There is need of the episodes possible in a novel or in an epic for deliberate portrayal of character. The premonitions of man's fall are given by the chorus in a song, a train of thought that Milton afterwards recast into the discussions in heaven of the plans to rescue man, and into the conversation in Eden of Raphael and Adam in the fifth and sixth books of *Paradise Lost:* thus did Milton later strive to justify the ways of God to man! Moreover by the brevity of the tragedy the magnificent figure of Lucifer is dwarfed, for we do not see him the " erectest spirit " of heaven astonishing all by his majestic beauty.

His dignity, pride, rebellion, and fall are reported by the chorus, too great a task as Milton afterwards decided, when he devoted all the deliberation and all the wealth of epic device to his masterly portrayal of Satan in *Paradise Lost*. Even now, when writing this third draft, he must have felt the impossibility of success in a tragedy that attempted to portray the heroic figure of God's protagonist.

The spectacular pageant displayed in the fifth act of the evil within and without, " both in their life and in the world," is marshalled by an angel and it is Adam's part to stand bravely his ground, face the grim spectres, and name them with an understanding of their meaning, though he shuddered at their menace to the coming generations of man. When he has endured this ordeal, Faith, Hope, and Charity minister unto him and the tragedy ends with a chastened calm over all. These evils that Adam is compelled to name are, in the fourth draft, caused to pass before his grief-dimmed eyes, " in shapes, a masque of all the evils of this life and world "; this treatment of the inevitable consequences of sin is nearer to that vision that Adam is shown by Michael in the eleventh and twelfth books of *Paradise Lost*, which in artistic method may show the influence of Camoens in the tenth book of the *Lusiad* as well as of Virgil in the sixth and eighth books of the *Æneid*.

The predominating characteristics of this third draft are more lyrical and epical than truly tragic in the artistic, literary sense. There is an effort, evident throughout, to reduce a complex plot to simplicity. In this respect, Milton's work is in sharp contrast to Andreini's spectacular tragedy, *L'Adamo*. There is noticeable in this third draft of Milton's tragedy a classical reserve and dignity and aloofness from realism. The effect is of a stately and impressive spectacle which suggests a musical setting of a religious type such as the *Parsifal* of Wagner, or to be rendered without spectacle as the *Creation* of Handel, or, better, to be incorporated in a symphony of Beethoven.

The fourth draft is the best of the plans made by Milton for a tragedy upon man's fall. There is a strengthening of the resistance of the good and the evil forces from the fact that Moses disappears from the plan altogether and prominence is given to Gabriel, who pervades the scenes. "By command from God," he not only keeps watch, " after Lucifer's rebellion," but on his own account he feels a deep personal interest in " the excellent new creature, Man."

Lucifer is better drawn in this fourth draft than in the other schemes for a tragedy sketched by Milton. His exultation over man's fall in the third act makes his antagonism to God stand out more glaringly. Adam and Eve are more vividly portrayed in the fourth act of this scheme than in any of the other plans, and the consequences of their fall are more realistically given. When Adam lays the blame for his loss of innocence upon Eve, Justice appears, reasons with him, and induces him to be gentle and fair-minded.

The conclusion is also better rounded in the fourth draft than in Milton's other plans for a tragedy. Mercy comes hand in hand with Justice; she comforts Adam and brings him promise of the Messiah, and thus strikes the note of the Christian epic. Adam is ready to go forth with Faith, Hope, and Charity to conquer evil, and in this courageous resolve lies the triumph of the good.

The lines of the tragedy in the fourth draft are more strictly drawn on the classic model, as may be seen in the relation of the actors to the chorus, not only in the case of Gabriel's explanation of the affairs of Eden in response to the inquiries of the chorus but in the retorts of Lucifer and in the answering notes of resistance to evil in the chorus. But Milton is not yet satisfied with his plan for *Paradise Lost*, or *Adam Unparadised*, the process of comparison, of reconstruction is still to go forward. It is probable that as the possibilities of the theme opened up more fully before him, he realised that only by meditation upon the philosophical basis of evil, upon the theories of literary art involved in the world's great masterpieces, upon the examples of great masters in tragedy and in the epic, could he build a firm foundation for his great life work. This he set himself to accomplish and, despite the long interruption of affairs of state and the hampering of his work by failing eyesight, he pressed steadily on to the goal of his great epic, " a work not of the heat of youth."

At least twice early in his career his pipe sounded " strains of an unknown strength," once in the impassioned burst of defiance [1] Satan hurled at the sun, and again in the

---

[1] Address to the Sun, 1642.

lament of Adam and Eve over their loss of Paradise.[1] These early passages, written some twenty years before the completion of the great epic.[2] of which they were the harbingers, reveal the two lines of development upon which he laboured:

He must depict the realm of the infinite, pressing upon the finite world, and the effect of evil choices upon two natures,—one defiant, impenitent, exultant, the other not " out of love with goodness " and bowed with human grief. He must attempt to solve the epical problem of God's relation to Satan and man and the problem both epical and dramatic of the characterisations of Satan, magnificent, individualistic, superhuman, and of the personalities of Adam and Eve as erring and human, but longing after God,—definite and at the same time universal types. The problem that confronted him, and not a chance quotation from Lancetta, surely inspired Milton to cast his discarded drafts into the heroic mould—but Lancetta's words have interest:

[1] Adam's and Eve's lament over loss of Paradise, near 1642.

[2] *Paradise Lost* begun according to Aubrey, 1658 ; finished, 1665. First edition, 1667.

God reveals himself to man by the intervention of reason and this infallibly ordains that reason, while she supports her sovereignty over the sensual inclination in Man, and preserves the apple of his heart from licentious appetites, in reward of his just obedience, transforms the world into Paradise.—If this were true, assuredly I might form an heroic poem worthy of demigods.

To this labour of Hercules Milton turned his hand.

V

OTHER VERSIONS OF MAN'S FALL

THE roots of Milton's philosophical ideas
upon the origin of evil are to be found in
the Bible, St. Augustine, and Plato, but the artistic structure raised upon those ideas owes
its existence not only to a latent necessity of
the theme, and not only as it appealed to Milton's peculiar cast of mind, but it also owes its
origin to a growth in his ideal of literary art.
Was there any aid for Milton in the preceding
literature upon Adam's fall?

As all of the world's great art contains a
note of discord from the warfare of good and
evil, or from an effort to resolve this strife into
harmony, the possible sources of Milton's artistic notions upon the conflict of Satan with
God are too broadly disseminated to be ex-
haustively traced, any more than one could
separate an Alpine torrent into the drops of
rain or of melting snowflake. At the outset of
such an investigation it must also be borne in

mind that Milton was one of the most learned men of his age, and of no single fact then available can we say with certainty "This Milton did not know." Although there are reasons for thinking that Milton was more interested in the ancient classics than in mediæval literature, he was certainly familiar with works of the middle ages, of the renaissance, of the preceding and of contemporary literature.

The field of interest for a student of Milton's *Paradise Lost* very naturally narrows itself into an attempt to comprehend the complete art product that Milton strove to perfect in *Paradise Lost*, and the details are of importance only in their relation to the whole work. There is interest in the pieces of literary art that might incite Milton to a quest for a fitting form: some of these works appear to be sources, others parallels and contrasts; some of these works might inspire him to effort by their own conspicuous lack of achievement, by their excellencies in fragments inharmoniously set, or as works of dignity and beauty on the same theme, or an allied theme, or on even a contrasting theme, where the problem of the artificer might be, at a given point, similar.

Such a study reveals that Milton's literary

tastes were individual. He grasped, after
years of thought, a conception of the art possibilities of the theme of Paradise Lost: he pro-
ceeded to elaborate this with every device that
he could invent: he borrowed here a scene, there
an episode or minor detail: an independent
thinker as he was, he brought himself into
harmony in the main, not with rules, but with
the underlying principles of Aristotle: he used
electively the great classics and recast some
of their beauty into his own original mould but
it was all changed; for there was little that he
touched that he did not Miltonise into something strange and new, with something of
sterner, loftier beauty than it had known
before.

The mythological fragments, the details of
cosmogony, and the folk tales upon man's fall
were crude and inartistic at best. The works of
theologians and the semi-popular treatises of the
church fathers were, in the main, no more than
raw material for future thought, that might in
turn become a basis of art. The process of
evolution was long and varied before clear-cut
characterisation and dramatic fire vivified the
story and it rose into the domain of art:
genius shed its light over the possibilities of

9

the theme and heightened it to the majesty of beauty and deepened it to pathos. The poet's voice wakened the echoes of universal human experience, and the world saw the consummation of the theme in *Paradise Lost*.

The poetical version of *Genesis*, long attributed to Juvencus, in the early part of the fourth century, but now believed to be the work of Cyprianus, attained no conception of the dramatic possibilities of the scene of the temptation and the fall. The poet was far more interested in nicely turned Virgilian lines, in pretty conceits, than he was in creating a work that would adequately clothe an important theme.

There is more literary art form in the works of Prudentius, a later fourth-century clerical writer. His work however is not at all important for any appreciation that he shows of the possibility of the theme of man's fall, which he has treated rather weakly in the *Dittochœon*, but for his literary sense in the treatment of the general theme of the contest of good and evil.

In the *Hamartigenia*, he discusses the origin of evil and powerfully depicts Satan under the influence of his ruling passion, that is, jealousy of the supremacy of God. Of more importance than this work is his *Psychomachia*. Prudentius here portrays, in an allegory with lyrical and epical characteristics, the combat of the soul with the forces of Satan. One by one the soul overcomes his foes through faith in Christ, and after the last victory, Peace and Faith advise the founding to the glory of Jesus Christ a temple, with all the beauties of Jerusalem the golden. In the conclusion of his epic Prudentius looks forward hopefully to the day when the good shall triumph over the evil in all hearts,—a promise of a regaining of Paradise. Prudentius is important in the development of the theme of the contest of evil with good, from the fact that the literary sense predominates in his work over the philosophical or the didactic aim, and he attempts not only to master a literary style, but to create an artistic whole.

For the same reason, there is interest in a later church father and poet, St. Avitus, whose Latin narrative poem, *De Mosaicæ Historiæ Gestis, Libri Quinque*, is of the first quarter of the sixth century. In the first book, *De initio mundi*, Avitus describes with poetical feeling the beauty of God's handiwork in creation. In the second book, entitled, *De originale peccato*, the narration grows in dramatic force. Satan, already fallen, is envious of the joys of man and declares that if he is doomed to everlasting fire, Adam and Eve must come to share the pain with him. He disguises himself as a snake and approaches Eve, whom he discovers alone. He without delay asks Eve to eat the apple from the forbidden tree and assures her that she is only denied this treat through the jealousy of God: for God fears that she, on tasting the fruit, will become a goddess. Eve is very easily won over by Satan and takes the fruit: at once the earth trembles, the snake glides away, and Adam returns. Eve urges him to eat the apple, for she insists that she feels greatly benefited and she incites him to be as courageous as she is.

Adam yields with very little resistance, and sadness falls upon them in their loss of innocence. In the third book, *De sententia Dei*, God comes to judge Adam and Eve, which book is a simple expansion into poetry of the Bible account of the expulsion from the garden after God's condemnation of man's sin.

There is in the poem of Avitus, in outline, material for the future work of *Paradise Lost*, but the possibilities of the twofold plot are not realised; for the warfare of good and evil is not presented as continuous, and from the lack of deliberation in the art, the motive for the fall is not adequately presented, and the character-isations of Satan and Eve are not complete.

As attractive as the poem of St. Avitus is in both its style and movement, it is evident that in the subordination of the plots and in clear characterisation it is surpassed by the work of a clerical writer of the seventh century. De-spite the fact that controversy has broken about the tenth-century manuscript of this earlier work, and the lines have been asserted to be not of uniform date nor of one authorship, the scene of the temptation has not been disproved to be the work of Cædmon. Beda states that Cædmon was ignorant; however, he may have known St. Augustine by tradition and he cer-tainly knew the Bible. In the rhymed para-phrase of Genesis there is poetical skill and imagination of no ordinary quality. The au-thor at once grasps the conception of the two interwoven plots, the fall of Lucifer, and the fall of man; he also seizes upon the dramatic possibilities of the scene of the temptation and makes an attempt to portray both motive and personality in his epical narrative.

The paraphrase of Genesis opens with the

insolence of the chief of the angels, who, lost in admiration of himself, believed that he had as many followers as God, and sought to set up a rival kingdom in the north of heaven. He with his followers, was banished to the misery of perpetual night, enhanced by intense heat and cold in hell. Thus his vaunt was empty, his hopes shattered, his beauty turned to ugliness. God now created the world and the earth and the garden of Eden and placed therein man whose race should replenish the empty halls of heaven. In a beautiful Paradise Adam and Eve lived with no evil desire and rejoiced in their love for God. They appreciated the dignity of their inheritance, for to them and to their children was given dominion over the land and the sea.

Meanwhile the banished angel, who of angels was once the brightest and fairest, now the king of hell and called Satan,[1] has other plans for Adam and he addresses his followers upon the subject. He confides in them that he finds his present abode too narrow and that he longs for a larger kingdom. He declares that they have been treated unfairly; for God has

[1] Notice agreement with St. Augustine in this distinction between the names, Lucifer and Satan.

no right to strike them down and to plan to re-people heaven with the sons of men, made of the dust of the earth. Satan longs for the power of his hands to right matters, but he is firmly chained and cannot free himself. It is useless, he declares, for the fallen angels to hope to re-enter heaven, but a plot may be devised to extend hell's sway into the earth if only he may corrupt Adam in his will. "We may," he suggests, "turn the children of men away from the celestial kingdom, and cause them to incur God's wrath, so that he will cast them down to be our vassals here in hell." Satan offers rich gifts to the daring one who shall pass through all barriers and reach Paradise to accomplish the fall of man.

The bold emissary of Satan reaches the earthly Paradise, enters a serpent, and twines himself about "the tree of death," and here in the temptation scene is given the interaction of the two plots, the fall of Lucifer, and the fall of Adam. The peculiarities of the story are the following:

1. He opens a conversation with Adam, not with Eve; and he shows no anxiety to find one alone, but attacks them together.

2. He boldly declares himself a messenger

of God sent to bring a divine command to eat of the fruit of the tree of knowledge, for increase in strength and in understanding. Adam firmly asserts his disbelief that God has sent any such command for three reasons:

(a) It is opposed to the former express injunction of God.

(b) The bearer does not look like any of God's messengers, and may have evil designs.

(c) God is not dependent upon a messenger: he can at will communicate directly with Adam.

3. The serpent now turns angrily to the woman and warns her of the wrath of God and the peril to her husband and family, if a heavenly messenger is sent away so churlishly. He advises her to use her influence to ward off this punishment. He suggests that perhaps she might set her husband a good example by eating the fruit, and she could then report to him how beneficial it is.

4. Eve, persuaded that it is her duty, eats and is cheated by such false visions that she is led to regard the fruit as very desirable. She urges Adam to hasten to obey God's messenger and to avert the wrath of God for his rudeness to his servant. She counsels prompt

obedience, " for," she says, " you know that we are dependent upon the angels." [1]

This deceiving of Eve into sin is a weak point philosophically and artistically in the narration. If Eve really were convinced that the serpent was a divine messenger and that upon her shoulders rested the responsibility of saving her family from the fatal mistake of distrust of God's messenger, she seems worthy of praise rather than of blame. She does not sin from a defect of will, but falls into a misfortune rather than into a sin. This weakness in the narration is far-reaching, for when Eve and the serpent have followed Adam about all day long, and finally, wearied with the contest, he yields and takes the fruit, we are not convinced of an evil motive in either Adam or Eve, and the punishment that follows does not appear as inevitable, as art demands.

The question arises did Cædmon fall into this mistake by the rapidity of his composition, upon the details of which he had not sufficiently reflected; or did he intend to throw emphasis upon direct spiritual perception and to embody the idea that Eve ought to have known both

---

[1] Adam had said that they were not dependent but could speak directly with God.

that this spirit did not look like God's messenger, and that God was not dependent upon a messenger; and therefore the consequence— God's punishment—is justified?

In both *Comus* and *Paradise Lost*, Milton also made important the possession of direct spiritual insight.   One of the sad consequences of the fall, in *Paradise Lost*, is found in the fact that Adam cannot discern Michael's approach.   Before the fall, he discovered Raphael afar.   Milton also discusses the relation of spiritual perception to free will, in the *Treatise on Christian Doctrine*.   If this obligation to retain perception is Cædmon's intention, the proofs lack clearness and become conjectures only, nor should a point so important in the plot be doubtful.

The immediate exaltation that follows broken law is soon succeeded by despair in Adam and Eve.   Shakespeare,[1] and Hawthorne [2] make use of this revulsion from triumph to humiliation for artistic effects, and so also does Milton in his depicting the manner of Eve, when she approaches Adam after her fall in *Paradise Lost*.

[1] *Macbeth:* Lady Macbeth before the knock on the door.

[2] *Marble Faun:* Miriam and Donatello on the death of the friar.

In Cædmon's narration, after the fall immediate discord arises between Adam and Eve. There are recriminations and self-justifications until Eve speaks to Adam with sweetness and dignity and true penitence. Cædmon depicts the penitence of Adam and Eve before God's voice is heard, but Eve shows no genuine penitence in *Adamus Exsul* until God approaches, nor in *L'Adamo*, nor in *Adam in Ballingschap*, nor in *Paradise Lost*. When they are summoned to judgment, Milton represents Adam and Eve as two sad culprits.

> Love was not in their looks, either to God
> Or to each other, but apparent guilt,
> And shame, and perturbation, and despair,
> Anger, and obstinacy, and hate and guile.[1]

Through the force given to the two plots, the work of Cædmon is conspicuously good among the simple narrative versions of the origin of sin, but there is need of a better balance of the celestial machinery in the second plot to make the resistance to evil more complete and to justify the outcome of the scene of the temptation. A more adequate portrayal of the divine interest in man and a clearer characterisation of Eve would dispel

[1] *Paradise Lost* (Book X, 111–114.)

the doubt that now obscures our knowledge of Eve's motives. She seems not fully instructed, and the question may be properly asked, whether on that point heaven has discharged all obligation? Likewise in Cædmon's story on the side of the evil powers there is a loss of force, for Satan delegates the important task of the temptation of man to a messenger; in *Paradise Lost*, the archfiend is eager to execute the plot himself.

Interesting as Cædmon's work is, it is evident that it could not aid Milton very effectively in his task of creating *Paradise Lost*. In so far as it makes, however, a definite artistic appeal, it may inspire the literary artist more than such other cruder clerical versions of the story as may be found in *The Story of Genesis and Exodus*, preserved in manuscripts of not later than the second half of the thirteenth century, or in *Cursor Mundi*, of the fourteenth. The temptation scene in these shows a clerical bias in the treatment of Eve that is not broadly human, and it reveals also no appreciation of the dramatic possibilities of the story.

The non-dramatic versions of man's fall reach a later evolution in such philosophical and didactic treatises as Tasso's *Sette Giornate del Mondo Creato*, in which the freedom of the will is dwelt upon, by which man's dignity is assured, by which also he fell. The temptation is given in the simplest, barest outline and the aim of the work throughout is doctrinal and it is not artistic in any creative sense.

So also in the work of Du Bartas, *Les Deux Premiers Jours de la Seconde Sepmaine*, there is little proof of creative imagination, no artistic grasp upon the dramatic possibility of the theme, and no artistic reserve. Du Bartas is an embroiderer of phrases rather than a constructive artist, and throughout his aim is philosophical and didactic rather than imaginative.

In the part entitled *L'Imposture*, Du Bartas recounts the details of the scene of the temptation and there is one point to be noted that is directly in contrast to Cædmon's method; Satan, when he is about to tempt Eve, decides that it is better to make use of a created body; therefore he tries several animals, as one might try a garment, and decides upon a serpent; for if he appears as an angel of light, he fears that this disguise would diminish man's fault, so Satan neither appears nor talks like an angel of light. There is a gain over Cædmon's method in this particular, but from a dramatic standpoint Du Bartas is inferior to Cædmon nor could he afford Milton aid in the important problem of the structure of *Paradise Lost*.

In Vida's *Christias*, which is a Christian epic, the temptation scene is colourless and non-dramatic. His theme is Christ's passion, not man's fall, and the influence of the work upon Milton's mind was not helpful in the larger problem of construction, but in the smaller details of finish. The influence of the *De Partu Virginis* of Sannazarro can be traced also only in such minor details as the descriptive passage of the flowers that lift their heads to greet the Virgin, as they also in *Paradise Lost* welcome the coming of Eve; the larger problem of the two works is not only different but the method is in strong contrast. So far, then, the help available to Milton from the preceding works of literature upon the contest of God and Satan was rather negative than positive. They might well impress Milton with the conviction that the vivid dramatic scene of the temptation, the towering figure of Satan stooping through defeat to subtlety and guile, the pathos of the lost innocence of Adam and

Eve and of all mankind had not found adequate expression in literary art.

There are however some dramatic versions of Adam's fall and of Satan's contest with God that are both interesting and significant for the light that they throw upon the distinction between the epic and the tragedy discussed in the foregoing essays, and for the influence that they may have had upon Milton's decision to write an epic rather than a tragedy upon the invasion of Eden by evil.

VI

MAN'S FALL IN TRAGEDY

"ADAMUS EXSUL," GROTIUS

AMONG the attempts to write a tragedy upon the fall of man there is one by no less a genius than Hugo Grotius. This "monster of erudition" turned his attention in his youth to the writing of poetry and attained a considerable degree of international fame for his short poems and for his three tragedies. Scaliger, Baudius, Lipsius, Vossius, and Casaubon were among those that praised his poetry, scholars whose praise was not thought to be lightly won. Among the three tragedies published by Grotius, the first was *Adamus Exsul*, printed at Leyden in 1601, when the author was in his nineteenth year. The fact that the author was only nineteen has no important bearing upon the value of the study of *Adamus Exsul*, for so great a prodigy was Grotius that ordinary conclusions are impos-

sible. The tragedy was held worthy of very
respectful attention and of flattering comment
in its day, and the interest in the work at the
present time has not died. The question that
confronts us in our study is not the precocity
of the author, but what are the defects in the
treatment of the theme reasonably to be attributed to his choice of an artistic form unsuited to his subject?

Despite his success, Grotius held a modest
opinion of his own poetical skill. On one occasion he expressed his surprise at the gra-
ciousness of Vondel, in translating the work of
one who wrote verses inferior to his own. On
another occasion in one of his letters Grotius
writes, " *Nos certe carminis gloria nulli non
cedimus.*" [1] Later when his brother William
proposed to collect and publish all of his poetical efforts [2] Grotius gave a reluctant consent,
but insisted that the juvenile tragedy *Adamus
Exsul* should be excluded from the
edition. [3]

As a consequence of this fact, possibly, the
tragedy does not appear in collected editions

[1] Epistle 5.
[2] Edition appeared in 1617; dedicatory letter to Vander-
mile is dated 1616.
[3] See *Vie de Grotius*, Burigny, vol. i, page 42.

of the works [1] of Grotius. The play, however, must have gone through a number of editions, for the only copy available is a London reprint of 1752,[2] from the fifth edition of 1601; that is of the first year of its appearance.

For the seven years between 1747 and 1754 the tragedy of *Adamus Exsul* was dragged into an unenviable publicity through the activities of William Lauder. But the question of Milton's indebtedness to Grotius was long ago a dead issue and hardly needed the offices of Doctor Johnson as chief executioner; for in any case there is no plagiarism " in bettering the borrowed." Our interest to-day is far different; we decide, despite Grotius's dissatisfaction with this work of his youth, that the tragedy is well worth study for itself and that while it was undoubtedly known by Milton, it presents more contrast than likeness to *Paradise Lost*, and our interest in it must be for the light that it may throw upon the treatment of the subject of the fall of man in a tragedy. Some considerations might be

[1] See edition of Holland Society, and see British Museum Catalogue.

[2] See Bibliography at end of this volume.

suggested that seem reasonable explanations
why this tragedy to-day is not better known.
The editions are few and the copies are
rare.

A seventeenth-century tragedy on the Sene-
can model in the Latin tongue is not likely to
be generally read to-day. It is probable, too,
that Lauder's claims that Milton had plagiar-
ised passages from *Adamus Exsul* have thrown
the work into some disrepute, as the *Lucifer*
of Vondel has also suffered from such a comparison with *Paradise Lost*. Fair criticism
should include a consideration of the author's
aim; the purpose of both *Adamus Exsul* and
of *Lucifer* differs from *Paradise Lost;* is
there any mistake in their aim. The consideration of that question alone is my purpose
in the study that here follows of this
play.

The tragedy of *Adamus Exsul*, [1] in five acts
with a chorus, opens with a speech of Satan of
two hundred and four lines about the fall of
the angels, the creation of the world, the
beauty of Eden, and the happy lot of man.

[1] Only translations found are:

1. In Dutch, in collected works of Vondel.

2. In English by F. Barham, mentioned in British
Museum Catalogue. London, 1839. 2d edition, 1847, no
copy found.

Satan shows that he is jealous of man, for he contrasts with Adam's manifold blessings his own hard lot, but he finds particular ground for resentment in the fact that man shall enter heaven. To quote the words of Satan, " Though man may cultivate Eden and aspire to my place in heaven, he shall not have it without war."

" Man despises my attacks in his confident hope of heaven."

" The shame, if I deserted my kingdom to have it given to another."

The archfiend displays not only pride, enduring in his fall, but resentment against God, for his banishment from heaven, and settled enmity against God and man. He has learned only caution by his former defeat. After the announcement of Satan's intention to corrupt innocent man and to set him at variance with God, the act ends with a chorus.

In scene i of the second act Adam talks with a wise and friendly angel very much as Adam in *Paradise Lost* converses with Raphael in the fifth, sixth, and seventh books. The topics discussed are also similar; Adam learns of the wonders of creation, of the cosmogony, of the music of the spheres, of the life of the angels in heaven, and of the conduct of the life of mortals on earth. There is, however, no allusion to Satan, for Adam and Eve are warned only of the subtlety of serpents.[1]

In scene ii, Adam and Eve rejoice in their great love for God and for each other and listen to a chorus of angels.

In Act III, Satan comes to execute his threat against man. He offers to make a bond [2] with Adam against God; by united resistance they may succeed in gaining the control of the heavens and the earth, and with Adam Satan promises to divide the spoils of war; but man unhesitatingly spurns the offer and puts Satan to flight.

Act IV. Thus frustrated, Satan devises a more careful plot for man's overthrow. He will practise all of his wiles upon Eve, and through her accomplish the downfall of Adam. To this end, he assumes the form of a beautiful serpent and approaches Eve whom he finds alone. Eve is amazed at the brilliant colours of the snake and exclaims, " I wonder if he can

[1] Notice that this warning against serpents implies lack of agreement with St. Augustine, Tasso, Du Bartas, in the theory that there is no evil in outward nature.

[2] This suggests bond in Marlowe's *Dr. Faustus*, also bond in Goethe's *Faust*.

speak." By this device, the author prepares our mind for Satan's first words. He marvels at her great beauty and inquires about her opportunities in her life in the garden of Eden. She expresses her gratitude for all the blessings that she and Adam enjoy, with one so slight restriction;—that is, they should not taste the fruit of the tree of knowledge, and if they do, death will be the punishment. It is noticeable that her thought is only of the wonderful benevolence of God, and that she throws no emphasis upon the restriction.

Satan at once shifts the stress and notices only the prohibition. He expresses great surprise at this command, for it is opposed to reason. The ground for the restriction is surely absurd, for the time of death is settled by heaven: no one has the power to shorten life but God. The fruit [1] cannot be evil for God created it, and since God is good no evil can emanate from him, therefore there can be no harm at all in the fruit. Even if there were harm, eternal death is impossible, for death is evil, and only good is eternal, as God alone is

[1] See the reasoning of Satan, *Paradise Lost*, Book IX, lines 679–703.

eternal. Eve clings closely to her text, what
she has stated is God's command and there can
be no discussion about it. Satan in reply insists upon the one idea that evil cannot come
of good, and he now gradually insinuates the
notion that since [1] the basis of the injunction
is untrue, the motive for the command is questionable. What can it be? The fruit must
be good, it looks most attractive, the command
is not based upon reason, and it is therefore
hard and unfair. After a long discussion
upon the nature of good and of evil and of
fate, he convinces Eve that God is indeed
jealous of her undoubted cleverness of mind
and of her transcendent beauty of form, and
he has forbidden her to eat the fruit solely to
prevent her from becoming a goddess. Satan
urges that if she will now be courageous and
take the apple, she will become divine, and she
will then have power to evade all punishment;
for she will be equal with God.

Eve, gradually persuaded of the truth of this
reasoning, becomes indignant at the injustice of
God in seeking to keep her from her proper
position as a divinity, and she boldly seizes the

[1] Compare *Paradise Lost*, Book IX, lines 703–717.

apple. Satan at that moment descries Adam approaching, and he flees.

Eve now hastens to meet Adam and urges him to eat of the fruit of the tree of knowledge. He unhesitatingly declares his loyalty to God and his horror of her disobedience. Eve thereupon rehearses all the arguments of Satan on the nature of good and evil and she shows how unreasonable is the command of God not to eat the apple and what deception is implied. She also points out the motive for this deception in the jealousy of God for their latent powers of the godhead, but she insists that it is unnecessary to submit to this envy of God, all that is necessary for freedom is courage. "Cast off the yoke of slavery, eat and with divine knowledge all punishment can be evaded." There is indeed no such thing as death, no one ever saw it, they cannot thus be frightened with an unreal phantasm. Will Adam, she asks, let a woman outdo him in courage? But Adam still stoutly resists all this sophistry, and Eve changes her tactics; for since the intellectual appeal has failed, she will try the emotional.

She asks what then is to be done? If Adam really supposes that the harmless little apple can bring death, is he willing that his wife should meet the punishment alone? She presents to him a dilemma most distressing to Adam: shall he obey God and desert his wife, or be loyal to his wife and disobey God? This artificial distinction blinds Adam's perceptions and causes him deep anguish. Eve pleads and rages like a Medea, and Adam very sadly yields to her demands, saying that he must cast in his lot with his wife, and he hopes that God will take into account his difficult position and will pardon him for his allegiance to the woman, whom God created for him and bade him to love and care for. Eve exults in her power, urges the fruit upon her husband, and assures him that now he shows courage; now he is a man.

But Adam's cheeks grow pale as he eats the apple and his strength fails. " Spare, oh spare man!" he cries, and the chorus laments the fall of man.

In Act V, scene i, Satan exults in his victory over God and man. He boasts that he now equals highest heaven, he now rules the earth; all created things are subject unto him. The punishment inflicted by God only makes him more powerful and as the exile from heaven was thus a blessing, he is mockingly grateful to God. The archfiend thus gloats over the fall of man and woman: "You now will go into exile, you alone will envy my lot."

In scene ii, Adam is completely unmanned, he trembles with terror; Eve, Medea-like, stands resolute; she assures him that there is no cause for alarm. To encourage Adam she repeats Satan's sophistry about fate and about evil, for as there is no evil, the apple was good and it was wise to eat it. Surely, she asserts, they are benefited by this act of disobedience and now they begin to live.

Unable to shake him from his abject despondency, she becomes personal and laments her loss of charm for him; in that, she declares, she is indeed unhappy. She suggests that he should cease to think about God and be satisfied with her approval. Again she seeks to set over against one another, love for her, and duty to God.

But the horror-stricken Adam thinks only of his lost innocence. He loathes life, it is better, he says, to die; but God may be yet more angry if he takes his own life. Eve rejoins that the only evil is fear; she begs him to be a man, to be strong, and take courage. But

Adam cannot be made to view his fall in any hopeful light and Eve is reduced to her last resort.

She says then:

If the first evil was the eating of the apple, as you believe, for that I am responsible, and on account of this act, life is impossible and yet you cannot commit suicide, however much you wish to die,—I will myself die by my own hand, or you may kill me,—will that improve matters? You then will be left alone !

Adam is not comforted but Eve gains her point; for he declares this to be no solution of his difficulty, he cannot live without her. He must be allowed to die first; she, if she insists upon dying, must at least outlive him. It is true that God may prefer to have him live, but life is intolerable. Thus the second time Adam declares his love for Eve in opposition to loyalty to the will of God.

All nature now groans, the trees bow their heads as at an earthquake shock, and God comes. In terror Adam flees and laments his shame. When God calls Adam, he replies that he is ashamed to see God face to face. Shame follows guilt; God declares he then must have sinned. Adam explains that Eve misled him and Eve urges, as an excuse for herself, that the serpent that God himself had created is really responsible. But God declares judgment upon them, after pronouncing his curse upon the serpent.

The judgment upon woman is mingled with a prophecy of Christ, which softens its severity. " Satan," he says, " shall not have dominion over woman, this ray of light shall lighten her future pathway, God shall take upon himself human flesh, born of a virgin, and shall bruise the arrogant head of the serpent," but upon woman " shall a curse fall, for her betrayal of man with crafty word;—even pain, and whimsical desires, and the imperious rule of man."

Adam's sentence follows and he is told in short that he is to be a leader, not a lackey in his home. He is to restrain the impulses of his wife and not to be her consort in perpetrating sin. In conclusion God enjoins this penalty " because you have esteemed less my law than the wit of a woman "—" with hard labour shall you win your bread, your body shall return to dust, and on account of your sin, you shall be condemned to hell, unless you receive the mercy of the righteous Judge."

Thus there is hope of salvation through mercy. God, after foretelling the race of

mankind that will be their descendants, gives
them clothes of sheepskin. Adam laments the
changes that sin had brought and God says,
with what strikes our ears as containing a
touch of pagan derision, " Seeking to be equal
with God, you have lost your pristine glory!"
In conclusion Adam and Eve are expelled from
the garden, and thus the tragedy ends.

The strong points in this tragedy are not
hard to find. The intensity of Satan's resentment against God gives a motive for his attack upon Adam and Eve, in whose beauty and
innocence God is represented as taking so
much pleasure. When he fails to make the
bond with Adam against God, and turns all
his energy to corrupting Eve, his scholastic
subtlety of reasoning and plausible explanations make her fall conceivable.

Eve's conversation with Adam, when she
plays the part of an ambassador of Satan, is
spirited and interesting and full of flashes from
human life. She is a bold, clever actress and
makes the situation theatrical, when she forces
the fall upon Adam as a knightly duty. In
our eyes, in a great measure, this justifies her
husband's perplexity. Adam seems worthy of
our respect; he has been hitherto an intelligent

companion of the angels; he has been upright and good from an appreciation of the beauty of holiness. He has unhesitatingly rejected Satan's overtures; for he has no ambition to supersede God in the management of the universe, nor to share this dignity with the fallen archangel. When Eve tells him of all the benefits of a freedom from allegiance to God, he is unconvinced. It is only when she thrusts upon him an artificial dilemma of her own making in the time-worn problem of a tragedy, the contest between love and duty,—then he hesitates and feels unequal to the solution. Eve has a motive now for passion, as Satan had for his intrigue, and she sweeps Adam on. He is too much moved by his love for her to be able to see clearly that in reality there can be no conflict between love for God and love for her, that the greater obligation includes the less; but he is persuaded blindly that he must choose between God and the woman. The movement of the tragedy is skilfully delayed here, until he has chosen a second time and avows again preference for Eve over God; then the punishment comes.

So far, the lines of the tragedy are correctly drawn and, with the dignity of style and the beauty of the chorus, the question may be

raised, why is it not a satisfactory tragedy?
The theme of the tragedy after all is the fall
of man,—has that been adequately treated?

Is the opposition of the good angels to the
bad angels as strongly depicted as the subject
demands? We find in this tragedy the two
interacting plots: Satan against God, and
Satan against man. The motive for Satan's
attack upon the innocence of man is, by means
of man's overthrow, to revenge himself on
God. The garden of Eden thus becomes the
battle-field of a spiritual conflict and Adam
plays a double part; he resists the attack
against God, by resisting the temptation of
Satan. For this reason, the first overture of
Satan to man is important for both plots, the
plot of the spirits of evil against the spirits of
good, and the plot of the evil spirits against a
good man, for man's resistance is necessary for
the intrigue in both plots. In *Paradise Lost*,
there is the opposition of the angels; Satan is
discovered by the heavenly sentinel before he
enters Paradise; he is later caught in Eden
by the guardian angel and put to flight. And
following fast thereupon, Raphael is sent down
to warn Adam very explicitly of the nature of
the peril that threatens him.

The angel's visit in the second act of *Adamus Exsul* does not clearly take the place of any of these devices for establishing the reasonableness of the story in the balance of the good forces against the bad angels. The angel messenger in Grotius's play gives no clear warning of the approaching contest of Adam with Satan. We do not, therefore, in *Adamus Exsul* feel that Satan has been sufficiently resisted by God. Nor does the garden of Eden seem so angel-visited and angel-guarded in *Adamus Exsul*, as Paradise appears to be either in *Paradise Lost*, or in *Adam in Ballingschap*. The lack of this establishing of probability in God's management of his kingdom detracts from the force of the conclusion. We are not convinced that the ending is inevitable for all men in like situation; instead we ask, has man fallen through his own free will in *Adamus Exsul*, or because God has been a little careless of his kingdom?

The inadequate presentation of the force of good reacts upon the presentation of the force of evil, for Satan does not have enough obstacles to overcome. Moreover, clever and seductive as his reasoning is, it cannot in itself reconstruct for our imagination the fallen

archangel, the great protagonist with God.
The cleverness of his words in the temptation
of Eve might emanate from Belial, or Mephistopheles, the emissary only, rather than the
Prince of Darkness; the outline of Eve's tempter in the play does not appear heroic to our
imagination. More episodes and great deliberation in the method are necessary to perfect
such a characterisation as that of Satan and to
present the convincing power of the story; but
these devices are questionable in a tragedy,
which should be closely unified and brief, and
the full intellectual stature of Satan must be
superhuman and could not be concrete in the
sense of the concreteness of a tragedy for it
would be grotesque.

The human side suffers from the incom-
pleteness of the balance of the spiritual forces
of the good and of the evil in two ways: first in
man; Adam is represented as a man worthy of
respect, unhesitating in his instinct for the
right; in the episode of the first conflict with
Satan he reveals no ambition to rival God, and
in the ordeal with Eve as tempter the only
problem that he admits as hard to solve is that
of the contest between love and duty. In the
moment of his fall, he pleads that God will for-

give him, because he is in such a very difficult position and must decide between these two conflicting notions, duty to God and love to Eve. The last words of God in the judgment scene come as a surprise therefore, from the standpoint of the dénouement of the tragedy. God says to Adam: " Seeking to be equal with God, you have lost your first glory! " There has been no trace of ambition in Adam—in the development of the tragedy, he has been a victim to family ties; in anguish of spirit, through the claim of his wife, he has lost clearness of perception—that is his part in the tragedy. If he were ambitious, we should have been clearly shown this defect.

The second loss in the human plot in *Adamus Exsul* is found in the character of Eve, who is in the human plot the chief actor, as Satan is in the spiritual plot. In order to throw the human characters into prominence for the exigencies of the tragedy, she is made too strong, not for the interest of the character in itself but for the theme. How could she be hitherto innocent of all evil?—for she seems experienced in guile. Adam is slow to fall into sin and immediately regrets it, but Eve shows rejoicing in her disobedience, and the only sign

of repentance that she shows seems merely a
form of fear. The character may not be
overdrawn for the tragic interest, but it is
exaggerated out of proportion for the reasonableness of the plot, unless Eve were really the
creation of Satan, rather than of God, a conclusion which is not in accordance with the
theme. Eve's character required the deliberation of the epic or of the novel.

We know next to nothing about Eve before
her fall; from that time on in *Adamus Exsul*
she is so bold, so hard, so unyielding, that she
has no prototype in literature except Medea.
From the talk with Satan at the foot of the
tree of knowledge on, she is mistress of the
situation; no compunction shakes her fell purpose, only the earthquake and the voice of God
bring her to her knees. Even in her reply to
God, there is a touch of impertinence,—" The
serpent that thou hast made," as though God
after all were responsible for her fall. The
episodes needed to prepare for so great a change
in her character belong essentially to the
leisurely devices of the novel, or of the epic,
rather than to the brevity of the tragedy; but
these details are particularly necessary in
treating a plot so remote from the usual, both in

persons and circumstances. The subject therefore seems unfitted to tragedy, and requires the epic method. Surely the battle of the good angels and of the evil angels demands the scope of the epic background, if it is to be adequately presented, and for such a task the epic method is indispensable.

VII

"ADAM IN BALLINGSCHAP," VONDEL

A MONG other tragedies upon the fall of
man is one of peculiar interest that was
written by Joost Van den Vondel, the great
poet of Holland, in his seventy-eighth year,
about ten years after he had produced his masterpiece, *Lucifer*.

Students of Dutch literature have ranked this
tragedy, *Adam in Ballingschap*,[1] as second only
in merit to *Lucifer*. The slow development of
the self-taught poet Vondel presents a contrast to Grotius, whose precocious mind received
every advantage of education. It was not
until Vondel was twenty-five, and not until
after he had produced his first drama, that he
turned his attention to the study of the lan-
guages, French and Latin, and not until he was
forty that he undertook the study of Greek.
Through perseverance he became not only a
scholar, but an imitator and a translator of the

[1] *Adam in Ballingschap*, 1664. See bibliography at
end of this volume.

classics, of Sophocles, of Ovid, and of Seneca, and he made Sophocles and Euripides his models in tragedy. Nor devoted as he was to study did he neglect his art of creation; indeed Vondel wrote in all thirty-three tragedies, eighteen of which were presented on the stage.

His dramas reveal a personality that is definite and vigorous. He was indeed an ardent champion of human liberty, and he was opposed to the intolerance of zealous reformers in his day in both church and state, who, he thought, were promoting no one's liberty except their own. He was renowned for his satires and his keenness in controversy, and while he made many enemies, his genius was recognised from his first published drama, and his life was full of honour and of appreciation. In 1653, his position in the world of art and letters was shown, when the painters, sculptors, poets, and architects gathered at an anniversary meeting at St. Luke's Hall, Amsterdam, and he was crowned with laurel and made king of the feast. To his contemporaries, Vondel must have appeared veritably immortal, for in his eighty-seventh year he was still writing, and not until he was ninety-one years old did he pay the debt to mortality.

In the great tomes that preserve for posterity
his work there are two separate tragedies upon
the themes that are combined in *Paradise Lost*.
Vondel knew well the work of Grotius [1] and
there are points of resemblance in the two tragedies, the *Adamus Exsul* of Grotius and *Adam
in Ballingschap* of Vondel; but on close observation the differences are more prominent than
the signs of similarity.

1.—In *Adam in Ballingschap*, the good and the
bad angels are more conspicuous and play
a more important part in the plot.

2.—This aids the reader to a clearer comprehension of the dignity and beauty of Adam
and Eve in their hours of innocence.

3.—The time of the play, *Adam in Ballingschap*,
is clearly defined; it is less than a day and
that the first day of Adam's and Eve's
" joyous entry " into Paradise, the day
of the celebration of their wedding.

In Act I, Lucifer rises from the abyss at
early dawn. He declares his thirst for vengeance on God for his banishment from heaven,
but he admits that there is need of the utmost
secrecy, for this second attempt against the

---

[1] Vondel translated *Adamus Exsul* into Dutch. See
collected works of Vondel.

majesty of God must not fail, as did the first trial in the battle in heaven. God, out of his vanity, has now created man and placed him in a garden full of beauty, but has been foolish enough to put there the means of man's overthrow in the forbidden tree of knowledge. Surely God is selfish and cares only for his own glory. At this point in his soliloquy, Lucifer sees Adam and Eve approaching and he hides.

Unmindful of any lurking foe, Adam and Eve walk down the garden path; enthusiastic as they are over the beauty of nature, they suggest singing; the question of a subject is discussed and Eve decides upon a hymn in the praise of God. A chorus of guardian angels join them. There are three songs and a " tegenzang."

In Act II, Gabriel, Rafael, and Michael appear flying toward the earth. They rejoice in the beauty of Paradise and they note the fact that the name Eden is given, in appreciation of the beauty of the garden. They reveal in their conversation that the object of their visit is to express their greetings to Adam and Eve, on the occasion of their wedding and man's joyous entry into his estate, as lord of the garden. Gabriel assigns to his companions their part in the ceremonious visit—Rafael is to bear the wedding wreaths of laurel adorned with rubies and diamonds; for here as elsewhere, Dutch customs of wedding fêtes are introduced.

The solemn marriage feast is to be spread for Adam, and throughout this scene there is apparent the utmost reverence for man's dignity,—indeed the reader feels that the angels regard Adam as a little their superior. That there may be no disturbance of the festivities, Gabriel directs Michael to remain on guard, to protect Adam and Eve from hellish spirits who may be plotting.

Adam and Eve watch the three angels approaching, and rejoice in their iridescent beauty of colour and their heavenly grace in motion. As they meet the angels, Adam is very dignified, but with stately cordiality he invites them to remain to the wedding feast. Gabriel makes a fitting reply, addressing Adam as "lord of these possessions by the grace of God," and directs Rafael to place the crowns on their heads. The reader is impressed by the good manners in Eden. Adam expresses his gratitude to God, for the delightful home in the

garden of Eden and for the charming companion he finds in Eve.   Throughout this scene
there is an atmosphere of a great occasion be-
fitting the entrance into a kingdom.

Now Adam calls upon the guardian angels
and the birds to join in a song for the pleasure
of the guests; meanwhile he directs all the animals to be quiet and listen.

These songs, like the classic chorus, are important for the development of the plot; for
they contain premonitions of evil.   There are
in the chorus two " zang," two " tegenzang,"
and a " toezang."   In every one of these songs
there is reference to present innocence and bliss;
and to the great loss to man if evil should enter
the human heart.   For example:

If mankind lost this gift, this privilege,
And had to depend on human power alone,
Nature could not alone support him.
The wedding garment would be in tatters, his glory
    would pass away,
Cherubim would grow pale at the thought.

Line 510—

In the angel songs, there is recognition of the
gift of eternal youth to Adam and Eve, also
of the quality of an angel and of a beast
joined in man, and there is a definite warning
at the end—

> "Preserve your privileges,
> Maintain the task imposed,
> Then no enemy can molest you,
> You may hold yourself safe from injury and grief."

Throughout the tragedy, there is prominent the Dutch seventeenth-century idea of feudal government. Adam holds his possession by the grace of God, he has sworn fealty and he loses all if he breaks his oath.

In Act III, Lucifer stamps on the ground and calls up from hell Asmodé to assist him in devising a scheme for man's overthrow. The nature of their plot may be best understood by a quotation from the text, Lucifer says:

> "We will, like bandits, eternally strive against God;
> We will by plot and guile work against God; if we cannot conquer,
> We will at least worry him."

But to our surprise, Asmodé soon takes the lead, while Lucifer's suggestions seem futile and altogether the would-be Prince of Darkness is dependent upon his confederate. Asmodé advises the use of the forbidden fruit to work man's woe. Lucifer objects that this is too open an attack; and begs Asmodé to think of a slower, safer plan, for there is fear of Michael and the heavenly guard for the wedding feast. In fact, he reflects that there is likely at this time to be a special vigilance on the part of the good angels, and an evil spirit might be quickly dragged from cover. Asmodé suggests that the tempter should take the shape of an animal to avoid discovery; after some discussion of the form of disguise of the elephant, of the eagle, of the dragon, the snake is finally decided upon; for its natural sly qualities are well suited to the guileful purpose of Satan. Asmodé also suggests approaching Adam and Eve, not together, but separately and strongly advises tempting first the woman. He reasons that she may fall more easily, and if she should fall, man would not hesitate to join her in her sin. Lucifer does not approve of attempting first the woman; for he thinks it is important that man should be corrupted without delay. Asmodé urges that "A little fondness for dainty things" can win women over through sight, taste, and smell, and he contends that since she is the easier victim, she shall fall first. He also recalls to mind that the angels fell through ambition to equal God, and it will be worth while to attempt to stir the same ambition in Adam.

Lucifer offers to call up from the abyss as many spirits as are necessary to execute Asmodé's design, a whole regiment shall quickly

appear if desired; but his accomplice assures
the archfiend that his armour-bearer, Belial,
is well fitted for the undertaking, and the service of no other spirit is needed. Belial is now
summoned and given the task of tempting Eve
with the fruit of the forbidden tree.

Meanwhile the wedding feast has been in
progress and now the guests are departing.
There is the atmosphere of reminiscent joy and
Adam and Eve sing in response to the farewell
of the angels. When now Eve suggests leaving
Adam for a little, he is unwilling and together
they watch the angels depart and wing their
way out of sight. Eve recalls the angels' conversation, " which pushed back," she says, " the
veil from human faces and showed them God
and heaven."

They dwell with joy upon the invitation
given by the departing angels to meet them at
a heavenly feast, which will be a stately return
of courtesies. Adam and Eve rejoice in their
happy lot and she in a burst of spontaneous enthusiasm assures him that she will delight in
carrying out his wishes in all things; no command of his can be a burden; but he rejoins
that the weaker is stronger, as the lioness rules
the lion, so he feels her sway. Adam now pro-

poses seeking solitude for a moment to pray to God, and Eve decides to sit at the foot of a tree to wait for him.

When Eve is left alone, Belial at once creeps up in the form of a snake, and compliments Eve on her surpassing beauty; he expatiates on her magnetic power over butterflies, dolphins, unicorns; like these, he also feels her marvellous influence. He thus gains her attention and then he asks abruptly, "Have you noticed these apples full of wisdom? I will pluck some for you."

Eve commands him to be silent; the fruit is forbidden. Belial is greatly surprised, he had supposed that Adam and Eve were in absolute possession of the garden. The prohibition upon this fruit is contrary to right and reason; the apple is not baleful but will give eternal youth. When Eve remains firm in her belief that the command of God is to be respected, the serpent urges that the fear of the apple is mere superstition; God could create nothing evil. No meat nor drink made by God can injure the body, much less can the soul be harmed by a material thing.

Eve now begins to doubt the grounds of the prohibition of God, and Belial offers to explain;

but it is dangerous to tell the secrets of the Almighty, and she must promise to be very prudent and not to tell. The fact is, God is jealous of the power that Eve would have if she ate that apple of wisdom, " for you would then be equal with God."

" Only an apple peel protects God! " he declares with a sneer. " Here, take the fruit before any one comes "; he adds flippantly, " I will shake the tree and let divinity fall into your lap."

Eve expresses fear, but the apple is attractive, she plucks and eats.

Belial exclaims, " Here comes Adam, he is apparently excited. Shall he be bidden to the feast?—how can he refuse what his bride asks,— I will help you win him over."

Adam approaches, soliloquising upon his secret communion with God. At length he notices Eve and she is eating some fruit; he is at once apprehensive. By degrees he learns that she has taken the forbidden fruit, which she pertly declares is " all the more to be desired, because it is forbidden." When Adam laments over her disobedience to the divine command, she assures him that she understands matters far better than he does. She is persuaded that he is superstitious, he must be cured of that weakness; she offers him the fruit as a first gift to her husband,—"Taste, and then judge with understanding," she urges.

When Adam resists, she becomes petulant and imperious.

"Will you oppose my wishes? this does not bring love. You did not promise to behave like this. Bear yourself like a man. Take God's own gift; by it shall you mount to the stars. Use your own free will and show me the first token of love, in obeying my first request. Your acquiescence brings peace between us."

Adam now shows a quick change of attitude. "What a change"—he exclaims "to use free will, instead of dragging the yoke of obedience!"

Eve boldly sets herself up as a divinity. "Use your own free will," she urges: "here earthly gods prevail."

Although Adam sees the attraction of the fruit, he still fears God's displeasure and cries out against the unnatural contest: "Shall I lose for ever the love of my wife, or turn the mercy of God into unmercy?" He decides that it must be a separation from Eve, rather than from God.

At this decision Eve becomes more imperious and exclaims, "You break at once the bonds of marriage. . . . You can devote yourself to naming the animal and get on without a wife. . . . Your heart will turn to ice "—and she bids him farewell and hastily leaves him.

Adam begs her to wait a moment, but over her shoulder as she departs she asks coldly, " Why? "—" We are already parted, you have never really loved me. Who is mated without love can separate without pain. May the Almighty shape you another wife, but if you cannot love her better, remain unmarried."

Adam cries out in agony, " How can I serve God and you! Father, can you forgive me this one misstep, that I for a moment content my wife? this is only a flag of truce. Give me the apple God will take away the venom from my disobedience."

Adam eats the apple and hears at once the wail from the angel chorus. Eve asks, " Why do you look so pale? I alone bear the burden of this act upon my soul."

The chorus philosophises upon knowledge,—

" Divinity knows itself, therefore knowledge is divine,
God would not exclude any one from mercy for a desire
    for knowledge.
He planted the tree, but those who seek the fruit in de-
    fiance

Are wrongly wise. There is the difference between wisdom rightly and wrongly won."

Act V, scene i.—Lucifer congratulates Asmodé upon his victory, and Asmodé depicts to Lucifer the present condition of Adam and Eve. They are hiding in a wood and Eden rings with complaints and recriminations. Adam cries out,

"I gave ear not to my bride but to an enemy. Alas, this comes from love of a woman. Woman's love cost me too much. I would not strike my flag before God's wisdom and ambition has caused my fall."—"The flesh now wars with the spirit in my members."

Lucifer reviles God, who makes laws in order to see them broken.

"I shall now sow churches to spite him. Man shall bow to idols and shall swear by the divinities of hell. I exchange now the burden of the origin of evil from my neck to the neck of my enemy. Out of sixty centuries, God will scarcely get a handful of souls. So I mount higher by my fall." . . . "God will now repent that he ever made man."

In scene ii, Adam and Eve still lament their fate and quarrel with one another. Adam blames his wife and deplores his marriage with her. Eve inquires what was his object in marrying her, and when she learns that it was to gain a helpmate, she feels that he was responsible for the fall, in not setting a good example.

She reminds him that, "A man should be strong in sturdy piety and not yield to the prayer or the threats of a woman."

But there comes a sudden change of mood and she is gentle and penitent and promises to deal no more in reproaches, but to try to comfort him. Adam rejects all of her consolation and calls upon Mother Earth to receive him, for "Timely dies he, who has no more to hope." He is sure that he has lived already too long, and to Eve's great distress he dwells persistently upon the different ways open to him of taking his life.

Eve seeks to divert his purpose to commit suicide, and begs him not to leave her alone in the garden. Adam is very severe upon her and implies that remaining with her is no inducement to live, for he declares, "You are the snake that gave me the blow of death."

Eve is very humble and begs to be allowed to die with him and at length Adam is softened by her misery and relents. He comforts Eve with these kind words—

"My love, it was my fault; I will prolong my life for
    love of you,
You shall not weep on your wedding day, alone."

A storm of wind springs up suddenly with

thunder and lightning and " divinity comes." Adam and Eve cry out and are beside themselves with terror.   Uriel appears, as the judge sent by God, and " In God's name," he pronounces the sentence upon them.   Uriel announces to them this comfort: " But ye shall see that God places mercy above justice," and there follows the prophecy of Christ's coming, born of a woman.   Otherwise, the sentence does not materially differ from that pronounced in the judgment scene in *Adamus Exsul*, the work of Grotius.

The culprits are now expelled from the garden of Eden, and Eve laments the loss of Eden and the consummation of her bridal song in the flames of Paradise but Adam is lost to present discomfort in pondering the purport of the divine message; he is convinced that it was not Uriel, but God himself, who had appeared to punish them " for seeking to soar above human limits."   And Adam at length bids farewell to Eden in these words:

" Farewell, Paradise, we must turn from thy gates to seek dry and thirsty lands.   Summer is past; winter is come."

Adam's lament closes the tragedy without a

chorus of the angels. We are given to understand that the heavenly host has fled from Eden
after man's fall.

There are features here that are more attractive than anything in *Adamus Exsul*, in some
respects. The machinery is better balanced,
the innocence of Adam and Eve is more charm-
ingly depicted, and there is a tragic force in
the reiteration of the thought that the joyous
entry into their possessions in Eden, their wedding feast, important both in Paradise and in
heaven, and their unhappy fall and expulsion
from their kingdom, all happen between dawn
and twilight; so quickly was their " summer
past."

The choruses have elevation of tone and convey thoughts that are needed for a correct interpretation of the events, as the author views
them. Indeed, the chorus plays thus, in part the
office of the narrator in the epic. In these points,
the tragedy is superior to *Adamus Exsul*.

Adam and Eve are very attractive in their
hours of innocence. They carry with them the
atmosphere of spring as they traverse the
shady walks of Paradise singing to the response of the angels, or of the birds, but their

joy is saved from exuberance, by a pleasing dignity, a consciousness of their high destiny, and of their kinship with God. Their association with the angels is characterised by stateliness without stiffness, and the reports of their conversation with the angels are vivid and free from didacticism and from improbability.

The fall seems not so well managed. Belial is flippant and has an air of not needing to exert himself, for his task is easy; nor are we greatly impressed with the resistance of Eve.

Wherein Belial's plea has merit, the arguments seem to have been learned from the Satan in *Adamus Exsul*. When Adam returns from his secret communion with God, Belial turns from Eve to look at him but shows no anxiety at the important approaching struggle, for he still seems jestingly, mockingly, at ease; this degrades the dignity of the contest between good and evil and makes Adam seem a less important personage even before his fall than the plot should demand.

When Adam reaches her, at the foot of the tree of knowledge, Eve is no longer the highborn lady that he had left a few moments before. He finds her indeed changed into a pert, unrefined type of woman; wilful and assertive, personal and theatrical. Her fall seemed too easily accomplished in the first place, so does Adam's in the second place. Her wiles, we feel, would mildly disgust the well-bred Adam of the earlier acts who received the angels as his fitting guests. The double motive for the fall of Adam, in ambition, and in a hopeless contest between love and duty, both appear here as in *Adamus Exsul*, but Vondel has prepared for this duality in the conclusion, by a more carefully suggested dual motive earlier in the action. Ambition is not, however, so prominent as love for Eve, and ambition still seems forced upon our attention through assertion rather than evident in the action.

The reasonable sensitiveness of characters new to sin is preserved by the treatment of the sincere penitence of both before " divinity comes," but there is loss of dignity, one may feel, in the prolonged quarrel of Adam and Eve in the first and second scenes of the fifth act, and by the harshness of their utterances to one another. There is in this family quarrel a suggestion of the early comedy. It would be difficult not to arouse satirical laughter in an audience by presenting this scene, and that marks a defect in the method of the tragedy.

There is a gain in Vondel's tragedy over the treatment of Grotius in the judgment scene, in the fact that mercy is emphasised as above justice, for when justice and mercy are not represented as identical, this is a wiser course.

The sending of Uriel as a delegated judge marks a connecting link between this tragedy of Vondel and his other great tragedy, *Lucifer*, and reminds us that, according to Vondel's scheme, the battle of the angelic hosts of heaven under Michael against the fallen angels under Lucifer was carried far outside the ramparts of heaven. A messenger returning to heaven announces to the waiting angels the victory of Michael and recounts the Homeric exploits of the heroes in the combat, but in the midst of the rejoicing, Gabriel arrives with the lament— " Our triumph is in vain—Oh, Adam 's fallen! "

Lucifer, then, we are given to understand, before he could be sealed in hell, had speedily accomplished this act of revenge on God, so that news of the victory is blended with the news of the defeat; and Uriel is sent at once to execute the orders for the expulsion of Adam and Eve from Paradise. As we shall see, Lucifer of the Morning Star is inconceivably changed in this short space of time. Indeed the characterisation of Lucifer is one of the weakest points in *Adam in Ballingschap.*

Although he comes himself to Eden to spy upon Adam and Eve, and to bring about their overthrow, he seems incapable of either devising or of executing the plot but he calls up Asmodé to help him. This device, at first sight, appears a very clever stroke on the part of Vondel, for Asmodé, the fiend opposed to the peace of the home, is an appropriate schemer against the bliss of Eden on Adam and Eve's wedding day.[1] But when Asmodé comes to Lucifer he takes the helm, and his chief's suggestions are so weak and futile that they are wisely overruled by his more skilful subordinate. Asmodé, in turn, delegates the execution of the perfected plot to Belial, so that Lucifer's share in man's fall seems in *Adam in Ballingschap* both indirect and remote. If this tragedy is read in sequence with Vondel's *Lucifer,* the weakening of the fallen archangel from the mightiest and fairest of the princes of heaven is inconceivable in the few intervening hours of Vondel's chronology. Milton's conception

[1] Asmodé, prominent in spectacular open air performances—early became a character for comedy. Asmodius is a character in the apocryphal book of Tobit, a fiend opposed to the peace of the home.

that he had not yet lost all of his original brightness is far more convincing. Nor is it reasonable to believe that the slow-witted Lucifer of *Adam in Ballingschap* could rule the denizens of hell.

Vondel has shown himself able to handle divine machinery in the tragedy of *Lucifer;* why has the defect arisen here?

Is it not reasonable to suppose that these considerations influenced him? He intended this tragedy to be placed on the stage and he was somewhat guided by stage traditions of Satan, for the problem confronted him, how are spirits and mortals to be presented on the same stage in artistic harmony? He may have felt that the nearer the fiends were brought to base man, the more they would blend in artistic detail with the human plot. At all events, that is what he has done, and there is a corresponding loss to the successful development of his theme. In the *Lucifer* his problem was somewhat different, for the tragedy moved on the stage of heaven.

Has not the *Adam in Ballingschap* lost by not being kept epical in elevation, while the tragedy of *Lucifer* is successful in so far as it is epical?

The defect of *Adam in Ballingschap* lies in a realism that is out of harmony with the theme and causes loss in dignity in scene, and reasonableness in characterisation, as well as convincing power in the conclusion. The theme required the elevation of the epic, the epic background, and the epic method, both for the dignity of the thought and for the character development.

VIII

"L'ADAMO," ANDREINI

THE tragedies examined in the last two essays incurred failure in the presentation of the theme of the origin of evil on earth, through too great concreteness: the operatic type of tragedy by Andreini now before us has not that defect in so marked a degree; but its chief fault is an element of grotesqueness that is out of harmony with the dignity of the theme.

This play, which appeared in 1613, is a work extraordinarily interesting for a number of reasons aside from any merit in the drama itself. In fact *L'Adamo*,[1] *Sacra Rappresentazione* of Giovanni Battista Andreini, is not the highest development of a not thoroughly artistic dramatic form.

The sacra rappresentazione was a fifteenth-century development in Italy of the earlier miracle play. The motive was usually re-

[1] See bibliography at the end of this volume.

ligious, the style declamatory, and there was a multiplicity of marvellous scenes from biblical subjects or from ecclesiastical legend to delight and amaze the spectators. This style of play became very popular in Florence, and throughout Italy, and thousands were produced before the end of the seventeenth century. Crude as they often were and devoid of all literary merit, such was not always the case, for Lorenzo de' Medici and Politian both employed their elegant style upon this hybrid type of play. Music was early introduced as an accompaniment, and the rappresentazione very naturally merged itself in the Italian opera of the seventeenth and eighteenth centuries.

The author of *L'Adamo* was a comedian as well as a playwright; and he was the son of a celebrated comedian, who was also an author and a leader of a travelling company of actors. Although he enjoyed a passing fame there are proofs that neither Giovanni Battista Andreini nor his tragedy *L'Adamo* made any lasting impression upon the age or upon the nation that produced them. Italian scholars to-day in both histories of the drama and of literature omit the work altogether, or give it brief mention only. From the standpoint of Italian literature, the play has, however, critical interest, in its not infrequent touches of Marinism; and in the history of the drama, it is worthy of note as the only sacra rappresentazione extant that approached the Spanish auto in its treatment of abstract subjects. For this reason, *L'Adamo* to-day merits the characterisation of " an isolated eccentricity." [1]

From the utterance of Voltaire in " *Essai sur la poésie épique*," and from the various comments made from time to time upon that utterance, there are reasons for believing that *L'Adamo* has had a degree of publicity outside of Italy since the first quarter of the eighteenth century that surpassed any interest it has ever aroused in the land of its birth. It is significant that Mickle, writing in 1775, expressed grave doubts as to the existence of either the play, *L'Adamo*, or of the author, Andreini, outside of the fertile fancy of Voltaire. Doctor Johnson dubs Voltaire's account " a wild, unauthorised story "; but Doctor Warton gave a summary of *L'Adamo* in his essay on the *Genius and Writings of Pope* in 1782, and Hayley made the analysis of every act and scene, which was included in the fourth

[1] Given by Dr. Garnett.

edition [1] of the Poetical Works of John Milton
in six volumes, edited by Rev. Henry John
Todd, and thence it took its place in the literature connected with the study of *Paradise
Lost*.

The substance of Voltaire's comment, it
seems to us, to-day, need not to have hurt the
sensitive feelings of the lovers of Milton in the
eighteenth century. He declares his belief that
Milton saw the poor attempt of Andreini; he
saw, too, the possibilities of the story and resolved to try a better development of the art
themes involved in that subject. Our interest,
to-day, is not to find out what Milton borrowed
from an obscure and unskilful poet, but to note
what light is thrown by *L'Adamo* upon the artistic treatment demanded by the subject itself.
To discover this, the summaries hitherto given
are inadequate [2] and we must turn to the
original work.

The *Sacra Rappresentazione, L'Adamo*, is a
play in five acts distributed in forty-six
scenes with the following cast of characters:
(1)—God the Father, the Archangel Michael

---

[1] Introduction.
[2] Hayley is frequently inaccurate, and changes the
purport of entire scenes.

and a Chorus of Seraphim, of Cherubim, and the Angels, a Cherub, on the side of the heavenly forces.

(2)—Adam, Eve—for the human characters.

(3)—Lucifer, Satan, Beëlzebub, Seven Deadly Sins, the World, the Flesh, Famine, Labour, Despair, Death, Vain-glory, Serpent, Volano, Chorus of Phantoms, a Chorus of Spirits, of fire, air, earth, and water—for the infernal forces.

There is noticeable here an odd lack of discrimination in the characters; for instance the distinction made in the name of Lucifer and of Satan, as two names for the same fallen archangel, is disregarded, and there is further confusion in the Serpent as a character not identical with Belial, as in *Adam in Ballingschap*, or with Satan in *Adamus Exsul*, and in *Paradise Lost*. The Seven Deadly Sins are not well discriminated from the World and the Flesh; nor does the list given at the beginning of the drama cover all of the characters introduced in the plan. The author's object is not to portray clearly defined characters, but a pageant varied and startling. There is dumb show, tableau, song and dance, as well as long declamation, and more solemn chorus.

Act I consists of six scenes. In the first, God creates the world and places Adam and Eve in Paradise; a chorus of angels extols the glory of God, and Adam and Eve declare their delight and gratitude in God's benevolence. The remaining five scenes present the forces of evil plotting against God.

In scene ii, Lucifer rises from the abyss of hell and reviles God, who, he says, is evidently tired of heaven and wants a new Paradise.

"But why," he mockingly asks, "did God create this earthly Paradise and place in it gods of human flesh?" The fallen angel feels that it is because his own revolt has desolated heaven; and he boasts that God may go on building new worlds all that he likes, but Lucifer will find means to destroy what God has made.

In scene iii, Lucifer is stirring up Satan and Beëlzebub to an open expression of resentment against God. He tells them that proud hearts cannot endure their punishment. For his part, he has resolved upon a change; he will no longer endure the darkness of hell, but the sun and moon shall shed their light into the abyss. He calls the devils to arms; for if

13

they will arouse themselves men made of dust shall not possess the stars.

Beëlzebub, full of wrath, shakes back the hissing snakes from his eyes, and Lucifer continues to fan the blaze of envious wrath. He reminds them that man is now very fortunate in Paradise and there are grounds for grave fears that his posterity will be raised to heaven. Satan expresses his apprehension of the power of "the incarnate word" [1] and Lucifer explains that through the incarnation of Christ the human race is destined to be raised above the angels. He calls now for concerted action against such a usurpation of heaven. If man can be put to death before Christ's incarnation, the hopes of the "God man" will be effectively crushed.

In the planning that follows, Lucifer takes the lead. He has already thought of a vulnerable point in man: Adam sustains life by food, and he shall be made to eat the forbidden fruit this very day; by this act shall he merit death.[2] Lucifer pauses in his plot to sneer at

[1] Lucifer fears Christ but has not the unity of plan of resistance to the Messiah that is elaborated in *Paradise Lost*.

[2] Lucifer knows all about man, is fully informed also as to the prohibition concerning the tree of knowledge;

God's foolishness in putting such a peril as
this in man's way. It looks, he says, as
though God were already tired of his new
amusement, man, and were willing to have him
destroyed. He has indeed made a poor piece
of work in the creation of a man so weak. Man
shall be forthwith destroyed; and when this
hope of Adam's race for repeopling heaven is
lost, God may decide to relent and to restore
the fallen angels to their proper place.

In scene iv, the plan for man's ruin takes
a more definite shape; Lucifer, Satan, and
Beëlzebub decide that Eve should be the first
victim of their plot. She shall be tempted
with Pride and Envy; Envy because she was
not created before man.

She shall complain against God that she, who is destined to be the mother of the human race, was not created
first and was not given dignity superior to Adam's. . . .
She thus shall lay down the law to God against his
actions.

Scene v is purely spectacular, indeed it is
a marshalling of the varied forces of evil, and
the allegorical characters are multiplied with

Milton follows the Rabbinical writers and makes neither
the angels of light nor of darkness omniscient. Satan in
Paradise Lost learns of the forbidden fruit from Adam's
own lips only.

a loss to logical clearness; not Pride and Envy as before planned, but Greed, Wrath, and Avarice are now sent to seduce Eve.

In scene vi, Lucifer, Satan, and Beëlzebub, with other evil spirits, set forth to tempt Eve, but the evil spirits differ from those mentioned in the last two scenes. In this scene, Envy and Luxury are the agents.

In Act II, scene i, a chorus of fifteen angels sing of the majesty of God and of his benevolence to man.

In scene ii, Adam and Eve are portrayed in Paradise; Envy, Gluttony, and Luxury lurk unseen, watching for an opportunity to assail Eve, but Adam and Eve join so fervently in praise to God that the evil spirits are put to flight. The inner resistance from the force of good in man, as well as the conflict of the outer forces of the angels against the powers of evil, is well marked in *L'Adamo*.

In scene iii, the Serpent, Satan, and Volano —literally Shuttlecock; Variableness or Frivolity would perhaps render the name—appear in Eden. The Serpent explains why he took the form of a snake: he did not desire to choose a shape that would bring him into contrast with the angels, nor in a human form did

he wish to meet Eve for she knew there was one
man, only, in Paradise. He did not choose the
form of a tiger, nor of a she bear, nor of a
lordly lion, because Eve knew that these could
not reason. But as a serpent, " she could not
know that I was a foe of the great God."
Therefore he has chosen to disguise himself in
the scales of a serpent, from the waist down;
the rest of his body is that of a beautiful
maiden.

Scene iv is purely spectacular; Volano, the
Serpent, some other spirits, and Satan announce to the infernal forces of hell the plan to
tempt Eve.

In scene v, Vain-glory, drawn by a giant,
Volano, the Serpent, Satan, and other spirits
enter Paradise. Vain-glory and the Serpent
conceal themselves near the tree of knowledge
to tempt Eve to eat of the forbidden fruit.

In scene vi, Eve rejoices in the goodness of
God and in the beauty of his work. Her soliloquy is interrupted by the sight of a beautiful
woman's face among the branches of the tree.
She is surprised to see what appears to be another human being,[1] with the eyes, face, and
arms of a woman and the rest of the body in

[1] The description suggests Keats's *Lamia*.

the form of a serpent with glittering scales. She exclaims at this wonder, and the Serpent remarks in an aside, " Evidently I am fortunate in my choice of a disguise! " He then begins an encomium upon her matchless beauty which amazes Eve and she asks who he is. The Serpent declares that he was appointed to be a guardian of the fruits in Paradise. He would like to show her some great beauties of Eden which she may not have discovered, and he claims the power to work wonders.

When Eve insists upon knowing this stranger's name, she is told " Wisdom." By degrees the Serpent avows his desire to see justice done to so beautiful a creature as she is; she ought to be exalted above her present condition. He wishes to see her adored as a goddess. He arouses Eve's curiosity by his strange words and then he offers her some of the fruit of the tree of knowledge. She promptly rejects this and tells him of God's commands. Thereupon the Serpent expresses surprise; the only explanation that he can surmise for this prohibition is that God is jealous of what she might become did she partake of this fruit. He tells her that she is superior to Adam, that justice demanded that she should have been created

before Adam as she was to be the mother of
the human race. Injustice was then shown to
her in her birth, and now there is further
ground for indignation, for the injunction
upon the fruit has no foundation except in the
desire of God to deprive her of her rights and
to compel her to remain a mortal when she is
by nature a goddess. He descants upon the
efficacy of the fruit to reveal to her the mysteries of God. Fully persuaded that proper
spirit demands from her indignation for her
wrongs and courage for the grasping of powers
that are her right, she takes the fruit. A
chill of horror warns her of broken law, but
she will not listen to her conscience and she
exults in her newly gained perceptions. She
rejoices that Adam is in her power; through
her, only, can he be exalted. Vain-glory now
sings a song of triumph.

In Act III, scene i, Eve goes to find Adam.
She meets him, on his return from a ramble,
and he is too enthusiastic over a discovery of
a beautiful waterfall to notice her changed as-
pect. She tells him that she has been frightened in her solitary walk and finds comfort
in seeing him. There are here long, tender
speeches very full of Marinism. At length

Eve produces the apple, which singularly enough Adam has not noticed before in her hand. He is horrified, for he recognises this fruit at once as a product of the tree of knowledge.

In justification of her deed, Eve presents a new view of her motive, for she now says that she took the apple in order to take wings to carry her husband to the sky. Adam is unmoved by her plea of wifely zeal for his aggrandisement. He declares that it is his duty to obey God, and he wonders that she did not grow pale at the thought of the death penalty. Eve replies, with her newly acquired satanic wisdom, that if the apple could bring death the Creator would not have planted it there, where life is given. Moreover, she argues, things good are beautiful and things beautiful are good, therefore the apple is as good as it is beautiful; but Adam is unconvinced and refuses to touch the fruit.

Eve now abandons all attempt at an argument and plays upon his feelings. "Then you do not love me," she says, and she declares her resolve to go away by herself. She gains her point, for Adam begs her to stay. She reiterates that he is very ungrateful for her courage in risking perils for his future glory,—" I who did so much to exalt man above high heavens,"—she pleads that it is very little for him to do to complete his emancipation from human fetters, and to eat the apple that she has brought. Adam is finally won over, and they eat the apple together. They, at once, feel deep grief, and they are persuaded that they are subject to death and a thousand ills.

In scene ii, Satan and Volano proclaim the fall of man, and call upon the infernal powers to strike up the bugles of victory.

In scene iii, Satan, Volano, and a chorus of spirits with ensigns and musical instruments celebrate the victory of Evil over Good.

In scene iv, the Serpent, Vain-glory, Satan, Volano, and other spirits dance and sing songs of rejoicing.

In scene v, the infernal dance continues, a pantomime of imps, the Serpent, Volano, Canoro, Vain-glory, and other spirits join in the dance, until the voice of God is heard and they all flee in terror at the sound.

In scene vi, God, some angels, Adam, and Eve appear as actors. God says that since Adam has chosen to listen to the Serpent rather than to him, "If I could repent, I do repent, that I have made man."

Since man has corrupted all, God announces that it is right that punishment should follow sin. God is justice, and Adam is called to answer for his sin at the bar of divine justice. Adam throws the responsibility of his sin upon Eve; and Eve says—"the Serpent made me sceptical about God's intentions." God proceeds to pronounce his judgments and Adam's sentence ends with these words, "You aimed at highest heaven and have gained instead lowest hell."

In the sentence upon Eve next pronounced, there is no hint of hope in the incarnate word but in the condemnation of the Serpent there is this significant passage: "Between the woman and the Serpent there shall be continual war. If one woman fell, that other woman [the Virgin Mary] shall be victorious and her seed shall bruise the Serpent's head." God then disappears into the heavens.

In scene vii, clothes are brought to Adam and Eve, and lamentations for lost innocence fill the scene. Eve is gentle and penitent and takes all the responsibility for the sin upon herself. But Adam is bitter, his ruin, he declares, came through his loyalty in love.

In scene viii, Michael descends to exile Adam
and Eve from Paradise.

In scene ix, some angels in a heavenly
chorus exhort Adam and Eve to repentance,
and proclaim hope of mercy and of joy
hereafter.

In Act IV, scene i, a chorus of spirits of
fire, of air, of earth, and of water express their
obedience to Lucifer in accordance with the
belief of demonology and of black art.[1]

In scene ii, Lucifer rises and denounces light;
the demons try to console him, but he insists
upon knowing what was the meaning of God's
words, in his condemnation of the Serpent,—
Who is it that shall crush his head? The demons suggest explanations, but he spurns their
reasoning and says that his vanquisher could
be no other than the " incarnate word," that is
the Christ. He feels that his plot has failed
and he devises new schemes to set God against
man, so that the omnipotent may destroy man
before " God in flesh " is born.

In scene iii, Lucifer tries his hand at creation
in derision of God. To this end the infernal

[1] Notice common belief in origin of black art after
man's fall—notice also belief in dominion of evil spirits
over forces of nature. See for instance in Tasso.

cyclops and Lucifer create monsters for troubling man and they despatch World, Flesh, and Death to tempt Adam and Eve. Lucifer here practises black art after the fashion of his later descendant Archimago.

In scene iv, Adam laments the loss of perfection in outward nature ensuing from man's fall.

In scene v, Adam and Eve fly to hide themselves from animals that fight and pursue one another.[1] Eve declares that to exist is no longer life, if they must thus be in the constant fear of death.

In scene vi, Famine, Thirst, Fatigue, Despair, explain in turn to Eve their significance, and she is terrified at the ordeal.

In scene vii, Death threatens to cut off the life of Adam and Eve, and dwells upon the fury of the elements, but it is noticeable that all are outward horrors, nowhere is suicide suggested, as Hayley implies.

In Act V, scene i, the Flesh, in the shape of a woman, tempts Adam, but he resists her blandishments.

In scene ii, Lucifer comes to the aid of Flesh

[1] Incorrectly given by Hayley; Eve nowhere advises suicide.

and exhorts Adam to yield and he promises him heaven, if he will surrender.

In scene iii, a guardian angel flies to the aid of Adam, and Lucifer and Flesh are put to flight.

In scene iv, World appears to tempt Eve,— this creation is not unlike Comus; there is a long description of his frivolity and finery. He urges Eve to make him her choice, but she does not yield.

In scene v, the ordeal of Eve continues, and the Comus element increases in prominence. World now offers to raise by magic a glittering palace which Eve is urged to accept.

In scene vi, some Nymphs are called by World to enchant Eve. They are about to enchain her, when Adam encourages her to resist and she prays for help and mercy.

In scene vii, Lucifer, Death, World, and a chorus of devils threaten to seize Adam and Eve, and they are about to bear away their victims.

In scene viii, to prevent this seizure, the archangel Michael flies to the rescue with a chorus of angels, and a spirited combat follows between the good and the bad angels. Michael is victorious and the evil spirits are put to flight.

In scene ix, Adam and Eve rejoice in their deliverance by Michael. The archangel cheers them with the promise of the renewed favour of God and of a future home in heaven. Praise of the Redeemer is the last note struck in the drama, not by a chorus of angels, as Hayley says, but by Michael himself.

The variety of episode useful in the epic is attempted in this work. The activity of Satan's followers is graphically portrayed; they crowd and pervade the scene and show impish delight in evil deeds. The resentment of Satan toward God and his unceasing resistance to the incarnation of Christ give unity to his motive throughout the play. From all this we conclude that the motive, the action, the resistance, and intrigue are clearly defined in *L'Adamo*.

The temptation of Eve has interesting and skilful management in certain respects. Her innocence is not so vulnerable as it appeared in *Adam in Ballingschap*, for there are two attempts to mislead Eve. In the first ordeal, Envy, Gluttony, and Luxury are all put to flight by Adam's and Eve's hymns of fervent praise of God's goodness. The next attack is not very confidently undertaken by the Serpent, Satan, and Frivolity, and other spirits later join them. At length when Vain-glory comes drawn by a giant, the spectator is made to feel that the power of evil is exerting itself to the utmost to accomplish a difficult and important task. Vain-glory and the Serent together await the passing of Eve. These elaborate preparations have advantages: they aid in the portrayal of the dignity of the human beings in the plot, for their fall is not easy to accomplish; they manifest the dignity of the conception of God, for the forces of evil were taxed to the uttermost to gain any foothold in this angel-guarded Eden, and they did not find free field for their activities. These details add force to the characterisation of the powers of evil in two ways: They are forced to use a variety of devices and they are unresting in their eagerness to do evil. Where one or two evil spirits are delegated to perform an errand a host fly to aid.

The reasoning of the Serpent in the scene of the temptation of Eve has some interesting characteristics. He stirs Eve's resentment toward God, because she has not been treated fairly; as the mother of the human race, she should have been first created and made in every way the important consideration in the plan of the universe. He points out that the prohibition not to eat the fruit of the tree of knowledge is another attempt to deprive her of her privileges. Surely, her wrongs ought to be righted, urges the solicitous and friendly Serpent, and the first step for her to take is to eat the apple boldly. After that act she will not be in this sadly dependent position, but will be able to see for herself what is true and to decide what should be done. All this strikes the spectator as likely to surprise and impress Eve, and might easily through curiosity and vainglory bring her downfall. It makes her fall seem reasonable without depicting her as in love with evil, or too vicious to be new in sin.

After the fall of Adam and Eve, when God has pronounced his judgment upon them, and they are expelled from Paradise, a chorus of good angels sing of repentance and hold out a hope of mercy and of joy hereafter. In the hope of salvation for man lies Satan's defeat, and in the next act we are not surprised to learn that Lucifer doubts his own success. He admits that there is still danger of Christ's incarnation, his task therefore is not accomplished, and he gathers all of his resources for

another plot. The World, the Flesh, and
Death are despatched to tempt Adam and Eve.
The conflict is desperate, but the earnest
prayers of man bring Michael to the rescue,
and the hosts of right gain no doubtful victory.
Adam and Eve rejoice in their deliverance,
and listen to the glad promises of hope that
they may regain favour with God, redemption
through Christ, and a home at last in heaven;
no longer can Lucifer doubt his defeat.

These are excellences in *L'Adamo* which reveal a broader, better balanced treatment of
the theme at these points than we have found
in the other tragedies, but are they of advantage to the play?

The breadth has been gained by a confusing
variety [1] of scenes and complicated allegorical
machinery, that might result in the effect of
a comic opera upon the stage. The multiplicity
of scene diverts and distracts the attention, and
the play becomes a spectacular and astonishing performance without the dignity that the
theme demands. Related rather than acted,
and through the use of the epic background
and the epic method, the varied episodes might

[1] *L' Adamo* has forty-six scenes and five acts. By variety of scene, I do not mean change of place *to 46 scenes*.

14

reach dignified elevation, and lend importance and reasonableness to the plot.

The difficulty with *L'Adamo* as a tragedy is found in the fact that instead of being impressive it becomes grotesque. It stands on the borderland of the miracle and the morality play with characteristics of the opera and of the epic. The thought emerges from the full epic background and requires the devices of the epic method for dignity in its presentation. Andreini doubtless possessed more ingenuity than elevation of genius, but not even a Milton could make the visual presentation of such an epic combat other than grotesque.

Not alone for the consideration of dignity, but also for reasonableness and force, is the choice of the epic form demanded by the theme of Satan's contest with God, as the next tragedy to be reviewed very eloquently sets forth, —that is, the tragedy of *Lucifer* by Vondel.

IX

"LUCIFER," VONDEL

THE best of the tragedies upon the origin of evil that were doubtless known by Milton is *Lucifer*, the acknowledged masterpiece of Vondel, which appeared in 1654 and was twice presented upon the stage. It is a classic drama built about the choral ode and shows the influence of Sophocles and of Euripides. The work has received a good deal of attention, through the services of George Edmundson, Edmund Gosse, and the admirable translation of Leonard Charles Van Noppen, and unquestionably deserves a wider popularity than it has yet received, for it is a production of power and of beauty, although its wide appeal is limited by local colour. Lucifer the Stadtholder [1] with his oath of fealty had reality and even satiric force in seventeenth-century Holland, but he is provincial and requires explanation to-day.

[1] See career of William the Silent, 1533–1584, Motley. See character of Philip II from his letters.

There can be little doubt that the tragedy of *Lucifer* struck with dynamic power burning questions at issue, not only in Holland, but in Europe in Vondel's day. To the author's disappointment, however, since the presentation of heaven and the angels was not in accordance with the notions of the clergy, the acting of the tragedy was caused to be discontinued by law. This statute was unrevoked and for two hundred and fifty years the work has taken its place in the long line of tragedies to be read, but not to be acted. However narrow-minded and partisan the opponents of Vondel may have been, one may raise the question to-day whether some fundamental principles of good taste were not involved in their opposition. Is the tragedy of *Lucifer* suitable for stage presentation, on artistic grounds alone?

Vondel, in *A Word to Follow Academicians and Patrons of the Drama*, has left us in no doubt in regard to his conviction of the didactic office of tragedy, which "Can drive the turbulent spirit out of a possessed and hardened soul." [1] After mentioning examples of the efficiency of tragedy in bringing about the

[1] See translation by Van Noppen.

conviction of sin and as a moral teacher generally, he discusses the objection of those who maintain that

"One should not play with holy things." He resolves this into an equivocation and thus concludes: " So that we, hereby encouraged, may, with greater zeal, bring Lucifer upon the stage, where he, finally smitten by God's thunderbolt, plunges down into hell,—the mirror clear of all ungrateful, ambitious ones, who audaciously dare to exalt themselves, setting themselves against the consecrated powers and majesties and their lawful superiors."

But this is not the ground to-day upon which we should either commend or censure the tragedy. It is not whether it contains a good moral lesson, or is likely to influence possible Cromwells in the audience to desist from sedition that interests us; the question here to be answered is, whether the theme can be artistically presented in a tragedy.

Vondel himself may be quoted against this attempt; for in the beginning of the letter quoted, he says:

The great Archangels, Lucifer and Michael, each strengthened by his followers, come on the stage, and play their parts. The stage and the actors are, in sooth, of such nature, and so glorious, that they demand a grander style and higher buskins than I know how to put on. No one, who understands the speech of the infallible oracles of the Holy Spirit, will judge that we present here the story of Salmoneus, who, in Elis, mounted upon his chariot, while defying Jupiter, and imitating his thunder and lightning, by riding over a brazen bridge, holding a burning torch, was slain by a thunderbolt.

A study of the tragedy will reveal that the many good points in *Lucifer* are " of a grander style and higher buskins " than are suited to a tragedy.   The play attempts in fact to present the epic background and the theme demands the epic treatment.

In *Paradise Lost* Lucifer will not submit to the supremacy of the Messiah.   By rebellion, he seeks to divide the kingdom of heaven. Expelled from heaven but unconquered in his spirit, he carries the same war against God into Eden, although he confesses that he has no feud with man.

In his Foreword, Vondel explains that Lucifer fell through pride and envy, and quotes St. Augustine's distinction of these emotions; pride is a love of one's own greatness, but envy is a hatred of another's happiness.   From pride, Lucifer sought to be equal with God; from envy, he conspired against man.[1]   In *Adamus Exsul* the motive of Satan in his plot

[1] See Vondel's introductory comments on *Lucifer*, translated by Van Noppen.

against Adam is primarily revenge against
God, and envy of man secondarily. In
L'Adamo, revenge against God seems the chief
motive, but very prominent was the determination to prevent the coming of God in human
flesh by causing the destruction of Adam and
Eve before Christ should be born. In *Adam in
Ballingschap* the motive of Satan is to defeat
God's decree concerning the incarnation of
Christ, and to check the growing dignity of
man. Lucifer carries on the same war in the
garden of Eden that he began in heaven; he
has changed his place and his methods, but the
determination to subvert the decree is unaltered, and he himself refers to the plot against
man as his second attempt in the campaign.
The first battle is on the plains of heaven, and
the imaginative appeal in this scene is not
suited to treatment in any other literary form
than the epic.

In this tragedy of *Lucifer* by Vondel the
Angel of the Morning Star is called heaven's
Stadtholder, who takes it upon himself to stand
firmly for the ancient hereditary privileges of
the angels. The decree granting man equal
and even superior dignities to the angels is an
innovation to be resisted. Lucifer, supported

by his accomplices, causes a revolt, raises the "Standard of God and the Stadtholder," and declares as his purpose both the preservation of the constitutional rights of the angels and the "locking of man out of heaven for all eternity." Throughout the play, Lucifer shows overweening pride. Before the creation of man he was peculiarly favoured by God; now man and the son of God, who shall take upon himself human flesh, menace Lucifer's supremacy, and this is the secret of his resentment.

Vondel has made an innovation in the story of creation; for he has placed the creation of the world and of man before the fall of the angels.[1]

We learn, in the opening of the first act of *Lucifer*, that there were mutterings of discontent in heaven. Beëlzebub, "the privy counsellor of Heaven's Stadtholder," is awaiting the return of Apollion, who has been despatched by Lucifer to spy upon the beauties of Eden and the blessings of man. The motive of this expedition appears to be curiosity and a latent unfriendliness toward man. When Apollion arrives with the golden bough from Eden his

[1] See Tasso's *Sette Giornate del Mondo Creato*. See also Milton's *Treatise on Christian Doctrine*.

report of earth's delights very evidently fans the sparks of envy.

Apollion's description is interrupted by the sound of a trumpet and Gabriel arrives with a chorus of angels to announce God's decree of Christ's incarnation and of man's future supremacy over the angels. The chorus rejoices in the executing of all the commands of God.

In Act II, Lucifer, whose character has been suggested by his favoured servants, now appears and his mood is no longer a question for conjecture. His pride and envy are revealed in these lines [1] :

> "Lo, the moment comes
> When Lucifer must set before this star,
> This double star that rises from below
> And seeks the way above, to tarnish Heaven,
> With earthly glow."

His glory, he fears, is to be overshadowed, and he sees a prophecy of a Götterdämmerung.

> "The shades of night
> Bedim the angels and the suns of Heaven,
> For man hath won the heart of the Most High,
> Within his new created Paradise.
> He is the friend of Heaven. Our slavery
> Now begins."

[1] *Lucifer* has been read in the original Dutch. Van Noppen's translation is quoted in this essay, after careful comparison with the original.

But as the Stadtholder, he will stand for their freedom and their ancient dignity and rights.

> "Let all yield
> Who will, not one foot shall I e'er retreat,
> Here is my Fatherland."

Nor is he without supporters apparently experienced in conspiracy and guile of long practice.[1]   Beëlzebub, who prods Lucifer to action, very much as Cassius incites Brutus, calling him the Angel of the Morning Star who from " heaven's face can drive the night away," urges him to espouse the cause of the oppressed, and pleads—

> "The Godhead once
> Set thee, the first in glory, at his feet,
> Then let not man dare thus our order great
> Profane, nor thus cast down these vested rights
> Without a cause, or all of heaven shall spring
> To arms 'gainst one."

Lucifer, who seems not to have been present when the decree concerning man was proclaimed in heaven, now meets Gabriel and asks him censorious questions about God's message, and, finally, he declares very frankly that he

[1] Lucifer refers to Apollion as the master wit in evil and to Belial as experienced and skilful in guile; see Act II, line 390, Van Noppen's translation.

considers the majesty of God debased by this decree.

Gabriel makes the characteristic reply of the good angels, that God—

> "The point wherein his majesty doth lie
> Far better knows than we."

As for the angels, their office is to obey. This conclusion Lucifer rejects and, when Beëlzebub again stirs the pride of Lucifer to action, the Stadtholder sends forth this challenge.

> "Let not a power inferior thus dream
> To rule the powers above."

He is now firmly resolved that he will set up his own kingdom above the stars, and he will grind to powder all that oppose him;—he even defies God's marshal, Michael himself. Indeed Lucifer will, if necessary, wreck the heavens and the earth and, in his insolence, he exults,—

> "Who dares, who dares defy great Lucifer?"

He now thirsts for battle and summons Apollion to take council on ways and means, announcing to him

> "I joy
> To storm this throne with violence, and thus
> To hazard by one strong, opposing stroke
> The glory of my state and star and crown."

Apollion rejoices to hear of the approaching contest, but he desires one point to be made clear:—against whom are they to fight?—surely not against the Omnipotent; for that were a useless warfare. Lucifer evades this issue, by replying that angels may fight against angels, and thus they may put the opposing forces to flight and take possession of heaven. When that is accomplished, further deliberation will be necessary. From which we infer that he secretly believes that he can conquer God and rule in his stead or divide the kingdom with the Almighty, but this he does not find it a wise policy to state frankly.

Apollion, convinced of the wisdom of the revolt, confers with Belial, and a plan of action is so arranged; the guard must be won over, the chieftains and the bravest troops enlisted under Lucifer's banner; but there is need of a clear statement of the question at issue and Belial suggests:

> "For all eternity,
> Mankind to lock without the gate of Heaven."

The line of the campaign is speedily decided. Apollion and Belial are to stir the smouldering fire of resentment among the angels. Beëlzebub

is first to address the assembly upon their
vested rights and upon their grievances. Lucifer, when indignation has reached its highest
pitch, is to appear, to deplore the need of rebellion, but to offer his mighty arm to right
the wrongs. The question of his wearing the
crown will be settled by the counsellors, who if
they deem this wise will draw up such a request
in writing and affix their seals. From this,
it is evident that Apollion gained no equivocal
idea of Lucifer's intention to rule in heaven.

In Act III, the rebellious angels, called
Luciferians, have formed themselves into a faction and their murmurings make discord in
heaven, for which the good angels are grieved.
They are solicitous to soothe, to cheer, and
finally to upbraid the Luciferians, when they
understand the full cause of their woe; " for
one to grieve o'er others' bliss shows lack of
love and scents of envy and of pride." They
assure the unhappy, envious spirits that
greater and lesser stars move harmoniously
in the heavens, that God's ordinances rule all,
and they have no cause for discontent.

Belial and Beëlzebub move among the hosts
as practised demagogues and swell the tide of
resentment, but at the same time they pretend

to be sorrowful and shocked at this outbreak in heaven. Beëlzebub even hypocritically begs the Luciferians, before they risk a battle with Michael, to send an embassy to God to see if they may not obtain their rights by a petition.

Meanwhile, the noise of the tumult has reached the ears of Michael and he comes sternly to demand the cause of the disturbance. He stands for absolute authority—" Who dares oppose or question God? " When he waves his hand, Michael expects instant dispersion of the rebels. They should lay down their weapons and retire, their assembly is unlawful.

The reply of the Luciferians, that they await the coming of Lucifer, greatly amazes Michael. Surely, he replies, they can expect no sympathy from Heaven's Stadtholder; there can be no question of his loyalty. The Luciferians obstinately stand their ground, and Michael departs to learn God's commands as to the method of quelling this insurrection in heaven.

Lucifer now arrives in the assembly of the dissatisfied angels, and he professes to be greatly shocked by this revolt; he admits that the angels have their grievances and he deplores the unpleasant situation in which God has placed himself. Lucifer assumes an air of grave deliberation; both submission and resistance are alike perilous. The assembled angels beg him to take his battle-axe and defend them and not cast them under the yoke of man, as Michael would gladly do.

Lucifer replies that in leading a revolt against God, he would break his oath of fealty.[1] The Luciferians assure him that he has the support of a third part of heaven, and Beëlzebub now frankly espouses the cause of rebellion, and openly urges the Stadtholder to revolt. Lucifer with well feigned reluctance yields to their combined entreaties.

Beëlzebub thereupon reveals the full significance of the rebellion. He causes Lucifer to mount a throne, and all the Luciferians swear allegiance to the Stadtholder. Lucifer calls them all to witness that he, constrained by necessity and compulsion, advances his standard to defend God's realm and to ward off impending ruin. The standard of the Morning Star is raised and all swear, " by God and Lucifer," but they now transfer to Lucifer the rites of worship peculiar to God's throne. The act ends with a chorus of Luciferians that sing

[1] Notice phraseology of William the Silent throughout.

a pæan, and a chorus of loyal angels that lament the premonitions of doom.

In Act IV, Gabriel brings God's command to Michael to proceed against the rebels and Lucifer. Michael again shows amazement that Lucifer should be found faithless, and he marvels over what can be the motive for his defection. When he learns of the desecration of the rites of God that have been appropriated by Lucifer, he calls for his armour and with the swiftness of thought stands in battle array. He calls for lightning and his standard and issues summons to war. Delegating his power in heaven in his absence to Gabriel, he goes forth to battle.

Beëlzebub, meanwhile, continues to flatter Lucifer; already, he declares, he sees heaven's crown upon the brow of the Stadtholder. Lucifer is visibly delighted and drops all subterfuge. He declares that there is no possible reconciliation with God; there is no course open but to overthrow the tyranny of heaven and to establish a condition of perfect freedom. He proclaims to the rebellious angels, "Adam's son shall not chain your neck." Again his forces swear allegiance, " to God and Lucifer."

Raphael with an olive branch in his hand is

now seen hastening toward the ranks of the
Luciferians. He comes to plead with Lucifer,
whom he sincerely loves, and he implores him
to desist from opposition to God and he brings
to him an offer of mercy. The former beauty
of Lucifer, his position of trust and of confidence in heaven are dwelt upon very eloquently
by Raphael, and he begs him not to lose all the
pristine holiness that has made the angels delight to honour him. Lucifer is unmoved and
replies that he deserves neither threat nor
wrath; he has done no wrong; and he has not
overstepped his commission for his troops have
sworn allegiance to " God and to Lucifer."
In short, he battles under God, for the defence
of these his angels, and for their ancient charter
and their right,—privileges assured by God to
them before the birth of Adam. " Take back,"
he says, " this message to the Father, whom I
serve and under whom I thus unfurl the standard of our Fatherland."

Raphael cries out, in astonishment, against
such an attempt to deceive Omniscience, and
when Lucifer is still obdurate, the indignant
angel turns a swift ray celestial upon the rebel
soul and interprets thus what he finds written
there:

"I shall mount up from here beneath, through all
The clouds, aye even above God's galaxies
Into the top of Heaven, like unto God
Himself ; nor shall the beams of mercy fall
On any power, unless before my seat
It kneel in homage down ; no majesty
Shall sceptre dare, nor crown, unless I shall
First grant it leave out of my towering throne."

Lucifer proudly rejoins, as in self-defence, that he is Heaven's Stadtholder, but Raphael reminds him,

"Thou rulest in His name."

" Only," grumbles Lucifer, " until Prince Adam comes." But again Raphael urges him not to attempt to oppose God's decree. The Stadtholder at once rejoins, " 'T is we that are opposed," and he insists that the Luciferians are about to be robbed of their inheritance.

Raphael protests against Lucifer's audacious attempt to lay down the law to the Omnipotent, and, after further explaining the constitutional law of heaven, concludes that a " vassal's power is no inheritance." In that case, Lucifer replies, their privileges are no boon. Raphael pleads so earnestly for peace with God, that the haughty Stadtholder for a moment wavers, balances gain on both sides ; —how can he retreat from his position, at the head of the rebel legions? but he sees the wickedness of his course. At that moment the trumpet sounds to battle, Michael approaches; Apollion hastens to Lucifer and asks, " Why this delay? " Michael is near, he urges, but " looks pale with terror "; and the die is cast, Lucifer joins battle with the forces of Michael. With divine solicitude, Raphael grieves for Lucifer, once so beautiful, stately, and noble. The chorus responds to his lament and the act closes with this prayer for the Angel of the Morning Star:

> "Oh, suffer not that soul to die
>
> •   •   •   •   •   •   •
>
> Oh, keep the archangel e'er in Heaven,
> Let not his guilt be unforgiven."

In Act V, there is rejoicing in heaven, over the tidings of Michael's victory over the forces of Lucifer. Uriel, in Homeric fashion, recounts to Raphael the exploits of the battlefield. Vondel also introduces here a device of his own, in that the monsters of the zodiac are represented as joining in the fray and are overcome, and Lucifer as he falls is changed into a hideous composite of the seven deadly sins. Raphael grieves over the fall of Lucifer. From their post on the wall of heaven,

Michael is now descried returning from the battle and he is hailed by a chorus of angels; Michael responds and the chorus concludes,

> "This is his fate who would assail God's throne,
> This is his fate who would, through envy, man,
> In God's own image made, deprive of light."

At that moment, Gabriel appears fleeing from earth with a lament. At once at the end of the battle with Michael, Lucifer had called a council and devised the plot to corrupt Adam and his seed so that he should incur God's wrath.[1] To accomplish this, Belial was immediately despatched to take the form of a serpent, and to tempt Eve with the forbidden fruit.[2] Thus the first parents had been speedily tempted and both had fallen, and God had already pronounced punishment upon them.

So swift has been the action here that when the angels first hear this startling announcement, there remain only the expulsion of Adam and Eve from Eden to be accomplished. Michael, at once, despatches Uriel to drive them from Paradise. Ozias he sends to cap-

[1] Notice that the implication here is that Satan has eluded God's plans. Compare method followed in *Paradise Lost*, lines 210–220, Bk. I, etc.

[2] Compare opening of *Adam in Ballingschap*.

ture the infernal animals, also the lion and
the dragon,—bind them neck and claw and
chain them in the bottomless abyss. Azarias
he delegates to guard the infernal prisons, and
Maceda he orders to light the eternal fires.

At the end of the tragedy, a chorus sings an
ode in praise of Christ, the deliverer, who shall
bruise the Serpent's head and who shall open, in
heaven, a fairer paradise for the souls of men.
Man shall rise to the place once held in heaven
by the fallen angels and Lucifer is defeated;
for the decree that man through Christ shall
mount to heaven is unaltered.

There can be no question that this masterpiece of Vondel is attractive from many points
of view. There is much that is majestic and
beautiful in the depicting of Lucifer, the Angel
of the Morning Star, the most important and
most favoured spirit in heaven. His defect
arises from his greatness; he has come to demand subservience to his beauty and power.
Since he was thus vainglorious what could be
more natural than his displeasure with the
newly created man, who seems a rival power
destined to supersede great Lucifer in the chief
place in God's favour? While these doubts and
fears are fomenting, there comes the decree of

the incarnation of Christ, and unrest becomes rebellion.

Lucifer evades the frank view of his own course. He declares that he is not rebelling against God, but upholding the ancient rights and privileges of the angels. He reasons that he is therefore attacked by God's decree and his resistance is unavoidable. Michael, Gabriel, and Raphael find such sophistry inconceivable, but Lucifer has much to strengthen his position; for one third of the angels of heaven resort to his standard and they are ready to resist with him now, and to serve him hereafter; and he resolves to break " the tyranny of heaven " and be king himself, if not above God, equal with God.

Lucifer's former dignity in heaven is shown by the incredulity of Michael; the loyalty of the Angel of the Morning Star cannot be questioned, for he can conceive of no motive for his opposition to the decree. The beautiful solicitude of Raphael reveals, also, Lucifer's high place in heaven.

Raphael's longing to reconcile Lucifer, his hero, with God, and to prevent his ruin and disgrace is vividly portrayed in a scene that is dramatic and where his emotions are subtly and exquisitely blended. It seems reasonable that even the obduracy of Lucifer should be for a moment shaken, and then the archangel makes his great final choice and loses all power to ever choose right again. There is undoubted skill in Vondel's art in this scene. Lucifer, Michael, Gabriel, Raphael are all clear characterisations in the tragedy, dramatic, brilliant, and poetical in their treatment.

The forces of evil that are aiding Lucifer in revolt are not so convincing in their characterisation. Beëlzebub, although he lives in heaven, shows no good traits, he is a demagogue skilled in sedition and unhesitatingly spurs Lucifer to action; nor is he alone, for Belial, we are told, is experienced in guile, and Apollion is consummate in deceit and in base political methods. Whence came they, why are they spirits of light? Before the fall of Lucifer they are old in sin and apparently not at all dependent upon the great protagonist for inspiration, but rather he relies upon them for plans for ways and means. There is no suggestion that they have ever had nobler employment than that of unprincipled political leaders; the only evidence in their favour is that they are not held as suspicious characters by Michael, the captain of the hosts of God and the promoter of order in heaven. But should not Michael have been on his guard? There is a gain in dramatic power in these clear-cut characterisations, but there is loss in philosophical consistency.

Arising from this lack of deeper consistency between dramatic characterisation and philosophical truth, there is likewise a failure to subordinate the good forces under an omniscient and omnipotent God, as well as to make the evil forces dependent upon the father of all evil.

In the scenes between Michael, Raphael, and the good angels and Lucifer, Beëlzebub, Belial, and the Luciferians it is impossible to feel that God is very clearly present in heaven; he seems remote and dependent upon messengers. This impression of his aloofness from heaven is equalled only by his detachment from the affairs on earth; and Vondel's treatment of the second plot, the fall of man, enhances this impression; for after the battle in heaven, while Michael is returning with songs of victory, before a command can be given to seal Lucifer in hell, the fallen archangel has called a council, evolved the plot against man, Belial has accomplished the fall of Adam and Eve, and God has judged them. Until Gabriel comes with his lament from Eden, the good angels have not had an inkling, even, of a peril menacing the denizens of Eden. Surely that is a defect. There is no reference to a warning to man; there is no effort of the good angels to be guardians of Eden, nor to resist the bad angels and to shield Adam from harm. There is no reference to any obstacle overcome by Lucifer in causing Adam's fall. The loss, therefore, in such a treatment is threefold, for God, for man, and for Lucifer. The dramatic shock in the last act of *Lucifer* is bought too dearly.

As brilliant as the production is, it is surely outside the domain of tragedy. If ancient Greeks with reason decided against the presentation of the *Eumenides* of Æschylus, modern as well as ancient theories of tragedy must count against Vondel's *Lucifer*.

The stirring, skilful scenes and spirited passages, that make the work deservedly admirable, belong rather to the epic than to the tragedy. The whole play is not concrete enough for tragedy, but too concrete for philosophical truth; for the concreteness of tragedy is at variance with the subject, composed as it is of divine machinery, which plays its part in the human plot, but is more important than the human plot. The effort to make the divine machinery concrete has brought loss both to the reasonableness of the characters, and of the theme; and the subordination of the plot in Eden has caused a loss in force in the plot of Lucifer's fall. All this might have been avoided by recognising the full epic background and by resorting to the epic treatment. The good points in this tragedy are of the epic nature rather than of that of the tragedy; all considerations point to the need of epic treatment for this theme of the origin of evil.

X

SOME EPIC SCENES IN EARLIER OR
CONTEMPORARY LITERATURE

IF Milton could find little direct guidance in
his quest for proper art form for the theme
of the fall of man, from these tragedies, there
were available to him passages from works on
allied or different themes that were significant.
Indeed there were many characterisations of
Satan in the sixteenth and the seventeenth
century that might arrest the attention of the
author of *Paradise Lost*.

From a list of works upon different themes,
a number, that were of undoubted aid to Milton
in the creation of the character of Satan,
should be noticed. If Tasso in *Il Mondo Creato*
had been of small service to Milton such was
not the case in his *Jerusalem Delivered*. In
the fourth canto, the superhuman figure of the
grim monarch stands forth boldly in his appeal to the imagination. Through description
of what could not be acted, and by epic speech-
making, the effects impossible to conceive of

in a tragedy are reasonable through the epic devices.

Pluto calls a council of the infernal powers.

Its hoarse alarm the Stygian trumpet sounded
Through the dark dwellings of the damned; the vast
Tartarean caverns tremblingly rebounded,
Blind air rebellowing to the dreary blast:
Hell quaked with all its millions; never cast
The ethereal skies a discord so profound,
When the red lightning's vivid flash was past;
Nor ever with such tremors rocked the ground,
When in its pregnant womb conflicting fires were bound.

The gods of the abyss in various swarms
From all sides to the yawning portals throng,
Obedient to the signal—frightful forms
Strange to the sight, unspeakable in song,
Death glares in all their eyes ; . . .

There follows a description of Satan:

They took their stations right and left around
The grisly king; he, cruel of command,
Sate in the midst of them, and sourly frowned,
The huge, rough sceptre waving in his hand.
No Alpine crag, terrifically grand,
No rock at sea in size with him could vie ;
Calpe, and Atlas soaring from the sand,
Seemed to his stature little hills, so high
Reared he his horned front in that Tartarean sky.
A horrid majesty in his fierce face
Struck deeper terror, and increased his pride ;
His bloodshot eyeballs were instinct with rays
That like a baleful comet, far and wide,
Their fatal splendour shed on every side ; . . .

We may notice that Tasso's Prince of Darkness speaks like Milton's Satan in some respects:

"Princes of Hell! but worthier far to fill
  In Heaven, whence each one sprang, his diamond throne;
Ye, who with me were hurled from the blest hill,
  Where, brighter than the morning-star, we shone,
  To range these frightful dungeons! ye have known,
The ancient jealousies and fierce disdains
That goaded us to battle; overthrown,
  We are judged rebels, and besieged with pains,
Whilst o'er his radiant hosts the happy victor reigns.

" And for the etherial air, serene and pure,
  The golden sun, the starry spheres, his hate
Has locked us in this bottomless obscure,
  Forbidding bold ambition to translate
Our spirits to their first divine estate;
  Then, ah the bitter thought! 't is this which aye
Stings me to madness,—then did he create
  The vile worm man, that thing of reptile clay,
To fill our vacant seats in those blue fields of day.
Nor this sufficed; to spite us more, he gave
His only Son, his darling, to the dead;

.   .   .   .   .   .

" And shall the myriad spirits who bestowed
Tribute on us, that tribute now disdain,
And o'er dispeopled realms abandoned Pluto reign?

" No! for our essences are yet the same,
  The same our pride, our prowess, and our power,
As when with sharp steel and engirding flame
  In godlike battle we withstood the flower
Of Heaven's archangels; we in evil hour
  Were foiled, I grant; but partial chance, not skill

> Gave them the victory,—still we scorned to cower ;
> Victory was theirs, but an unconquered will
> Nobly remained to us—it fires our spirits still !
> . . . .
> "Let what I will, be fate ;"   .   .   .

The effect of Tasso's Satan in oratory is as potent as Milton's upon his followers:

> Ere yet the anarch closed his fierce harangue,
> His rebel angels on swift wings were flown,
> Glad to revisit the pure light ; a clang
> Of pinions passed, and he was left alone.

A less skilled poet than Tasso had written also a spirited description of Satan and composed for the defiant foe of God an impious speech.   Milton unquestionably knew this work in the original Italian, and he could hardly have failed to read Crashaw's version of *Sospetto d'Herode*, which is the first book of *Strage degli Innocenti* by Marino.   This kind of speech was not confined to the epic.   It is true that the heroes of Homer and Virgil make long impassioned speeches that give life to the council scenes in the epic ; but Euripides and Seneca had also written elaborate heroic speeches in their tragedies, Shakespeare and Marlowe adopted the method of Euripides in this respect, and Sir John Denham had composed

[1] J. H. Wiffen's translation.

speeches in the *Sophy* upon the classic model.
Milton saw the advantage of such speeches for
the portrayal of Satan, but he saw also that
he required utterances in keeping with a superhuman creation only whose outlines could not
be adequately given without the deliberation
of the epic and its varied devices.

Marino's lines are more excited but less con-
vincingly strong than those of Tasso's composition. Satan, in the passage from Marino about
to be quoted, is enraged at the news of Christ's
birth; so that the time presented is possibly
two thousand years later than *Paradise Lost;*
but the opposition of Satan to God is unchanged by time, his memory of his defeat is as
stinging as when he first arouses himself after
the battle in heaven.

"O me!" thus bellow'd he: "O me! What great
    Portents before mine eyes their pow'r advance?
    And serve my purer sight, only to beat
    Down my proud thought: and leave it in a trance?
    Frown I: and can great Nature keep her seat?
    And the gay stars lead on their golden dance?
    Can His attempts above still prosperous be,
    Auspicious still, in spite of Hell and me?

"He has my heaven, what would he more? Whose bright
    And radiant sceptre this bold hand should bear ;
    And for the never fading fields of light
    My fair inheritance, He confines me here

To this dark house of shades, horror and night
To draw a long-lived death, where all my cheer
Is the solemnity my sorrows wear
That mankind's torment waits upon my tears.

"Dark dusky man, He needs would single forth
To make the partner of His own pure ray
And should we pow'rs of Heaven, spirits of worth
Bow our bright heads before a king of day?
It shall not be, said I, and clomb the north
Where never wing of angel yet made way:
What though I miss'd my blow?   Yet I stroke high:
And to dare something is some victory."

.   .   .   .

"Art thou not Lucifer? he to whom the droves
Of stars that gild the moon in charge were given?"

.   .   .   .

"If Hell must mourn, Heaven sure shall sympathise;
What force cannot effect, fraud shall devise."

"And yet whose force fear I!   Have I so lost
Myself?   My strength, too, with my innocence?
Come try who dares, Heaven, Earth, what e'er dost boast
A borrowed being, make thy bold defence;
Come thy Creator, too, what though it cost
Me yet a second fall?   We'd try our strength.
Heaven saw us struggle o'er as brave a fight
Earth now should see and tremble at the sight."

A stronger speech from Satan is to be
found in the work of a seventeenth-century
English poet, Sir Joseph Beaumont, whose
wearisome *Psyche*, a second *Psychomachia*, has
furnished " many flowers " to greater men's
gardens.   There is a hideous description of

Satan followed by a well composed speech of
God's unyielding foe. There are many re-
miniscences of those words in the oratory of
the archfiend in *Paradise Lost*. Satan, though
fallen, boasts an unconquerable mind, and a
courage unshaken. He encourages his followers by assurance that chance only took from
them the victory; and in the next encounter, experience will reinforce their strength in arms.
Their highest boast now may be that they have
once engaged God's army in conflict; even
though they failed, they should not despair, for
in a second onslaught, they will find God vulnerable through man.

> "I yield not yet: Defiance Heaven," said he,
> "And though I cannot reach thee with my fire
> Yet my unconquered brain shall able be
> To grapple with thee: nor canst thou be higher
> Than my brave spirit: know, though below I dwell,
> Heaven has no stouter hearts than strut in Hell."

. . . .

> "Courage, my Lords, ye are the same who once
> Ventured on that renowned design with me
> Against the Tyrant called Heaven's righteous Prince.
> What though chance stole from us that victory?
> 'T was the first field we fought; and He being in
> His own dominion might more easily win."

. . . . . . ,

> "I am resolved to find Him work as long
> As He and His eternity can last.

"My spirit never must forget that wrong
Which me into His hateful dungeon cast.
Nor need I fear Him now, since I can be
Victorious yet—in my unconquered will,
Were pow'r but mine, I would defy Him still."

.   .   .   .

"Once more with brave confed'rate dæmons rise
And grapple with the Tyrant of the skies."

, ...

"Yes Lucifer, thy every subject boasts
He fought the armies of the Lord of Hosts."

.   .   .   .   .   .

"But yet in man, His darling care,
Yes, we shall find Him vulnerable there." [1]

In Cowley's epic, *Davidëis*, Milton found not
only descriptions of hell that took his thoughtful attention, but scenes also in heaven. Beneath the silent chambers of the earth, beneath
the waves, where no dear glimpse of the sun's
lovely face illuminates the solid darkness, Cowley placed his mighty captive, Lucifer. Milton
changed the cosmogony and conceived of hell
as outside of earth and of the solar system altogether, but there is similarity in the picture

[1] See also *The Glasse of Time in the two first ages
divinely handled by Thomas Peyton of Lincolne's Inne,
Gent.*, London, 1623; Strafford's *Niobe, or Age of Tears*,
1611, Humphrey Lownes's press.

of the fallen archangel persistent in his defiance:

Proud 'midst his woes, and tyrant in his chains.

He is surrounded by his myriads of followers, whom Cowley like Milton, also, suggests rather than describes; but Milton has surpassed him in the impressionistic art of the portrayal of the spirit world.

Here are Cowley's words:

Myriads of spirits fell wounded round him there ;
With dropping lights thick shone the singèd air.
Since when the dismal solace of their woe,
Has only been weak mankind to undo ;

.   .   .   .

And, though no less he knew himself too weak
The smallest link of strong wrought Fate to break ;
Yet would he rage, and struggle with the chain ;
Lov'd to rebel, though sure that 't was in vain.

.   .   .   .   .   .

Thrice did he knock his iron teeth, thrice howl,
And into frowns his wrathful forehead rowl,
His eyes dart forth red flames, which scare the night,
And with worse fires the trembling ghosts affright.
A troop of ghastly fiends compass him round,
And greedily catch at his lips' fear'd sound:
" Are we such nothings then ! "

.   .   .   .   .   .

" Oh, my ill-chang'd condition !   Oh, my fate !
Did I lose heaven for this ? "
With that, with his long tail he lashed his breast,
And horribly spoke out in looks the rest.

The quaking powers of night stood in amaze,
And at each other first could only gaze.
A dreadful silence fill'd the hollow place,

. . . .

No hiss of snake, no clank of chains was known,
The souls amidst their tortures durst not groan.

Thus Satan raged against young David,
from whose seed Christ was to be born. Meanwhile
David slept peacefully, and Cowley continues
in these lines:

Sleep on, rest quiet as thy conscience take,
For though thou sleep'st thyself, thy God's awake.

And there follows a dignified, suggestive description
of heaven:

Above the subtle foldings of the sky,
Above the well-set orb's soft harmony,
Above the pretty lamps that gild the night;
There is a place o'erflown with hallow'd light;

. . . .

For there no twilight of the sun's dull ray,
Glimmers upon the pure and native day.

. . . .

Nothing is there to come, and nothing past,
But an eternal now does always last.
There sits th' Almighty, First of all, and End,
Whom nothing but Himself can comprehend.

Not only has Cowley thus depicted Lucifer
and God, but he also attempts the spirits of
heaven:

When Gabriel (no blest spirit more kind or fair)
Bodies and clothes himself with thicken'd air.
All like a comely youth in life's fresh bloom,
Rare workmanship, and wrought by heavenly loom;
He took for skin, a cloud most soft and bright,
That ere the midday sun pierc'd through with light :
Upon his cheeks a lively blush he spread ;
Wash'd from the morning beauties' deepest red.

The tendency in Cowley is to the diffuseness of over-elaboration rather than to condensed energy. The imaginative effect of certain lines certainly reaches toward epic height, and the range is also epical. However, to the sensitive ear of Milton there must have been much to desire in the sweep of the lines ; for the melody instead of expressing the elevation is frequently at variance with it, and may well have hastened Milton's conclusion in his prefatory note to *Paradise Lost*, on " The Verse ":

The measure is English heroic verse without rime, as that of Homer in Greek, and of Virgil in Latin ; rime being no necessary adjunct or true ornament of a poem or good verse, in longer works especially, but the invention of a barbarous age, to set off wretched matter and lame meter ; grac't indeed since by the use of some famous modern poets, carried away by custom, but much to their own vexation, hindrance, and constraint to express many things otherwise, and for the most part worse, than else they would have exprest them.

Nor are the pictures grasped in these passages from Cowley, but the effect is suggested by surroundings or atmosphere.   There was still much to be done before the epical material could emerge in the clearer outline attained in *Paradise Lost*.

There are passages of greater power that bear in themselves proof of their influence over the mind of Milton in his construction of *Paradise Lost*.   For instance, the guardians of hell's gates in Milton's epic are found also in the *Apollyonists*, a Spenserian poem by Phineas Fletcher, written against the power of the Jesuits in England.   Here Lucifer appears as the father of the Jesuits, he calls a council in hell for which the iron gates are flung open.

The porter to the infernal gate is sin,
A shapeless shape, a foule deformed thing,
Nor nothing, nor a substance; as these thin
And empty formes, which through the ayer fling
Their wandering shapes, at length they'r fasten'd in
The chrystall sight.   It serves, yet reigns as King·
It lives, yet's death : it pleases, full of paine :
Monster ! ah who, who can thy beeing faigne?
Thou shapeless shape, live death, paine pleasing, servile
    reigne.

When the spirits have assembled, Satan sits aloft:

To be in Heaven the second, he disdaines :
So now the first in Hell, and flames he raignes,

Crowned once with joy, and light: crowned now with
    fire and paines.

In another work of Phineas Fletcher's, the
Latin poem *Locustæ*, there is a speech of Satan
nearer in some respects to the oratory of the
fallen Lucifer in *Paradise Lost*. Like Satan in
the first book of Milton's epic he spurs his dis-
mayed army with irony and ridicule:

> " Can you degenerate souls, inactive lie,
>   You, who have shook the empire of the sky?
>   Can you, who grasped at Heaven, and greatly fell
>   From slaves above, to reign supreme in Hell?
>   Who fac'd the thunder in a burning show'r
>   And fought intrepid 'gainst the Almighty pow'r,
>   Can you, thus lame, behold your abject fate
>   Nor prop the ruin of our falling state? "

    .   .   .   .

> " But you, perhaps, forget your ancient feud,
>   And pious slaves, degen'rate into good.
>   Best seek those honours you enjoy'd before
>   Suppliant with pray'rs, the thunderer adore,
>   Perhaps you'll shine with cherubim again
>   And Heaven relenting break the eternal chain ;
>   Once more with flaming ministers enrolled
>   The effulgence of Divinity behold.
>   But could Repentance deprecate my crime,
>   Or were my tortures limited by time,
>   And tho' by base submission, it were given
>   Once more to gain yon abdicated Heaven,
>   Rather than fawn, or sink so meanly low
>   I'll howl amidst infinity of woe.
>   Once more to gain yon abdicated Heaven

That easy God I'd scorn, whom now I hate,
    If he had punished with a milder fate." [1]

The management of such attributes as justice and mercy in Giles Fletcher's *Christ's Victory and Triumph* may have aided Milton in his conclusion to fuse all the allegorical elements into the method of *Paradise Lost,* in the eleventh and twelfth books.

Stronger than all these influences, was the result of Milton's long meditation upon the great literature of the classic world, as may be seen from his introduction to Book IX of *Paradise Lost:*

No more of talk where God or angel guest
With man, as with his friend, familiar us'd
To sit indulgent, and with him partake
Rural repast, permitting him the while
Venial discourse unblam'd : (I now must change
Those notes to tragic); foul distrust, and breach
Disloyal on the part of man, revolt,
And disobedience : on the part of heaven
Now alienated, distance and distaste,
Anger, and just rebuke, and judgment given,
That brought into this world a world of woe ;
Sin and her shadow Death, and Misery
Death's harbinger: sad task, yet argument
Not less but more heroic than the wrath
Of stern Achilles on his foe pursu'd
Thrice fugitive about Troy wall ; or rage
Of Turnus for Lavinia disespous'd,

[1] Sterling translation.

Or Neptune's ire or Juno's, that so long
Perplex'd the Greek and Cytherea's son:
If answerable style I can obtain
Of my celestial patroness, who deigns
Her nightly visitation unimplor'd,
And dictates to me slumb'ring, or inspires
Easy my unpremeditated verse:
Since first this subject for heroic song
Pleas'd me, long choosing and beginning late;
Not sedulous by nature to indite
Wars, hitherto the only argument
Heroic deem'd, chief mastery to dissect
With long and tedious havock fabled knights
In battles feign'd; the better fortitude
Of patience and heroic martyrdom
Unsung; or to describe races and games,
Or tilting furniture, imblazon'd shields,
Impresses quaint, caparisons and steeds;
Bases and tinsel trappings, gorgeous knights
At joust and tournament; then marshal'd feast
Serv'd up in hall with sewers, and seneschals;
The skill of artifice, or office mean,
Not that which justly gives heroic name
To person or to poem. Me, of these
Nor skill'd nor studious, higher argument
Remains, sufficient of itself to raise
That name, unless an age too late, or cold
Climate, or years damp my intended wing
Depress'd, and much they may, if all be mine,
Not hers who brings it nightly to my ear.

With this as Milton's conclusion, we are
brought to the end of our quest, to *Paradise
Lost,* and in the next essay we shall note Milton's finished art in the epic.

XI

GOD, SATAN, ADAM, AND EVE

*P*ARADISE LOST represents the work of a lifetime.[1] Even after there is reason to believe that Milton had decided to write not a tragedy, but an epic upon man's fall, he laboured seven years more to produce his masterpiece. In his fifty-eighth year, the poem was ready for the press, and two years later, in 1667, appeared in its first edition in ten books. The argument of every book and the note on the verse were added in a reprint.

In the second edition, in 1674, the epic was published in twelve books,[2] and fourteen years later Tonson produced his beautiful folio known as the Somers edition, containing twelve plates; among them Milton's portrait with

---

[1] Address to the Sun, 1642.

Adam's and Eve's lament over loss of Paradise near the same date.

Paradise Lost begun according to Aubrey, 1658. Finished 1665. First edition, 1667.

[2] Books VII and X enlarged and divided.

Dryden's lines engraved below.[1] In less than a hundred years after its first appearance *Paradise Lost* reached its fifty-sixth edition, and it had been translated twelve times.

Milton's version of man's fall has not only absorbed the student, but it has delighted the reader for art's sake. It has been seized as a creed by the multitudes, and it has rooted itself as folk-lore among the ignorant; the range of its appeal is therefore wide. Indeed, before his epic had attained translation into more than eighteen tongues, the words of Milton in *Epitaphium Damonis* were justified; for surely he was not in this aim over-boastful, that he should " be read from yellow-haired Ouse to the wave-worn shores of the far Orkneys," for he was known beyond all realms of this dream of his youth far " in the land of the stranger."

As Milton has himself written the arguments for every book of his great epic, it would be a

---

[1] Three poets, in three distant ages born,
Greece, Italy, and England did adorn.
The first in loftiness of thought surpassed,
The next in majesty, in both the last.
The force of nature could no farther go ;
To make a third she joined the former two.

Lines printed under the engraved portrait of Milton in Tonson's edition of *Paradise Lost*, 1688.

work of supererogation to more than outline the
plan of *Paradise Lost*. Upon his grasp of
the epic background, we have already sufficiently expatiated in essays one, two, and three,
of this volume. It must be the chief purpose
of this essay to indicate his skill in *Paradise
Lost* in the characterisations of God, of Satan,
and of Adam and Eve, and to note his dependence upon the epical method for his measure of
success.

Milton has found the epical invocation an
artistic aid in several ways; for instance it
renders it reasonable for the author to relate
what he could not be supposed to know without
help divine, and it makes prominent the domination of God through the entire epic, which
is important from both an artistic and a philosophical point of view in *Paradise Lost*. The
invocations also promote the stately elevation
of the style.

Aside from these considerations, the invocations are of interest to the student of *Paradise
Lost* from the fact that they reveal a peculiarity
of Milton's mind, for he adopts no convention
of the epic blindly, but all devices interest him
from a philosophical point of view,—therefore
no matter how much he may borrow, he is

always essentially original. To Milton the heavenly muse is not only Urania, but she is the holy spirit that revealed the mysteries of God to Moses; she is the light that may irradiate his mind so that he may see and tell of things invisible to mortal sight. Milton's tendency is more modern than classic in this philosophical bent toward a comparative view of religions.

After his first invocation, Milton introduces the important theme for the unfolding of which he needs superhuman aid. In a tragedy, man may grope for the forces that are at play; in an epic, they are relatively clear and so Milton propounds his question, What caused the first parents to sin? and he proceeds at once, after invoking the aid of the heavenly muse, to answer it. It was the infernal serpent stirred up with envy and revenge, who after he was cast out of heaven deceived the mother of mankind. Thus at the outset of the epic the powers opposed in combat are perfectly defined: Satan at first against God alone, afterwards against God through man; and the two plots of the fall of Lucifer, and of the fall of man are the logical outcome of this situation and supply the twofold plot for the epic.

The rebelling archangel becomes the bond of unity between the two plots, and the temptation scene, the point of intersection of the two episodes, is for this reason the dynamic centre of the epic. Lucifer originates the action in both episodes but he is not therefore the hero. Not even in a classic epic did he who originated the action become necessarily the hero; but quite as often the resistance to the initial action marks the hero. The whole structure of Milton's epic is reared to show how, by resisting Satan's scheme, the Son of God triumphed as the hero of *Paradise Lost*.

Milton spared no pains to paint the magnificent display of God's power, when the Messiah cast the rebellious angel out of heaven and returned amidst the songs of triumph of the hosts of loyal angels to his seat at God's right hand. Now defeated in heaven, Satan carries his war into Eden, and by subtlety rather than with courage for open battle, he attacks the dweller in Paradise. Adam and Eve are thus acted upon by Satan, and they at first resist the evil influence; but a latent vanity in Eve at length weakens the defence, she yields to the blandishments of the serpent; then the growing blindness of passion in Adam for Eve makes possible his surrender, and Satan triumphs in their fall; but the war is not at an end, for man is not given over to Satan.

Endowed with free will, man had fallen through an unworthy choice, but through a nobler choice he might yet obtain salvation and thus triumph over evil; divine love hastens to man's rescue and the Messiah's resistance to Satan assumes even a deeper spiritual significance in the contest in the garden of Eden than within the realm of heaven. Upon Milton's genius here, lies the burden of clothing in epical action the philosophy expounded in the *Treatise on Christian Doctrine*. Through remorse, even despair, through a consciousness of a sin that he would fain escape, Adam makes his way to repentance and a persistent desire for a right relation with God. It is true that retribution falls upon the erring ones, for they must leave the earthly Paradise; but the penalty, after all, enhances man's dignity, for he enters into an appreciation of his high birthright through the dignity of suffering, and his inheritance is worth a contest to regain.

Meanwhile Satan does not gain dominion over mankind. The decree of God that to his Son every knee should bow is unrevoked, and his proclamation that men should people the depleted halls of heaven is valid; Satan, therefore, is defeated in both plots against God's authority, and Christ is triumphant, both in heaven and on earth. But Christ's victory is not the kind of triumph most often found in the classic epics, for through a sacrifice that most eloquently sets forth divine goodness, Christ is victorious, and through a display of dark passions that can bring only degradation, Satan meets defeat. Beauty and goodness carry triumph in their train; and this is Milton's Christian Platonism.

Paradise Lost is a Christian epic and Christ is the hero. Milton has laid the classic epic under tribute for details that adorn a new and in most respects modern type. There were two artistic problems involved in his attempt: how was he to present God, omnipotent, omniscient, and omnipresent, and how was he to clothe in action, both artistically and efficiently, the theories of man's free will?

Milton was aware that the characterisation of God was an impossible undertaking; for in the *Treatise on Christian Doctrine*, he has stated his belief that to a finite mind God was incomprehensible. How can the unknowable be

definitely enough conceived for the clearness
required by art? that was Milton's problem,
and his consciousness of this unattainable goal
stiffened his style when he set about a portrayal
of God. However he made a gallant attempt;
and he very wisely called to his aid the Bible
phraseology, for the language of religious association would be invaluable in promoting the
elevation of his style and it would lend dignity
to his effort.

Milton had not attempted a portrayal of
God in his plans for a tragedy. The effort
made by Grotius in *Adamus Exsul* had not
been successful, for God appeared to be neither
omniscient nor omnipotent. The attempt made
by Vondel in *Adam in Ballingschap* and in
Lucifer had not convinced the reader that
God had sufficiently warned Adam of danger
or adequately guarded Eden. Indeed if in
these tragedies the plotting fiends do show
some apprehension of discovery by the angel
guests, they have no very consistent fear of
the all-seeing eye of God. Moreover, even in
heaven, God seems dependent upon the report
of the loyal angels for knowledge of what is
taking place. Otherwise the sedition under the
leadership of Lucifer could not have made such

progress before God appears to have had any
inkling of the rebellion.   Indeed, wrapped in
mists and aloof from His kingdom, both in
heaven and on earth, He has other interests and
other cares apparently.   Milton has changed
all this.

In *Paradise Lost* God dominates all.   He
not only sees every movement of Satan, but
long before his intrigues knows what he will
attempt.   The Almighty Father discusses all
the problems of government with His Son.   He
knows that Satan will attack man and find him
vulnerable through his free will, which makes
possible the choice of good or of evil.   Adam
cannot be deprived of his free will without
the loss of power and of dignity.   He must
learn to choose wisely, and here is the universal
human problem.   How can man choose wisely?
Milton's Paradise is not a background for an
artificial Adam surrounded with toy angels,
but it is man's life in epitome.   Milton's conclusion that Adam must learn through suffering is inevitable, and his triumph must be like
Lear in the assurance that he has learned to
discriminate good from evil.   Even Eden then
is not so important, because anywhere they
could " sing like birds in a cage."

The underlying plan in *Paradise Lost* is convincing; God is unresting in his fatherly care of man, He inspires the loving sacrifice of the Messiah. The angels are ministers of God's pleasure and are manifestations of His gracious solicitude for men. There is no flaw in their discipline, there is no defect in their zeal to discharge their duty, there is no weak point in their resistance to evil, and there is no loophole of escape from the responsibility of Adam and Eve. They fall from no one's carelessness nor inefficiency, but from their own free will. Of that the reader is so convinced that when the guardian angels, on the day of man's fall, rise mute with dismay to God's throne, their acquittal by God of any charge of negligence seems inevitable. "Force against free will had there no place" and all else had been tried. True, the angels were not omniscient, that was an attribute of God alone.

The words put by Milton into the mouth of God in the third book, for instance, are not, however, so fortunate and detract much from the beauty and dignity of his characterisation of God. The reader may accept every conclusion in *Paradise Lost*, while he deplores a presentation of God that represents him as ego-

tistical, as mindful of his own dignity, and as
guarding himself against the attack of the
schoolmen. The poet seems to have too vivid a
memory of theological disputes not to introduce a polemical spirit into heaven. This atmosphere of debate and of self-justification is
at variance with the majestic sweetness that we
may believe sits there enthroned.

Milton was dominated by " the old dispens-
ation " as well as the new; but in certain respects, he had not fused them into unity. As
proof of this, in the *Treatise on Christian
Doctrine*, justice is treated with a degree of
enthusiasm that far surpasses the somewhat
perfunctory comment upon mercy. In fact,
intellectually, as he more than once asserted,
Milton had accepted a union of justice and
mercy, and he had even declared that he put
mercy above justice, but in his heart he was
prone to put justice above mercy, for this
both his polemical writings and *Paradise Lost*
would indicate. This peculiar twist of his nature affected his art and made inconsistent his
characterisation of God.

The conception that he that sits in the
heavens shall laugh, God shall hold them in derision impressed him, and not alone the logical

inference from Christ's teachings that enjoin
not an eye for an eye but pity for the evil-
does. Milton may declare as his belief that
the curse of evil is continuance in evil, but
would he picture a wronged and suffering Prometheus striving to remember the words of that
curse that, in his first pain, he hurled against
his torturer? The conviction had come to the
Titan that Zeus suffered enough in being evil;
Prometheus had learned to pity the tyrant; and
now he would retract the words of hate. In
this regard Shelley and Vondel are superior to
Milton, for there is no doubt that Vondel, too,
better comprehended divine love, as may be
seen in his portrayal of the solicitude of Raphael for the erring archangel [1] Lucifer. Of
all the bright throngs of Milton's heaven, no
one pities Lucifer in his fall,—and yet he had
been the most influential of all the starry
hosts. There are indications that Milton is
as stern as Dante without his violence, but without also his convincing tenderness.

Impossible as a perfect characterisation of
God must be to the finite mind, it is evident that
the defects in Milton's portrayal are not
all essential to the attempt to present the

[1] See the ninth essay of this volume.

infinite, but that they are in part blemishes that are conditioned by his peculiar turn of mind.

The second difficulty in *Paradise Lost* is allied to the portrayal of God, that is the attempt to treat in art the problem of man's free will; and this entails perplexities in itself. All trains of thought indeed in *Paradise Lost* must lead to the conclusion of the responsibility of man's free will. Milton was aware that all dogma imperilled the life of the epic and he has spared no pains to throw his philosophical principles into action; for this end he has enlisted every epic device that might give vigour to his difficult theme. There is however a degree of impossibility involved in the material as he conceived it, and in this respect he shows the baleful influence of contemporary thought. The passages of discussion of foreknowledge and free will have not been all fused by emotion and imagination, but remain unepical dogma. Here Milton was doomed to failure, but he was right in feeling that his hope for success in his theme lay first of all in the strength of the characterisation of Satan and Eve, and in this phase of his art he has won the greatest measure of triumph.

The first step in an adequate presentation of

Satan was taken in his portrayal of God. The poet has not failed to present an all-powerful, all-seeing God whose opposition to the machinations of Satan is continuous. In his drafts for tragedy, Milton had failed to present Satan fully. In *Adamus Exsul*, God's foe might have been Mephistopheles, the ambassador of the archfiend, rather than that great adversary in person. In *Adam in Ballingschap*, and in *Lucifer*, only the name remains to identify the base bandit with the commanding figure of the former angel of light, and his power is not sufficiently put to the test in Eden, for his victory is too easily won. In *L'Adamo*, the fiends crowd and jostle one another to the loss of the conception of the figure of God's great protagonist. All these difficulties Milton overcame in *Paradise Lost*. In the characterisation of Satan, Milton has indeed shown the highest order of genius. He has created a spirit worthy once to be an angel of light, endowed with great powers of mind and heart; he fell through a defect that was allied to his virtues, and degenerated into a fiend, possessed not of alien characteristics, but of qualities that result from a consistent downward development. The poet has created an enlarged psychology for Satan; he is never a man but superhuman always, all of his capabilities of mind and heart are on a larger scale than human. This achievement is a triumph of epic art.

First of all, in the portrayal of Satan, Milton concluded that the fall of Lucifer, the most beautiful spirit in heaven, into outer darkness should not be passed over hurriedly. The Angel of the Morning Star, reverenced by his fellow angels for his beauty and strength, came to admire his own splendour and to trust his own power. The lurking danger, here, needed only a motive to develop the defect. When God's decree went forth that every knee in heaven should bow to Messiah as reverently as to God, Lucifer resented the revelation herein conveyed that he no longer stood second only to God in heaven, and he was jealous for his privileges.

His former virtues helped him to a following among the good angels. With the reasonable pretext that he will prepare for a suitable reception of the Messiah, he withdraws with his hosts to his own subordinate kingdom of the Morning Star. He now stirs up a rebellion. He insinuates that " knee tribute too much to one " is now doubly exacted. Where will the

infringements of the angel dignities cease?
Will not this innovation result in tyranny?
Thus he comes more directly to the point than
Vondel's Stadtholder, and there is less Dutch
provincialism in heaven. As it may be reasonable to suppose, not all of the listening angels
fail to pierce this sophistry. Indeed Abdiel
makes a spirited resistance. The angels, he
insists, have no privileges not held in trust
from God. In his reply to Abdiel, Lucifer then
first develops the spirit of negation. "Who
knows? Who saw God create the angels?
Who knows that they are dependent upon
Him?" Abdiel indignantly warns Lucifer of
his impious folly but the rebellious archangel
balances servility and resistance, and he de-
liberately chooses war with God.

Lucifer after this evil choice can no longer
remain the trusted archangel of heaven but
becomes now Satan, God's adversary. There
remain three terrible days of conflict before
the Messiah sweeps God's foes from heaven into
the bottomless pit of hell, and Satan begins
to understand. Here Milton opens his epic.
The poet thought it not reasonable that the
fallen archangel should all at once comprehend
his inward change; nor should he lose all traces

of his original brightness. He should be not less than archangel ruined, and he should feel his own degradation.

Milton conceived him, at the outset, in the first book of *Paradise Lost* as suffering through his sense of beauty. The surroundings in hell repel him by their ghastly ugliness in sharp contrast with the radiant beauty of heaven. However he is resolved that he is unchanged, and he trusts still his own strength,—and seeks relief in activity. His sense of generalship awakes, for he thinks of his loyal followers. Satan is not enwalled by a petty ego—but his egotism is vast in its scope. Skilled in leadership he knows how to appeal to the dejected spirits, by a commendation of their past exploits, by jeering at their present abject condition, and by spurring them to hope and action to see what resolution can be wrung from despair. In his speech he minimises God's victory, for the Almighty won by the concealed weapon of the thunderbolt an unsportsmanlike advantage and, therefore, the armies met in no fair field. There should be a further test of strength.

At the council, in the second book, Satan shows the power of silence while the fallen

angels speak their minds freely, as though the
question of peace or war lay entirely in their
hands for decision.   True the mighty potentate
of hell upon his throne, that far outshone the
splendour of Ormus or of Ind, assumes great
pomp, but he skilfully wards off all envy by
reminding his followers that,—

> "no strife can grow up there
> From faction ; for none sure will claim in hell
> Precedence, none, whose portion is so small
> Of present pain, that with ambitious mind
> Will covet more."

He is wise in directing the debate, for he
announces clearly the purpose of this meeting.

> "Whether of open war or covert guile,
> We now debate ; "

He listens to hot-headed Moloch, " whose sentence is for open war " and who scorns slyer
methods ; to the urbane and plausible Belial,
who " could make the worse appear the better
reason," and now counselled " ignoble ease and
peaceful sloth " on grounds that they might
make matters worse, if they attempted to resist ; and he hears without comment, the practical advice of Mammon, who states that they
cannot disenthrone the Omnipotent and while
God reigns the outcast angels could have no

wish to re-enter heaven where they would be compelled to celebrate His throne with warbled hymns. It were better far to keep by themselves, to develop the resources of hell, to raise a rival kingdom, and to dismiss all thought of war. But Satan had no thought of ceasing his warfare with God, and at his instigation Beëlzebub arose to propose an indirect attack on God through a plot against man. To this end the fallen angels should bend all their powers to learn about this newly created man and woman,

> " And where their weakness, how attempted best,
> By force or subtilty."

. . . .

> " who shall tempt with wand'ring feet
> The dark unbottom'd infinite abyss,"

who shall avoid the strict sentries of the watchful angels, and accomplish the difficult task, upon which the last hope of the fallen angels relies? The ground for Satan's supremacy in Pandemonium is clear, for he does not, as in *L'Adamo*, and *Adam in Ballingschap*, send a messenger to execute this important mission on earth, but first in courage, as first in power, he goes himself.

Undaunted by the perils of his voyage to

the world, he displays *finesse* with Sin and
Death and diplomacy with Chaos and Old
Night, and leaves them all allies. When at a
loss to find his way, he decks himself in the
guise of a reverent young angel and dares to
dupe Uriel on his watch tower in the sun. His
audacity and his holy mien mislead the guardian angel, who is faithful but not omniscient,
and Satan's very plausible request to see God's
handiwork that he may the better worship the
Creator wins for him the needed directions for
reaching Paradise.

After Satan has gone triumphantly on his
way, has leaped insolently over the wall of
Paradise, and has learned from the lips of Adam
and Eve the means of their undoing, the archfiend even looks about for more angels from
whom he may gain details that may be useful
for his plot " to confound the race of mankind
in one root." So far he seems triumphant in
his strength, and might well deceive not only
himself but the readers of *Paradise Lost* into
thinking him a dauntless hero; but it is all a
fine bombastic show, he carries the reason for
defeat with him.

His deception of Uriel is shortlived; for in
prospect of Eden, the archfiend falls into a

contortion of dark passions, when he hurls defiance at the sun that brings him remembrance of that state whence he fell. The good angel recognises evil negatively; Uriel realises that no angel of light was ever thus tempest tossed with conflicting emotions.

Thereupon the guardian angel speeds on his way to warn the angelic guard of the invasion of Eden by one of that rebel crew, and later a detachment of the heavenly host search out the archfiend in the shape of a toad squatting at the ear of Eve. A touch of Ithuriel's wonderworking spear uncloaks the evil spirit. Satan starts up with a bold attempt to confront the good angel, but his heart sinks within him before the awful beauty and strength of holiness which he knows now that he has lost, and that all of his boasting was an empty vaunt.

A rebel and an outcast from God, bereft of his celestial beauty, he still had clung to his former titles and to the dignity of heaven. Though doomed to become the father of all guile, he had not lost at once all of his noble heavenly bearing, and he at first took more naturally direct methods as suited to his past high position; slyer methods were the result of his situation. He was resolved to win, if not

by old devices, he will adopt new; but he did
not naturally crawl.

The encounter with Ithuriel and Zephon reveals to Satan that great Lucifer despite a
regal port can be no longer recognised by his
former subordinates in heaven. Now he loses
his royal air, heaven's scales show him his
doom; never more can he meet the forces of
God in open combat, no single angel of light
can he openly face again. A fugitive from
good, crawling is his only course, and herein
lies his defeat. This is a kind of defeat that
appeals most in its force to the Anglo-Saxon
love of open-minded, fair play. Surely no
genuine Englishman is likely to misunderstand
Milton's study of Satan here, nor to think him
the hero of *Paradise Lost*.

Both from his speeches and his behaviour it
is possible to see that Satan's course is con-
tinuously downward in *Paradise Lost*. He
degenerates through a series of choices. Endowed with fine intellectual powers, he has
capacity for clear and deep reasoning; but a
study of his many brilliant speeches in the epic
proves that it was his doom to see clearly good
and evil and to choose the evil. Created with
good impulses, it is now his curse to have all

trains of thought end in evil. His high sense of beauty remains with him to the bitter end, and it is a means of enhancing his suffering and of forcing him to acknowledge his overthrow in his losing contest with God; for he realises in the ninth book, when he lifts his impious voice in derision of God, that hideous shapes and sights unholy are his only heritage.

Satan's fine intellectual powers are displayed in his famous apostrophe to the sun. He understands and admits with perfect frankness his own wrong-doing, but with eyes wide open to all that evil means, chooses to be evil. [He realised that God had created him, given him high eminence, and loaded him with benefits, " yet all of his good," he says, " proved ill in me."

> " And wrought but malice ; lifted up so high
> I 'sdeined subjection, and thought one step higher
> Would set me highest, and in a moment quit
> The debt immense of endless gratitude
> So burdensome, still paying, still to owe ; "]

In his rebellion Satan admits that God deserved no such return for all of his benefits. With a realisation of his moral weakness he suggests that it might have been fortunate if destiny had ordained him some inferior angel;

but he reflects that, even then, he might have
been ambitious.

> " . . . but other powers as great
> Fell not, but stand unshaken,
> .   .   .   .
> Hadst thou the same free will and power to stand?"

Now Satan seems very near to penitence, but
there comes the sad twist in his reasoning that
is characteristic.

> "Thou hadst, whom hast thou then or what to accuse,
> But Heaven's free love dealt equally to all?
> Be then his love accurs'd, since love or hate,
> To me alike, it deals eternal woe:"

An outcast from divine love by his own elec-
tion, he realises, however, that this choice brings
him only despair. "Which way I fly is hell,
myself am hell." But there is no way to gain
repentance and pardon except by submission
and that he spurns through his own pride and
his dread of shame among the fallen angels.
Satan reminds himself that his followers rely
upon his promise to subdue the Omnipotent;
surrender is impossible. On weighing all these
conditions Satan becomes reckless.

> "So farewell hope, and with hope farewell fear,
> Farewell remorse: all good to me is lost;"

He knows for a certainty that even were he
again in heaven, he would again rebel.

But Satan did not mislead himself into supposing that he had any feud with man. He admits with perfect magnanimity that it is shameful to visit his hatred of God upon these innocent victims, for he has no reason in the world to wish them ill. He keeps still his high taste, for he is sensitive to beauty. Paradise is enchantingly lovely, and Adam and Eve delight him with their beauty; but this train of thought brings to his mind in sharp contrast the memory of the horrors of hell, and his uncontrolled resentment flashes up and from it emerges envy. With a sneer he says Adam and Eve when brought under his thraldom may not enjoy hell as much as they now delight in their earthly paradise, but let them thank God for the gift that they will soon receive, for Satan will after all only pass on the Almighty's bounty to them. Since he has obligations to his followers he must not recede. " Public good " demands that he should set up his kingdom on earth, thus with necessity, the tyrant's plea, he concludes that man must now be corrupted and made subject to the kingdom of darkness.

Nor does Satan make his evil decision once for all; but, tempest-tossed, he continues to feel

remorse yield to revenge. In all these pro-
cesses of thought, the starting-point is love
of beauty, and beauty is always joined by
Milton to thoughts of God and heaven, therefore as foe to God, Satan is a destroyer of
beauty.

When, after his ignoble defeat read from
heaven's scales, Satan fled from Paradise, he was
long in gathering courage for the second attempt on his victims in Eden. Now no longer
so confident, he creeps back to Eden at nightfall; he makes his way under the wall of the
garden under cover of a mist and crawls into
the mouth of a serpent. In adopting this disguise Satan admits his humiliation. Like an
erect angel of light how gladly would he have
paced the walks of Paradise, as he explored its
beauties, but he adds sadly, " If I could joy in
aught," and he continues, mindful of the disgrace that evil has brought:

> " O foul descent ! that I, who erst contended
>   With gods to sit the highest, am now constrain'd
>   Into a beast, and mixed with bestial slime,
>   This essence to incarnate and imbrute,
>   That to the height of deity aspir'd ;
>   But what will not ambition and revenge
>   Descend to ?   who aspires must down as low
>   As high he soar'd,"

. . . .

"Revenge, at first though sweet,
Bitter ere long back on itself recoils:"

He is not untouched by the loveliness of Eve, which brings to him fresh wonder every time he sees her. Now, " veiled in a cloud of fragrance where she stood," her graceful innocence over-awed his malice and for the time he remained " stupidly good," but here, as elsewhere, it is his sad lot that all of his good impulses are merged in evil.

He reminds himself that save what pleasure he can find as a destroyer, all his joy is lost. He sets about the execution of his fell design to subjugate the human race, and Eve here meets the most skilled and dangerous tempter of all the temptation scenes of literature.

He first arouses her wonder by his serpentine grace and iridescent colouring. He is in no hurry to execute his plot, for according to Milton's view of this scene, the power of hell uses deliberation and exerts itself to the uttermost for this difficult and important attack on God. At length, the serpent speaks, lost in admiration of Eve. When he has gained her attention, he insinuates that she is not appreciated; she should be adored, a goddess among gods with numberless angels in her train. When Eve has overcome her amazement sufficiently to ask how a serpent can speak, he explains that far away in the garden is a magical tree whose fruit quickens all the senses and reveals mysteries; of this he has eaten. Eve realises that she has not yet explored the whole of the garden, she does not yet know all of the trees of Paradise. When Satan offers to show her the way, she goes gladly to see this marvellous tree. This device breaks the abruptness of the fall, as, for instance, it is given in *Adam in Ballingschap.* After a walk of some appreciable length, they approach the forbidden tree of knowledge.

Now, with a sudden revulsion of feeling from anticipation to disappointment, Eve recognises the interdicted tree. When she expresses her regret at his waste of time in conducting her here to this spot, for this tree is not to be touched, and to eat the fruit will bring death, Satan falls into an attitude of indignant surprise. After a dramatic silence, he ignores Eve, for a time, and addresses the tree, extolling its virtues and deploring the false charge against it: "Death indeed! I have eaten and live." He then turns to Eve; surprise, indignation, solicitous regard for her welfare are so well feigned that she is swept on by forcible words to the conclusion that envy could be the only motive for God's injunction. Satan uses this *a fortiori* argument; if a serpent is made to speak through the efficacy of this tree, how much more will a mortal woman be lifted by its powers. She should become an angel. God's envy is not so strange, since she is worthy to be adored in heaven.

Satan employs fewer words than in *Adamus Exsul*, but he wastes no power, and Eve is incited to cast off God's tyranny. If this fruit brings death, it may be a death to be desired, the casting off of mortal for immortal dignity.

When Eve took and ate the fruit nature gave signs of woe, " that all was lost, and back to the thicket slunk the guilty serpent."

Still Satan, though creeping, has outward signs of victory for a time. Sin and Death have prepared a triumphal march for him back to hell, and have made ready for traffic with the world. Eager for his coming they advance to meet him. Sending on these grim harbingers as his regents on earth, Satan speeds on to Pandemonium, enters the council in disguise, mounts his throne, and flashes out his diminishing glory upon his astonished subjects. They receive him with adulation. The arch-fiend announces his victory; he exults, for he is persuaded that he has conquered God, and he pits against the thunderbolts of the Almighty the power of the puny apple. He jeers at God's folly in devising such a scheme as a forbidden tree which has brought the ruin of his handiwork. The denizens of hell are transported with joy and lift their voices in applause, when their triumph is turned to humiliation and they fall headlong, hissing serpents, and view this change with horror. They climb a tree with the semblance of the tree of knowledge and their mouths are filled with ashes. Satan's only applause is a prolonged hiss, his only satisfaction turns to ashes on his lips. To be a corrupter of beauty, a foe to love, and the adversary of God is his perpetual doom. Indeed, that the curse of evil is continuance in evil, is the conclusion of Milton's masterly characterisation of the fallen angel.

Second only to Milton's power in the portrayal of Satan is his skill in the delineation of Eve. As we have seen in Milton's plans for a tragedy, there was little opportunity for the development of the personality of Adam and

Eve, for they were not presented to us until after their fall, and we do not see them under the ordeal of their temptation.   In any case there are two fundamental difficulties in the delineation of these characters in a tragedy: transformations from perfect innocence to opposition to righteousness, from sullen despair to penitent hope requires the deliberate method of the epic or the novel; and another difficulty is found in the fact that if Adam and Eve must seem to us all men, not one man and one woman, the epic elevation is more efficient than the tragic vividness, for carrying conviction.

In the tragedies, *Adamus Exsul*, *Adam in Ballingschap*, and *L'Adamo*, there is a failure in the unity of the motive of Adam as well as in a consistent characterisation of both Adam and Eve.   The realism of these works is not only out of taste but at the same time prevents the validity of the conclusion, for Adam and Eve do not carry conviction to our minds that they are prototypes in any sense. As our faith in Adam and Eve is not established, we reject the author's tacit claims.

Adam and Eve are better developed in harmony with the theme in *Paradise Lost*, for Milton never loses sight of the notion that these characters should clothe the fable of how evil entered the world. The poet is convinced that sinless people could not suddenly fall into error without some tendency to deterioration in their hearts, which had either been disregarded or cherished. Moreover, some premonition of their vulnerability to the shafts of Satan should be given for the sake of the convincing reasonableness of the art. In *Paradise Lost*, Adam and Eve are less provincial than in the works of Vondel but better individualised and play better their part in an epic of human life. Milton decided that for this end they should never seem bad, but at the worst erring people, not for a moment unworthy of respect, sympathy, and love.

The opinion has been not infrequently advanced that Milton was unfriendly to Eve; the reasons have been adduced that the poet's own unhappy domestic experiences had distorted his art, and that, in general, Milton displayed a tendency to view with such vividness his own griefs that they became for him universal human experience. A careful study of his other works and of Milton's life goes to prove that there are grounds for the conclusion that to this mistake, Milton was by nature liable.

There is also no doubt that if this defect should appear in a work of art, it is too significant to be justly ignored, for an author should rise above personal considerations to the calmer and serener viewpoint of universal humanity. It is well however for us to remember that literary gossip is not literary criticism. So great a poet as Milton might find correction for his defects of impulse in his force of thought: every charge must be tested, not by reference to a generalisation, however plausible, but on its own merits.

There is a difficulty involved in the plot itself of *Paradise Lost* which it would be unfortunate to ascribe to Milton's hypothetical prejudice against women. In all the stories of man's fall, the immediate tempter was Eve. The question that confronts us at once is,— how could the first woman created tempt her husband to fall and yet be a fair specimen of womanhood, a prototype? This perplexity was not of Milton's invention, it was fundamental in the story, and it is neither just to hold the poet responsible for this situation, nor is it reasonable to demand that he should reform it altogether. It is only fair to examine critically his shaping of the unalterable situa-

tion into literary art and to ask the question,
—was he in this process at fault through unfriendliness to Eve?

I do not think that such a charge can be
substantiated, for much turning over of other
versions of man's fall must compel the conclusion that Milton's Eve is the finest characterisation of them all; a nobler, more lovable
woman, with truer instincts and higher taste;
a far more universal type than the other Eves
of art and story.

Milton has created an Eve divinely fair and
possessed of fatal charm; the flowers spring to
greet her; the animals seek her gracious influence; the angels delight in her beauty, even
Satan forgets his evil plots, lost in wonder at
her loveliness, and Adam adores her and questions whether he does not worship her. Worthy
as she is of love, does she take unconsciously
the adulation of all, or has it bred in her latent
vanity?

Woman fashion, she reveals herself in her
relation to Adam her husband. She is by nature impulsive and generous. She had fallen
in love with Adam at first sight, and with social
tact she delights to lead him to display his fine
powers of mind. She is a good comrade, by

no means unthoughtful herself. In proof of
her power of understanding abstruse subjects,
Milton takes pains to state that when the angel
Raphael came to Eden for a long visit to discuss with Adam and Eve the affairs of heaven
and earth, she is very graciously hospitable; to
his high discourse, she listens attentively for
nearly three books, and then, not because she
was tired, nor because she failed to comprehend
his condensed treatises, but because she had confidence that Adam would report to her all the
important details, she rises and goes to tend
her flowers, reflecting how much better after
all than the angel Adam could talk.

There is no subjection superimposed upon
her in Eden from without, but if it be here, it
is from a law of her emotional nature and emanates from within. There is a note of triumph
in her avowal of her love for her husband and
she scorns self-seeking reservations. Indeed
she is proud to admit to him that neither
breath of morn, nor charm of earliest birds, nor
rising sun, nor dew, nor fragrance after show-
ers, nor silent night, nor moonlight, nor star-
light " without thee is sweet."

On that very night Satan came to squat at
her side and to breathe into her ear an evil dream.

Hitherto Eve had seemed without defect, but the substance of the dream gives on this point some grave cause for doubt; for how could Eve conceive of the flattery and conceit implied in her vision of the night?   Does Milton adopt the notion of dreams as an art convention; does he really believe that both God and Satan may appear to mortals in dreams, when the will is off guard; or does he intend to imply that the material for the dream might be found in Eve's thoughts and that, in spite of her ideal simplicity, she was getting a little spoiled? Upon this question the text gives no help beyond that suggested by Adam that the dream was a fantastic reproduction of disjointed fragments of their evening talk, but he says:

> "nor can I like
> This uncouth dream, of evil sprung I fear:
> Yet evil whence?   in thee can harbour none,
> Created pure."

He feels confident, however, that she is free from defect.

> "Evil into mind of god or man
> May come and go, so unapprov'd, and leave
> No spot or blame behind; which gives me hope
> That what in sleep thou didst abhor to dream,
> Waking thou never wilt consent to do."

Whatever Milton exactly intended, he certainly gained definite artistic effect by the episode of the dream. It aids the deliberation of the method of the epic, and prepares our minds for the fall.

On the morning of the temptation, the dream again recurs to our mind. In her determination to go away by herself among the flowers, Eve's waywardness is most dramatically portrayed, and the scene reveals wider possibilities in both Eve and Adam than we have seen before. The conversation is piquant and human, the range of emotion interestingly portrayed, but Eve is changed. She has not the artless simplicity of the woman who was more interested in Adam's personality than in her own, for she now enjoys wielding her power. She is not at all ill-bred in her manner, she expresses herself still with a pretty deference, but she appears bent on having her own way simply from the pleasure of watching its effect upon Adam. The scene throughout chronicles a bit of coquetry, our minds instinctively revert to the dream, and, like the witches in *Macbeth*, it puzzles the interpreter. Did the vanity here originate with the tempter, or was it latent in Eve?

The plea of Satan at the foot of the tree of

knowledge gives further ground for reflection.
He is a skilled advocate, he knows how to present his plea, he looks for a weak point in Eve,
and he makes an appeal to her love of self. It
is further significant that when Eve has eaten
the fruit and gains, as she believes, all knowledge, she wonders if it will not be well to keep
this superiority over Adam.   How delightful it
will be to explain to his ignorant but docile
mind the mysteries of life! The question of
whether she is wise, or stupid, is not here the
issue, but the mental attitude is significant.
Pride of intellect, brooding consciousness of
intellectual superiority is, as Milton points
out, the most anti-social and ungracious of
traits. There is no doubt that Eve falls
from vainglory.

While she is balancing in her mind the de-
sirability of keeping her advantage over Adam,
she suddenly reflects that there may be punishment for her disobedience.

> " . . . if God have seen
> And death ensue? then I shall be no more,
> And Adam wedded to another Eve "

With this intolerable thought in her mind, she
resolves:

> " Adam shall share with me in bliss or woe:
> So dear I love him,"

And she does not seem to see the flaw in her conception of love.

Adam, meanwhile, is not lacking in responsibility, for he may have deprived Eve of the highest spur of a love built on truth,—he has idolised her. The defect in both Adam and Eve appeals to universal sympathy, because it is so human. At the time of Eve's false exaltation at the foot of the tree of knowledge, Adam was unhappily counting the moments until she should return to him. Loath as he had been to let her go away alone, her pride in her own strength had been a delicate matter to resist, and her implication that she longed for solitude was unanswerable. But now that the hour for her return drew near, he wove a garland for her head and came eagerly at noontime to meet her. Near the tree of knowledge, he descries her; with flushed cheeks and excited manner she is walking swiftly toward him. While still at a distance, she begins to speak and she is very voluble. She has news for Adam: the forbidden tree is not death-giving, the fruit is indeed magical and he must forthwith eat it with her.

The garland falls unheeded from Adam's nerveless hand;—he is silent with dismay.

" Surely some one has deceived you," he exclaims. Surely it would be impossible for Eve to intend to do evil. Then the thought of the fatal consequences comes to him, and he declares without a moment's hesitation—

> " with thee
> Certain my resolution is to die :
>
> .   .   .   .
>
> from thy state
> Mine never shall be parted, bliss or woe."

Adam in Milton's version of the fall has no struggle between love and duty, he sees no duty but in love.

Eve exults in this glorious trial of exceeding love, but she adds an apology that is insincere in view of her avowed intention to make him share her lot in weal or woe; she now says that she surely could not wish him to take the fruit, if it were not helpful, but she knows from experience that it is beneficial. Lost in thought Adam seeks excuses for Eve's disobedience of the divine decree, and tries to take her point of view. But she hastens him on to his doom, from her own experience she recommends the marvellous efficacy of the fruit, and Adam loses his clearness of thought. He reasons, had not the serpent already defiled the tree, and under

19

these circumstances God may no longer desire to reserve the fruit? If this be so there are strong reasons for desiring to taste the apple and to become gods or demi-gods. Nor can he believe that God will destroy his creatures; he would thus lose his reputation for wisdom, and Satan would exult. At all events with Eve Adam will live or die. Without delay; he takes the forbidden fruit.

After Adam and Eve have eaten the forbidden fruit, they feel exalted above all law and are as gods. They do not notice nature's signs of woe but wish that there had been ten forbidden trees instead of one.

> innocence, that as a veil
> Had shadowed them from knowing ill, was gone.

The reaction swiftly follows, bad passions well up in their hearts.

> anger, hate,
> Mistrust, suspicion, discord and shook sore
> Their inward state of mind,

The quarrel that follows is less violent and more truly tragic, in the dignity of their misery, than the contention, with comedy elements, given in the seventeenth-century dramas. This difference arises from two sources: the reader has a clearer comprehension of the characters,

from the variety of their conversation, and
from the deliberation gained from the number
of episodes; both Adam and Eve are more
clearly defined characters from the standpoint
of the plot in Milton's epic, but they are less
realistic than in the tragedies considered in the
foregoing essays.

After the fall in *Paradise Lost* there is a
change in both Adam and Eve; for Eve loses
every touch of vanity, and Adam for a time
shows an extreme revulsion of feeling from
his idolatry of Eve. The adjustment after
this shock to their relations is slow and tragic.
Adam exclaims if Eve had only listened to his
warnings and not wandered away seeking admiration even of a serpent, then they might
still be happy. Eve thinks this is severe; fate
decided all, therefore she might have fallen
quite as readily with Adam near. She then
asks some rather inconsistent questions: Was
he never to move from his side? Why had he
not been firm and insisted upon her remaining?
Evidently she does not yet assume frankly her
guilt.

Adam, who has shown before the fall conspicuous magnanimity and self-forgetfulness,
now becomes pettily personal and quotes his

own generosity, but after all with some measure of justice:

> "Is this the love, is this the recompense
> Of mine to thee, ingrateful Eve? express'd
> Immutable when thou wert lost, not I,
> Who might have liv'd and joy'd immortal bliss
> Yet willingly chose rather death with thee?
> And am I now upbraided, as the cause
> Of thy transgressing?"

He drives home the conclusion, it was her own fault, he had warned her of her danger, but of course she had free will to act.   He blames himself that he had so much admired her, and he closes with a wholesale denunciation of woman, which is more reasonable here than in the other versions of the story, as it has been prepared for by his over-exaltation of Eve; both extremes were alike dangerous and unjust.

But why should this denunciation be declared to voice the author's own personal view? There is no question about the personal basis of the divorce pamphlets, nor the soreness of wounded feeling that expresses its anguish in strange cries, but what bearing have these facts precisely upon *Paradise Lost?* Shall we then conclude that after his unhappy marriage with Mary Powell, Milton became a woman hater and lost no opportunity of expressing his detestation of at least one half of the human race? That conclusion is easy, but is it scholarly? I think not. The question here is not one of biographical criticism but of sterner art values. In *Paradise Lost* Eve has not been, up to this point, unsympathetically conceived by Milton. Adam has worshipped Eve and he now degrades her; the hope must be that out of the two extremes will emerge the happier mean of loving her as human. Adam does not here speak out of character, nor does Milton shield him from blame for his harshness to Eve. Moreover, how is it possible that Eve's abject misery should sadden the reader, unless there were pity in the heart of the composer of those lines?

What is more, before Milton's unhappy domestic experiences, he conceived the idea in his drafts for tragedy that Adam would naturally have a violent revulsion of feeling after his fall, that he would be harsh in his denunciation of Eve, and loud in his own self-justification, and the youthful Milton decided to introduce an angel of justice who should upbraid Adam for his persistent pride and for his unfairness to Eve, and this angel of justice should lead him to be gentle and reasonable and to accept nobly his share of the blame.   In *Paradise Lost* Adam's cynicism is reproved both by God and later by Michael.   Why then do these words of denunciation of woman seem to be more characteristic of Milton as a poet than those lines upon Eve's sweetness and loveliness? Euripides and Shakespeare have also suffered from this form of unrestrained biographical criticism.   I must confess great distaste to criticism that begins thus at the wrong end; for it is not important to note what the student finds in biography that can be transported bodily into the art of an author, but it is significant to discover what he finds in the literary art that is in harmony with biographical fact. Milton had not only a very striking personality, but he was well known in his lifetime and had many enemies, and from the first year of the appearance of his epic, until the present day, Milton's personality has loomed as the essential fact in *Paradise Lost*.   It has followed as a natural consequence that if one did not like the personality of Milton, or what somebody said was his personality, he did not like *Paradise Lost;* but the power both of Milton's character and of his work has been admitted.

In *Paradise Lost*, I find proofs of a larger

Milton than in the Jeremiad of the *Divorce Pamphlets*. Nor do I believe that it is possible for a man to sum up the whole world in his ego and be at the same moment a genius of universal power. It is enough for us to admit that Milton was sometimes like the writer of those pamphlets, and in greater moments rose to the creation of *Paradise Lost*. I should not call the two Miltons inconsistent but different. Who would judge his dearest friend's character at the moment that his sensibilities were stinging from injustice?—and least of all should one judge a poet's character at that crisis.

But to return to Adam's denunciation of Eve. In *Paradise Lost*, we have a gain over other accounts of the fall, for when Adam is upbraided by God for his sin, there is a revival in Adam of the past habit of magnanimity; he does not bear witness to God against Eve without a struggle; he says:

" . . . in evil strait this day I stand
  Before my Judge, either to undergo
  Myself the total crime, or to accuse
  My other self, the partner of my life;
  Whose failing, while her faith to me remains,
  I should conceal, and not expose to blame
  By my complaint;"

The sense of his own injury conquers and he continues indignantly:

> "This woman, whom thou mad'st to be my help,
> And gav'st me as thy perfect gift, so good,
> So fit, so acceptable, so divine,
> That from her hand I could suspect no ill,
> And what she did,[1] whatever in itself,
> Her doing seem'd to justify the deed;
> She gave me of the tree, and I did eat."

But the God of love does not accept this plea; "was she thy God?" he asks—and Adam stands convicted on his own defence. He had lacked the high truth of the greatest love.

After the judgment is pronounced by God, there follows a period of remorse without repentance, and Adam is very harsh in his resentment toward Eve. He calls her a bad woman, a serpent, the cause of all his misery, and Eve reaches the climax of her suffering. But it is remedial, for all thought of self dies, and we see the true woman purified from the defect that too great adulation had fostered. The scene is painful to read when she crawls to Adam's feet and begs for pity. She avows her sin against God and him, and prays eagerly that all punishment may fall upon her. As she can never hope to regain Adam's affection, she feels that through loss of love there is nothing in life and she longs for death. Adam is touched, his old-time gentleness and generosity return, and he vies with Eve in self-sacrifice. He declares that upon his shoulders only shall the burden of sin fall, and, to comfort her, he insists that matters are not past hope. Out of remorse, now comes true repentance, and the inner harmony of life returns.

When the penitent prayers are borne to God's throne, Michael is sent down with a retinue of angels to announce God's commands to the dwellers in Paradise. Because they are penitent, death shall be long delayed, salvation through Christ will insure them hereafter a home in heaven, but they must forthwith depart from the garden of Eden. At the thought of Paradise lost, Adam is awestruck, but he answers the angel with manly courage:

> " . . . gently hast thou told
> Thy message, which might else in telling wound,
> And in performing end us ; "

With a woman's natural love of home, Eve laments her bridal bower, her beloved walks, and her flowers—and such flowers can never grow out of Paradise. Adam grieves to leave the places so often hallowed by God's presence ; but Michael comforts them with the assurances that God goes with them and that with one another all places are alike home.

Adam is shown grounds for faith and hope for his future descendants in a series of visions of man's life until Christ's shall come. Meanwhile Eve has a fair dream that joins her in experience with the Virgin Mary, and she too ponders upon Christ's divinity deep in her heart; and both Adam and Eve become full of hope and quiet confidence. The angelic guard now closes about them and they are escorted to the gate of Paradise. Like pioneers, of high resolve, they go to prove their souls, and, wiser than in their days of untried strength, they set forth attended with the respect and confidence of God, angels, and reader.

Milton has created a consistent psychology for these two actors in a profoundly interesting human drama. This work does not present the distorted view of a petty egotist, but lays hold of universal human experience. Eve is no monster, but a sweet though erring woman, who as eagerly repents as she impulsively sins. Purified by her sorrows, her case is not hopeless, she may yet attain beauty for ashes.

Paradise Lost is not so much universal because it is great, as we are often told, as it is great because of its hold upon the universal human heart, and it shadows forth for the reader the relation of man's emotions to the epic background of mystery. The quest of the lost ideal of an earthly Paradise is not alone the heritage of the poet, but is a latent romance of most men. To this longing of humanity Milton speaks, and if we throw aside hearsay and listen sympathetically to the poet, his heralded severity melts in benignity. In our next essay, we shall note the touches of personal confession in *Paradise Lost*.

XII

THE EPIC SOURCE OF THE LYRICS

IN *Paradise Lost*, there are frequent bursts into pure lyric poetry and the examination of the source of these lyric strains and of their relation to the epic opens to the reader a train of thought of importance for a sympathetic appreciation of Milton both as a man and a poet.

The delicately organised mind of a poet seeks beneath the outward show of life for its deeper significance. From this seerlike tendency of the poet arises an insistence upon contrasting the imperfect reality with his ideal. His spiritual perception of life's possibilities brings about within him a struggle of the ideal beauty of his inner vision with the spectacle of the existing imperfections of life. The poet's belief that ideal beauty is attainable by humanity, and his sorrow over the failures of the quest most often and most deeply inspire the lyric: so it comes about that the spoiling of the lovely garden of Eden by the entrance of sin is a lyric theme, and the lament of Adam and Eve over their lost Paradise has become a heritage of poets.   Modern poets do not, as a rule, trace back their inherited impressions to their root but this Milton does with amazing thoroughness; for in *Paradise Lost* Milton struck the source of all lyric.

No poet has displayed so clearly before our eyes the pristine beauty of life, nor has shown with greater force the pathos of lost ideals, nor has sounded more inspiringly the appeal to mankind to return to Eden.[1] He has convinced his reader that there was involved in the fall of Adam and Eve more than their individual happiness.   Their joys and sorrows chronicle universal human experience, and for this reason, the lyric motive is lifted above the personal joy of Adam and Eve in the fresh morning of the world, or above their personal grief for their ruined Paradise, to the greatest and

[1] The train of thought in this essay has nothing to do with the literal acceptation of the story of Adam and Eve. The essay does not concern itself with the thought that the human race has tended upward since the days of the troglodyte and before. Pristine is a term employed here only in the sense of the fresh unspoiled vision of the ideal, and that the story of Eden typifies.

most universal of themes, that of life's ideal.

The story brings to the poet confidence in his own inner vision and revives his longing for its realisation. While Milton's sorrow for the loss of Eden finds expression in the lyric lines, the scope of the epic merges them in its sweeping onflow. Indeed the movement in *Paradise Lost* is from the epic to the lyric, and the lyric swiftly vibrates to the epic.

As Milton's theme of man's pristine perfection supplies the imaginative basis for idealism, it gives not only the dynamic centre for the lyric strains in *Paradise Lost* but to all poets, whether influenced by Milton or not. But the power of his genius has been far-reaching, and the nature of a poet's or a prophet's influence in other lands throws light upon what qualities may be forgotten at home.

On examination of the many lyric fragments in England's greatest epic, the revelation comes, with the force of a surprise, that Milton's influence has been both romantic and lyrical, not only from *L'Allegro* and *Il Penseroso* but most of all from *Paradise Lost*.

In the eighteenth century, when the poems of Milton were translated into French and German, they aroused unusual enthusiasm for

their presentation of the dignity of man and
for the freshness of their descriptions of nature.

In fact, Milton appealed to pre-revolution-
ary France as a romantic poet, championing
the dignity and the high destiny of man who
was born to be the friend of God and of the
angels. The same type of mind that afterwards turned to Rousseau as a liberator and to
St. Pierre as an interpreter of an earthly
Paradise found in Milton a thinker opposed
to artificial restraints, who saw clearly man's
place in the scheme of the universe, and sang
of the intimate relation of man and of nature, and of the unspoiled primitive man in
Eden. Everywhere the minds wearied with
trivialties of form found Milton abounding in
sentiment for nature, in high seriousness, and
in respect for his own emotions, and confidence
in their expression.

It may be doubted whether Milton's own
countrymen, without careful deliberation, would
turn to the author of *Paradise Lost* first of
all as a poet of democracy, or as a poet of
nature; Walt Whitman and Swinburne, Coleridge and Wordsworth rise readily to the mind
of the English reader to-day for these rôles,
and was England ever without her poet of na-

ture and of liberty? The splendour of the Empyrean, the horrors of hell, or the dramatic figure of Satan, impress most vividly the average English reader of *Paradise Lost*.

Born to the heritage of Chaucer, Spenser, and Shakespeare, the English people unconsciously demand of their great poets a strong grasp upon nature. From the classical tradition that held England for a brief space only, and developed a prose, rather than dominated successfully poetry, the reaction came so quickly and completely that the personal enthusiasm for nature may be claimed as an unbroken tradition, practically, in English poetry. Though Cowper, Young, Gray, Wordsworth, and Coleridge are among the many who have seen nature under Milton's guidance, it is not strange that the English people, as a whole, with the magnificent structure of the great epic before them, have centred their attention upon the epical or the dramatic, the theological or the philosophical, the biblical or the classical problems, that presented new questions for literary discussion.

In order to understand the interest taken in the eighteenth century by German and French readers of *Paradise Lost*, one must consider the

forces at work.   About 1715, there came a reaction from England upon France through
Holland.   Five years later, Lamotte-Houdart
in his protest against the formalism of Boileau
directed the line of attack.   Voltaire, in his
essay upon *Paradise Lost*, written while he was
in England, had extolled the genius of Milton ;
Voltaire had also made adaptations of Shakespeare's plays, and while seeking to improve the
uncouth Englishmen had caught the divine
ardour for naturalism and had copied sufficient
innovations of classical laws to justify a literary revolution.   Though the intellectual king
of his day, he could not prevent his radicalism
from becoming the conservatism of the following decade.

The reaction from the artificiality of a
school, discussing forms rather than creating
thoughts, brought with it an insistence upon
a man's individuality, upon the seriousness of
living, of feeling for nature, and of interest
in one's own feelings.   The result was essentially a lyric influence, whether expressed or
implied.   It was true enough that Shakespeare appealed not so much as an author, as
the embodiment of a movement for liberty of
self-expression.   Letourneur declared that the

20

Frenchmen, bound by rules, had lost the power of being themselves, and he advised an emulation of English literary ideals. At this time, English authors were widely translated and read, in fact, Shakespeare, Addison, Thomson, Gray, Young, Hervey, Macpherson, and Milton joined the forces in France against artificiality and hastened the transition from Boileau to Chateaubriand, from the classic to the romantic domination.

Meanwhile the influence of Shakespeare and of Milton was a disturbing power in Germany; but the movement was less significant than in France, where the insistence upon self-expression passed into politics and became a revolution. The day came, indeed, when a performance of *Julius Cæsar* aroused Paris to open revolt from tyranny; but in Germany, wise rulers foresaw the danger of revolution and compromised with the growing spirit of freedom. Therefore the romantic movement did not there accompany nor inspire a revolution; but it remained a literary movement, only, and the war a war of words between Bodmer, Breitinger, and Gottsched and their disciples. However, the romantic school aided by Addison dominated, and here as in France the dig-

nity of man and a sentiment for nature were
the ruling ideals.

Milton's influence in Germany and France, it
is evident, was not only romantic, but his appeal was, in the last analysis, largely lyrical;
for he helped to inspire the tendency of self-
expression. This view of Milton must again
surprise the average English reader, who turns
to *Paradise Lost* neither for nature poetry, nor
for a lyrical influence, but simply accepts the
work as the noblest epic of his mother tongue.
But it would not surprise the writers of English poetry from Milton's day to our own;
for what lyric writer has not felt the spell of
the master hand and not sought to catch
his strains, nor has not seen that " star that
Milton's soul for Shelley lighted " ?

A study of *Paradise Lost* and of Milton's
prose works reveals the grounds upon which
this eighteenth-century view of Milton is justified, and throws light upon his inevitable influence upon English lyric poets. Milton's
lyrical influence takes its source in his conception of nature as the manifestation of God.
We are often told that Milton believed in a
limited, definite universe; that he soared, in
imagination, to the blue empyrean, thence, look-

ing down upon the vast expanse of the universe, saw all things marked out clearly below him, and with unquestioning confidence set the boundaries of the world. This idea of Milton's scheme of the universe arises from a misunderstanding of his art. The passage most often quoted to prove Milton's belief in a limited universe is from the eighth book of *Paradise Lost*, when the Son of God, upheld by wings of cherubim, rode forth in paternal glory into chaos, followed by the stately train of angels to behold the wonders of his might,

> Then stayed the fervid wheels, and in his hand
> He took the golden compasses
>
> . . . .
>
> One foot he center'd, and the other turned
> Round through the vast profundity obscure
> And said, "Thus far extend, thus far thy bounds,
> This be thy just circumference, O World."
> (Book VII, 224-231.)

The definite effect of this passage it is asserted is enhanced by the details that follow. The world is hung from heaven, from which it is distant by the length of its own radius. The portion of space embraced by the world consists of ten concentric spheres moving about the fixed earth; the first is that of the moon, the second is that of Mercury, the third, of Venus, the fourth, of the sun, the fifth, of Mars, the sixth, of Jupiter, the seventh, of Saturn, the eighth, of the fixed stars, the ninth, of the crystalline sphere, and the tenth, of the Primum Mobile. Above this universe, is the empyrean, or heaven, and around is chaos, where elements are violently combining with their affinities, or meeting in vehement opposition those for which they have no valence. Below, at the distance of once and a half the diameter of the world from heaven's gate, are the gates of hell. Upon this definite scheme of the universe with its apparent accurate measurements, emphasis has been thrown, and the conclusions have been drawn that Milton had Homer's attitude toward nature, that sense of ease and at-homeness that precludes all mystery, and that he had adopted in *Paradise Lost* the Ptolemaic system. There are reasons for thinking that this is not true.

When Milton wrote his *Paradise Lost*, Newton had not yet found his audience, and the poet reveals that he is not an expert scientist, but that he has the judgment of the intelligent men of his day. Indeed he is boond to no system. One may easily see his open-mindedness by comparing the work of Milton with the work of Du Bartas by Sylvester. In his *Divine Weekes and Works*, Copernicus is mentioned, but his theories are dismissed as absurd; in *Paradise Lost*, there are nine references to Galileo and one to Copernicus, and their theories are either accepted as a belief or referred to as reasonable or possible, if not yet proved. Milton met Galileo in 1638, and felt sympathy for his independence of thought. In the *Areopagitica* is this reference: "There it was that I found Galileo, grown old, a prisoner to the Inquisition for thinking in astronomy, otherwise than the Franciscan and Dominican licensers thought."

The references in *Paradise Lost* show Milton's familiarity with his theories and his respect for his work. He accepts the notion of the movement of the planets about the sun, but, like Brahé, he hesitates to loosen the earth from her permanent place in the universe, for fear of undue liberty in interpretation of the cosmogony of the Old Testament. He believes in the diurnal movement of the earth and admits that it seems absurd that the heavier bodies should move about the lesser. He can only resort to mediæval mysticism, on this point, in a passage that shows his hold upon past methods of thought, and that, on this subject, he was well informed but unwilling to be strictly scientific.[1]

An examination of Milton's mental attitude from *Paradise Lost* and from the *Treatise on Christian Doctrine* reveals some important details, for the understanding of his literary art. Milton was dowered with unusual intellectual force, a keen reason, but his imagination was stronger than his reason and his emotion was sometimes at variance with reason. The result is inconsistency. There is little doubt also that Milton sought to justify his imagination by his reason where he had no data, and that led to inconsistency. His imagination inspired him to dwell upon definite pictures, but his reason made him sceptical of what had not been proved; he was critical of pictures too definite to be in harmony with an abstraction, or with universal truth; the result is the peculiar phase of art found nowhere in such perfection as in Milton and justifying a paradox, for, with a few exceptions, the pictures are both definite enough for our imagination, and often indefinite enough to satisfy our more critical

[1] See Book VIII., 25–38, 71–178.

reason, and the final judgment is, that they seem more definite than they are.

In so far as Milton engrafted the Ptolemaic system, as expounded by Dante, it is probable that he was influenced by these reasons:

First, both a study of *Paradise Lost*, and of Milton's prose works, reveals that he sought to hold to the verbal inspiration of the Scriptures, and the Ptolemaic system was more easily reconciled to the Bible account. Second, the imaginative material from the utterances of Plato, of Aristotle, of Homer, of Virgil, and of Cicero seemed embraced in their essential details in the Ptolemaic system. There is a certain sequence in great works of art; poets of universal power are interested in the heritage of poets, which passes into devices for an imaginative appeal. Literary artists make use of these devices for mental pictures and do not hold them as opposed to reason. This consideration blends with the third,—the Ptolemaic system was an aid to startlingly clear pictures, a not insignificant artistic aid to Milton, who had attempted the super-Promethean task of rendering vivid the abstract, of making an epic purely of abstrac-

tions.   There were these reasons for adopting
the Ptolemaic system in *Paradise Lost*.

But for the following reasons, Milton did
not adopt the Ptolemaic system: First, in
Paradise Lost Milton desired to follow literally
the Bible account, but this he fails to do.   With
his critical reason, here, as elsewhere, he judges
for himself, and proceeds to admit fragments
from Copernicus, from Kepler and Galileo,
that are at variance with the literal reading of
the Bible verses, and that subvert the Ptolemaic
system.   Second, although Milton, like all
artists of universal power, is undoubtedly interested in the classic past and is sensitively
alive to the beauty of the classics and to
the appreciation of their imaginative appeal,
still a closer study of his work reveals that he
forces all the classic material through a creative process into a new product, conforming
to his own individual taste.   This is true, not
only in great matters, but in minor touches,
and these differences all point to a different
conception of the universe.   Third, Milton's
pictures always strike the reader as clearer
than they are, like the images in dreams.   This
literary effect is a result of his great power of
will and of the mastery of his art.   We are under

the influence of the great magician; he moulds his material before us, like the true artist makes us see what he wishes us to see and depends upon his atmosphere for the correction, so that when one holds the product up by reflection to the critical light of reason, it gains in universality by a lack of definition. This makes a peculiar poetic atmosphere in Milton's work that is potent, even though, from not being understood, it is not sufficiently appreciated.

Milton gains in artistic power by one phase of his inconsistency in the plan of his cosmogony. If Milton uses the Ptolemaic system, in part, he redeems his universe from the definiteness that detracts from infinitude by admitting the vast and the unknown in the domain of Chaos and Old Night, beyond which lies hell, and by putting his heaven above the universe altogether. The earth, enclosed in concentric circles and shut off by an impervious wall from the warring elements of chaos, hangs from heaven by a golden chain. It is only possible to enter the world from the upper portion near heaven. Still Satan, after his daring voyage through chaos and his eluding of perils by the way, after he has accom-

plished the fall of man and returns in triumph
to hell,—finds a bridge built across chaos, and
the infernal gates wide open for traffic with the
earth. From the super-mundane heaven, angels have been daily visitors, have walked and
talked with Adam as friend with friend; the
celestial spirits have ministered and advised,
warned and condemned and comforted man.
Whatever we are told of the cosmogony, therefore, the plain picture that appeals to the imagination is an earth hung in limitless space,
open to the visitors from heaven above and
from hell beneath, and never for an instant in
the entire work are we permitted to conceive of
the world by itself, but always in its relation
to the infinite heaven and the boundless abyss.
In this scope Milton is not unlike Hawthorne,
who views the seen always in relation to the unseen, or Shakespeare in *Macbeth* and *Hamlet*,
where invisible forces press upon the finite
world.

In Homer, the abode of the gods is on a
mountain top; and Hades is in the dark re-
cesses of the earth. In Virgil, earth, heaven,
and Hades are joined, likewise, within dis-
tances that can be traversed by man.

In the *Divine Comedy*, the excursion into the

spirit land is extended and leads to abstract speculation, but Dante merges the material with the spiritual world, shirks the question of the dualism between mind and matter, and forces the spiritual interpretation of all by his symbolism. Accepting the more complex notions of his day, resulting from the fusion of the ideas of northern and of southern races, Dante constructs his hell. By the hole under Jerusalem, at the spot where the "sinless Man" died, guided by Virgil, he makes his way to Lucifer at the centre of the earth. Climbing up through a fissure in the rock and led by the sound of a rivulet, he mounts to Purgatory, upon whose summit Adam and Eve dwelt in their happy days in the terrestrial Paradise. As after man's fall, no mortal had entered the southern hemisphere, Dante startles the spirits of ante-Purgatory by his material body. Virgil says to them, "Marvel not thereat, but believe that not without power that comes from above, he seeks to surmount this wall."

In this way, the poet strives to restore the reasonableness to his story. But the scaling of the wall is too hard for Dante, and Lucia comes and bears him, sleeping, to the height, from whence he makes his perilous way to the earthly

Paradise. Later, the author of the *Divine Comedy* meets a greater difficulty in this attempt to translate a material body to the abode of spirits, and he is obliged to resort to the potency of the river Eunöe, which prepared Dante for the ascent of heaven by causing the force that draws him upward to be stronger than the power that draws him downward. Thus the spirit becomes supreme over the body, and, by means of this power, he mounts above the starry heavens to the Primum Mobile and to the Empyrean where is the Rose of Paradise and the Beatific Vision.   Milton's universe differs from Dante's.

By putting both heaven and hell outside of the world, Milton gains consistency as well as sublimity.   His fundamental ideas about nature are to be found in his prose work, the *Treatise on Christian Doctrine,* compiled from the Holy Scriptures. Nature is the manifestation of the glory of God, for in the heavens, he reads this declaration, " I am Jehovah, that maketh all things, that stretcheth forth the heavens alone; that spreadeth abroad the earth by myself." This is the explanation of the peculiar power of Milton, as a poet of nature, every phase of nature is approached from the standpoint of the universe, and creation is the manifestation of the " High and Holy One that inhabiteth eternity, whose name is Holy, dwelling in the light which no man can approach unto, whom no man hath seen, nor can see."

These are the texts upon which Milton bases his fundamental conception of nature. This spiritual domination was not only the condition at the time of creation, but Milton maintains that God still governs the world, " Upholding all things by the word of his power." Milton asserts ;

The ordinary providence of God is that whereby he upholds and preserves the immutable order of causes appointed by him in the beginning. This is commonly and too frequently described by the name of nature: for nature cannot possibly mean anything but the mysterious power and efficacy of that divine voice, which went forth in the beginning and to which, as to a perpetual command, all things have since paid obedience.

Milton's conception of nature as the manifestation of the glory of God, and therefore not comprehensible by man, classifies him with those who believe in an infinite universe with those who hold that complete knowledge of nature will never be attained. Therefore the Ptolemaic system was opposed to Milton's mental attitude. Milton's idea of nature bears in itself an epic attitude of mind and makes nature a fit background for the scope of his epic of *Paradise Lost*. This harmony is fitting to the epic for as Dryden has said in his essay on epic poetry, " Even the least portions of them [the epic] must be of the epick kind, all things must be grave, majestical and sublime."

Milton's approach to nature is reverent. There is no trace of ease and of familiarity, but rather of the attitude of the high priests who approached with awe the Holy of Holies. From this reverence, as a poet of nature, he gains his two striking characteristics, sublimity and mysticism, two phases of one attitude. It is interesting and significant to compare with these utterances of Milton, a passage from the cosmogony of Kant:

Two things there are which, the oftener and more steadfastly we contemplate them, fill the mind with an ever new, an ever rising admiration and reverence ; the starry Heavens above, the moral law within, and both are God's—of Whom and to Whom and through Whom are all things—Who is over all, God blessed for ever.

Here the poet joins hands with the philosopher, but Kant is not usually mentioned as showing Hebrew influence, nor is Plato, nor Shakespeare in *Hamlet* nor in *Lear*, nor Dante in the *Divine Comedy*, nor Wordsworth in the *Ode on Immortality*. Still the attitude is the same as that of the Hebrew prophets. A sense of the mysterious power of that divine voice, which went forth in the beginning, is present with them all, but this elevation of mind is a characteristic of the minds of many who see into the heart of things. It is not an influence that falls upon one from without and that is engrafted into one's own thought, but it is an attitude inseparable from some great natures, whatever the range of manifestation of power, from Michael Angelo to Beethoven. This type of mind does not stop with so-called realism, but " leads us to the edge of the infinite and lets us look into that." It does more, it sometimes starts from the infinite and views life only in its relation to God.

Universal reality emanates from this higher mysticism,—not the mediæval mysticism, not the mysticism of the worshipper of Isis or of Baal, not the mysticism that is the mother of superstition, but the power that spurs one's reason, fires one's imagination to reach toward the infinite, with, however, the wide vision that

sees there is a shadowy line between the finite
and the infinite, between limited reality and
limitless reality. Tyndall, Spencer, Darwin,
as well as Galileo, Kepler, and Copernicus recognised the infinite in mapping out their world
of thought, but their interest was in clearing
up the mists, the Cimmerian deserts, in the re-
gion of the known and in pushing out the bord-
ers into the former unknowable. However,
long study of some particular manifestation
did not so absorb their powers that they became men of limited vision, and lost their sense
of proportion. They did not feel that the veil
of the innermost temple of nature had been rent
in twain and that there was an end, or could
be an end of all mystery. Milton, at heart,
had the same interest in truth as these men
of science—his approach was different, his
method sometimes faulty; his desire was to
dwell in those regions of thought beyond the
transitory, where a man sees things as God
sees them. This is distinctly the epic
attitude.

From this elevated conception of nature,
arise the lyric bursts in *Paradise Lost*, starting from the epic and returning to the epic.
In fact, the conception of nature as infinite sup-

21

plies the dynamic force to the nature lyric not only in *Paradise Lost*, but to all poetry of nature. The momentum is greater in the lyric that arises from the mystery of the infinite than in the lyric that starts lower, or that aspires to a lower pitch.

We have seen then that the fundamental idea of Milton's attitude toward nature is gained from his use of the cosmogony he had inherited from poets, from the changes he made, and from his poetical and artistic reasons for these changes; but it is from the descriptions of nature in *Paradise Lost*, or from the exquisite descriptive similes, that we naturally gather details for comprehending his thought and feeling about nature. The first conclusion that one must draw from an examination of these passages is, that Milton has a peculiar tendency to view every detail in relation to the whole, and this is an epic tendency.

The descriptive passages often move from the vast and proceed to the more specific detail, as may be noted in the first view of the world, or from the minor phases of nature toward the infinite. Exactness, in these passages, arises from the force of imagination, which tends to paint vivid pictures and seizes upon the details for that purpose. The whole effect, however, is not grasped by the reader as a picture with a finished outline, for the edges fade off into the infinite. In the passage descriptive of Satan's flight to the earth may be seen Milton's emphasis upon the imaginative grasp of details, also the poet's brooding upon the stars, upon the mystery of night and of measureless space. These phases of nature aided him in the describing what he had not seen.

With a vivid memory of the scenes of hell, through whose gates Satan has passed into the abode of Chaos and Old Night, the reader watches his flight toward the world. The venturesome spirit sees at last his former home, empyreal heaven, with opal towers and battlements of living sapphire, and fast by, " hanging in a golden chain, the pendant world in bigness as a star." By these details we are shown the relations of the world to heaven, to hell, and to chaos, and the earth in relation to the world. In the third book, after a scene in heaven contrasting with the description of hell, the attention of the reader again turns toward the perilous journey of Satan, and he again sees the relation of the world to heaven and hell:

Thus they in heaven above the starry sphere
Their happy hours in joy and hymning spent.
Meanwhile, upon the firm opacious globe
Of this round world, whose first convex divides
The luminous inferior orbs inclos'd
From Chaos and th' inroad of Darkness old,
Satan alighted walks : a globe far off
It seem'd, now seems a boundless continent,
Dark, waste, and wild, under the form of Night,
Starless expos'd, and ever threatening storms
Of Chaos blust'ring round and inclement sky ;
Save on that side which from the wall of Heav'n
Though distant far, some small reflection gains
Of glimmering air less vex'd with tempest loud :
                    (Book III, lines 416–429.)

In both of these passages the scope of the
thought is essentially epic, and the style is in
key with the whole poem. If Milton's fundamental idea of the universe is vast in its scope,
so also is his conception of the smaller details
of nature: the spirit is rarely classical even
though the elements chosen are very frequently
the same as those used by classic authors if not
directly suggested by the writers of Greece and
Rome. In a very familiar passage, usually
selected to show Milton's tendency to appropriate the words of others, there is an interesting development of Milton's progress from the
definitely realistic as seen in,—

                    As bees
In springtime, when the sun with Taurus rides,

> Pour forth their populous youth above the hive
> In clusters ; they among fresh dews and flowers
> Fly to and fro, or on the smoothed plank,
> The suburb of their straw-built citadel, —

to the purer realm of imagination, moving toward the vast, with a grander sweep of melody :

> while overhead the moon
> Sits arbitress, and nearer to the earth
> Wheels her pale course; they, on their mirth and dance
> Intent, with jocund music charm his ear;
> At once, with joy and fear his heart rebounds.
>
> (Book I, 768–789.)

Milton's conception of the vastness of nature gives the dynamic power creating the lyric impulse. The majesty of nature may terrify and dwarf the lyric impulse, but not when the thought of the dignity of man keeps pace with a sense of the sublimity of nature. This greater power of the lyric carried to its fullest development merges with the epic. The force is too great to remain personal and passes into a universal uplift toward the abstract. This is the play of the lyric, we constantly find in *Paradise Lost*. It is not to be explained alone by the epic theme, by the fact that Milton is so perfectly the artist that he blends all parts of the epic into harmony, but it is characteristic of Milton, in his conception of God, of nature, and of man, as is revealed in his prose as well as in his poetry. There is the latent lyric attitude where it is not expressed, and it takes its rise at the very source of the epic itself, that is the dream of Eden spoiled by the entrance of evil.

The greatest lines in Coleridge, in Wordsworth, in Shelley, and in Byron have the Miltonic ring, not because these poets were imitating Milton, but because the author of *Paradise Lost* struck the philosophical basis of the greatest lyric, and they, with less power, now and then hit the same key, or near it.

Some selections may show the relation of the epic and the lyric in Milton's *Paradise Lost*. The display of so wide a background is in itself epical; earth, heaven, and hell are kept within our field of vision and a lyric sometimes helps to preserve the entirety of the scene. The connection of the earth with the infinite is kept by the celestial spectators, who applaud or deplore the drama acted in the world; cohorts of angels attend the Son of God on his way, when he planned the universe; angelic music applauded the works of creation in a passage that suggests a suppressed chorus for

a tragedy on the model of Æschylus or of
Euripides:

> "Open, ye everlasting gates," they sung,
> "Open, ye heavens, your living doors; let in
> The great Creator, from his work return'd
> Magnificent, his six days' work, a world!"
>   (Book VII, 565–568.)

> Thus was the first day ev'n and morn:
> Nor past uncelebrated, nor unsung
> By the celestial choirs, when orient light
> Exhaling first from darkness, they beheld
> Birth day of heaven and earth; with joy and shout
> The hollow universal orb they fill'd
> And touch'd their golden harps, and hymning prais'd
> God and his works: Creator, him they sung
> Both when first evening was, and when first morn.
>   (Book VII, 252–260.)

The beauty of earth is enhanced by the
thought of the divine presence, and elevated by
a comparison with ideal beauty, as is seen in
this passage, a type of many:

> with high woods, the hills were crown'd;
> With tufts the valleys and each fountain side
> With borders long the rivers: that earth now
> Seem'd like to heaven, a seat where gods might dwell
> Or wander with delight, and love to haunt
> Her sacred shades.
>   (Book VII, 325–331)

The divine presence is not withdrawn from
the world after it is created, but one might

meet the messengers of God face to face in Eden in the hush of noontide, or in twilight calm.   Adam calls Eve to enjoy the beauty of the approach of the angel:

> " Haste hither, Eve, and worth thy sight behold
> Eastward among those trees, what glorious shape
> Comes this way moving, seems another morn
> Ris'n on midnoon;"
>
> (Book V, 308-311.)

Angels come, as the messengers of God, and man looks up to the divine visitor, as to a wise friend, to whom he offers hospitability and from whom he is unwilling to part.

> " Go, therefore, half this day as friend with friend
> Converse with Adam, in what bower or shade
> Thou find'st him, from the heat of noon retir'd
> To respit his day-labour with repast
> Or with respose;"
>
> (Book V, 229-233.)

Adam urges the angel to remain in Paradise,—

> " Suspense in heaven,
> Held by thy voice, thy potent voice, he hears
> And longer will delay to hear thee tell
> His generation and the rising birth
> Of nature, from the unapparent deep:
> Or if the star of ev' ning, and the moon
> Haste to thy audience, Night with her will bring
> Silence, and Sleep listening to thee will watch,
> Or we can bid his absence, till thy song
> End and dismiss thee, ere the morning shine. "
>
> (Book VII, 99-108.)

The cherubim form an angelic guard, as may be
seen in words that are descriptive of light in
the heavens at nightfall:

> Now had Night measur'd, with her shadowy cone,
> Half way up hill this vast sublunar vault,
> And from their ivory port, the cherubim
> Forth issuing at th' accustom'd hour, stood arm'd
> To their night watches, in warlike parade,
>> (Book IV, 776–780.)

Or as may be noted in the passage descriptive
of sunset, when Uriel came to warn the guardian angels of Satan's invasion of Paradise.[1]
All heaven takes benignant interest in the
nuptials of Adam and Eve, and joins with
earth's epithalamium:

> ... all heav'n
> And happy constellations, on that hour,
> Shed their selected influence : the earth
> Gave sign of gratulation, and each hill ;
> Joyous the birds ; fresh gales and gentle airs
> Whisper'd it to the woods, and from their wings
> Flung rose, flung odours from the spicy shrub,
> Disporting, till the amorous bird of night
> Sung spousal, and bid haste the evening star
> On his hill-top, to light the bridal lamp.
>> (Book VIII, 511–520.)

The divine influences are not only prominent in
the life of Adam and Eve in Eden, but all of

[1] Book V, 540–560.

their deep experiences are joined with thoughts of nature, as may be seen in Adam's reminiscence of his first day of life:

> "As new wak'd from soundest sleep
> Soft in the flowery herb, I found me laid"
> (Book VIII, 253–254.)

In Eve's memory of her first moment of life,

> "I first awak'd and found myself repos'd
> Under a shade on flow'rs,"
> (Book IV, 450–451.)

or in Eve's beautiful lyric of love, we may notice the same memory of nature:

> "But neither breath of morn, when she ascends
> With charm of earliest birds, nor rising sun
> On this delightful land, nor herb, fruit, flower
> Glist'ring with dew, nor fragrance after showers,
> Nor grateful evening mild, nor silent night
> With this her solemn bird, nor walk by morn
> Or glittering starlight, without thee is sweet."
> (Book IV, 650–656.)

In their morning prayer, Adam and Eve call upon all the works of God to join them in praise. The superiority of man is asserted over the lower animals, who gambol about Adam and Eve, at sunset, and seek their attention; but into their bower,

> Beast, bird, insect or worm durst enter none
> Such was the awe of Man.
> (Book IV, 704–705.)

In the passages that have been quoted from Milton, it is evident that not all have the lyric freedom. The movement is from the vast moving with momentum toward a free expression of the emotion, which is a personal enthusiasm for the beauty described.

Frequently, the lines do not reach their full enthusiastic expression, and they do not, therefore, become truly lyrical. In the cases where the free lyrical note is attained, the duration is very short. The tendency in *Paradise Lost* is everywhere epical; the return to the epic comes so quickly that the lyric outburst must be brief, for it loses itself in the universal elevation. This is the range of the lyric in *Paradise Lost*, arising from the epic and returning to the epic.

In general in lyric poetry, there are two movements: from the universal to the more narrowly personal—which is usually the personal feeling of the poet; or a movement from the particular phase of emotion—which is usually the personal feeling of the poet—toward the universal experience of man or toward the infinite.

Both these types are found in Byron. His habitual mood is personal, for he modifies the universal human feeling by interpreting the general experience of man in the terms of his own peculiar emotion. There are however many lines in his work where the effort is to rise out of himself toward universal nature, or God:

> I live not in myself, but I become
> Portion of that around me ; and to me
> High mountains are a feeling.
>> (*Childe Harold*, III, 72.)

> Are not the mountains, waves, and skies a part
> Of me and of my soul, as I of them?
>> (*Childe Harold*, III, 75.)

> And this is in the night ; most glorious night!
> Thou wert not sent for slumber ! let me be
> A sharer in thy fierce and far delight,
> A portion of the tempest and of thee !
>> (Canto III, 93.)

The poet's longing to be one with nature suggests Shelley's lyric cry:

> If I were a swift cloud to fly with thee ;
> A wave to pant beneath thy power, and share
> The impulse of thy strength, only less free
> Than thou, O uncontrollable !
>> (*Ode to the West Wind*)

The desire to rise toward the infinite is more fully expressed in these lines from Shelley:

> That Light, whose smile kindles the universe,
> That Beauty, in which all things work and move,
> That Benediction, which the eclipsing curse

Of birth can quench not, that sustaining Love,
Which thro' the web of being blindly wove
By man and beast and earth and air and sea,
Burns bright, or dim, as each are mirrors of
The fire, for which all thirst ; now beams on me,
Consuming the last clouds of cold mortality.

> *(Adonais)*

The lifting of the personal toward the universal finds more articulate expression in these lines of Wordsworth:

And I have felt
A presence that disturbs me with the joy
Of elevated thoughts, a sense sublime,
Of something far more deeply interfused,
Whose dwelling is the light of setting suns,
And the round ocean, and the living air,
And the blue sky, and in the mind of man;
A motion and a spirit, that impels
All thinking things, all objects, of all thought,
And rolls through all things.

> *(Tintern Abbey.)*

This is an epic movement in the lyric and is fundamentally the type found in *Paradise Lost*. When the starting point of the lyric is higher, the momentum is greater than otherwise and that gives a superior force to the lyric bursts in *Paradise Lost*.

There are three stages that may be noted in all lyrical expression:

First, that in which reason predominates to

restrain the lyric impulse and to direct it toward prose;

Second, that in which reason is partly fused by imagination and emotion; and this is a stage of lyric development usually found in the English poets;

Third, that in which the thought, starting in reason, has been brooded over and passed on, a completed intellectual product, to the imagination and the emotion, by which it is perfectly fused and finds expression as a sublimation of reason and emotion in the lyric. When this perfect fusion has taken place the expression in words or in music is accidental, the intellectual product is the same. It is a lyric idea or a musical idea depending upon whether the self-same process has taken place in the brain of a Schubert or of a Shelley; a Beethoven or a Milton; the rest is technique.

The first stage finds exemplification in much of Milton's poetry. The author of *Paradise Lost*, together with most English poets, experiences the difficulty of merging the rational element with the lighter lilt of pure emotion.

The greatest men have been distinguished for clearness of thought, force of imagination, and wide range of emotion. Such men were Michael

Angelo, Leonardo da Vinci, Shakespeare, Goethe, and Milton. Few men, in all the world's history, have achieved a balance of these powers of their nature. The tendency of one power to escape from control and to dominate all others forms an interesting study in the life and the works of men of genius. The highest development of the lyric arises from the concentration of thought that has inspired the imagination; so that, free from conscious thought, but not opposed to reason, it passes on in sublimated form, through emotion, into the clear lilt of song. The three stages of this rise into lyric power are often discernible in one passage from Wordsworth, or from Milton.

The most conspicuous passages from *Paradise Lost* that drop proseward are doctrinal sections, where Milton's mind is busy with theories of theology or with material of past and future controversy. There are other lines in which his lyric impulse is chilled by fear, for two reasons: first, because he has too deep an insight, too clear a judgment, not to perceive that a finite being cannot grasp the infinite with sufficient clearness to portray God; second, because in his attempts to portray heaven and God's direct commands to his celestial ministers, he fears that he may fall into inconsistency and present a vulnerable spot to the theologians. It is true that Milton had not avoided theological controversy, but it is also true that, in most fundamental principles of Christian faith, he was more conservative than his bold utterances might lead us at first to believe. These considerations make his muse conscious and check the freedom of his verses. When Milton turns from these difficult attempts to depict God, to portray the adoration of the angels, there is a rise in poetic power into the second stage, wherein the rational element is partly fused with the emotional, and this stage, in varying degrees of predominance, marks the usual lyric power of Milton and of all poets. It is only in rare touches that Milton attains the highest lyric lilt, in which the conscious rational element disappears altogether, while the influence of the reason remains in the justification of the emotion, and these passages always express enthusiasm for nature.

Paradise Lost, since it was written after Milton had become blind, opens up an interesting field for research in the poet's attitude toward the details of nature. The poet can no longer go forth to the wood and the fresh fields to view the dawn, or the twilight, the tempest, or the calm stars. The nature of *Paradise Lost* is accurate in detail, but it is a broadly personal world suffused with a sentiment for nature. There is sublimation of detail arising from the maturity of intense feeling; from the remembered joys of that happy time before his loss of sight had debarred him from new impressions. This fusion of details into a suggestive picture may arise also from his habit of relating all particular impressions to man's more universal experience. Some of Milton's descriptions of nature are classical in richness; there are touches that have the outspoken frankness of the Renaissance, and nowhere is he ascetic, or negative, but he enters into the enjoyment of nature with fulness of life. His earth is not however the earth of Ovid, nor of Hardy, but a place where angels walked and talked with man and there is a holiness in its charm. When man by sin put to flight the angels, earth was less beautiful, and thus Milton viewed nature ideally, for a veil of higher sentiment, like a mist in the valley of Grasmere, suffuses all nature.

It is interesting to see what experiences of

22

nature, stored in his mind in more fortunate days, he draws upon in his years of blindness. The phases of nature that recur most frequently are: dawn, the early hours of morning, noontime, sunset, evening, the moon, stars, mirage, eclipse, thunder, lightning, tempests, volcanoes, echoes among rocks, wind blustering, sound of waters, of trees, of birds. Most of these were to him an actual experience, of others he had read. These phases of nature fall into two general classes,—first, those that have the beauty, not so much of majestic sweetness, as of terror, where, however, force passes toward sublimity rather than toward sensationalism. There is, in these passages, an exultation in might that may inspire a Byron, although to a strain less grand than that of his master. In English literature, the only passages descriptive of nature that can be compared in force are to be found in the works of Shakespeare, in *King Lear*, in *Macbeth*, and in *Hamlet*. There is a suggestion of this style of description of nature in the thirty-eighth chapter of Job.

In the following lines, from the speech of Satan to inspire Beëlzebub to courage, one may notice that the details that appealed to the

imagination of Milton are to be found in a
thunderstorm, and it is difficult to recall in any
poetry a passage more eloquent of delight in
power:

> "But see ! the angry victor hath recalled
> His ministers of vengeance and pursuit
> Back to the gates of heaven ; the sulphurous hail
> Shot after us in storm, o'erblown hath laid
> The fiery surge, that from the precipice
> Of heaven received us falling, and the thunder
> Wing'd with red lightning and impetuous rage
> Perhaps hath spent his shafts, and ceases now
> To bellow through the vast and boundless deep."
>
> (Book I, 169–177.)

In a spirited passage chosen from the council of the infernal powers there may be found
another description of a tempest in which
lightning, whirlwinds, and the boiling ocean
are suggested with terrific vigour:

> "What, if all
> Her stores were open'd and this firmament
> Of hell should spout her cataracts of fire,
> Impendent horrors, threatening hideous fall
> One day upon our heads ; while we, perhaps
> Designing or exhorting glorious war,
> Caught in a fiery tempest shall be hurl'd
> Each on his rock transfix'd, the sport and prey
> Of wracking whirlwinds ; or for ever sunk
> Under yon boiling ocean, wrapt in chains ;

> There to converse with everlasting groans,
> Unrespited, unpitied, unreprieved,
> Ages of hopeless end ? "
>
> (Book II, 174-186.)

If we compare with these lines Byron's description of a storm, we notice that the lack of height and depth makes his poetry less free in lyric force, while the lines are more oratorical:

> The sky is changed.—And such a change ! Oh night,
> And storm, and darkness, ye are wondrous strong,
> Yet lovely in your strength, as is the light
> Of a dark eye in woman !   Far along
> From peak to peak, the rattling crags among
> Leaps the live thunder !   Not from one lone cloud,
> But every mountain now hath found a tongue ;
> And Jura answers, through her misty shroud,
> Back to the joyous Alps, who call to her aloud !
>
> (*Childe Harold*, III, 92.)

A storm on the ocean is again portrayed by Milton in a selection remarkable for its imaginative grasp of the fury of the sea:

> On heavenly ground they stood, and from the shore
> They viewed the vast, immeasurable abyss
> Outrageous as a sea, dark, wasteful, wild,
> Up from the bottom turn'd by furious winds
> And surging waves, as mountains, to assault
> Heaven's height, and with the centre mix the pole.
>
> (Book VII, 210-215.)

Other similes in *Paradise Lost* are borrowed

from the terror of an eruption that shatters
the side of "Thundering Ætna," from the popular fear of an eclipse "that perplexes monarchs with fear of change," or from the
mysterious course of meteors.

Under the second class of the phases of
nature, selected for treatment by Milton, are
those that have the charm of tranquil beauty,
often majestic, blending with the sublime and
in certain lines tending toward the first class
of beauty with terror. The best example of
this tranquil type is found in the description
of morning in the garden of Eden, as lovely as
"when fair morning first smiled on the world,"
an ideal for poets, who view nature through the
golden light of poetic sentiment. Under this
division are similes of "the morning star that
guides the starry flock," descriptions of when—

> Morn,
> Wak'd by the circling hours, with rosy hand,
> Unbarr'd the gates of light.
>
> (Book VII, 2-4.)

.   .   .   .

> and now went forth the morn
> Such as in highest heaven, array'd in gold
> Empyreal; from before her vanished night
> Shot through with orient beams.
>
> (Book V, 12-15.)

In freshness and purity Wordsworth's frequent lines upon morning supply interesting ground for comparison.

The sky rejoices in the morning's birth.[1]

. . . .

Never did sun more beautifully steep
In his first splendour valley, rock, or hill ;
Ne'er saw I, never felt a calm so deep.

(Sonnet.)

In Milton's portrayal of evening there is an exquisite companion picture that compresses into twelve lyrical lines all that is most suggestive of poetic sentiment dwelling upon twilight and evening. With this passage we may compare a selection from Wordsworth that rises towards Miltonic power. In Milton's lines one finds colours at sunset, sounds of evening falling upon palpable silence:

Now came still evening on, and twilight grey
Had in her sober livery all things clad,
Silence accompany'd ; for beast and bird,
They to their grassy couch, these to their nests,
Were slunk, all but the wakeful nightingale ;
She all night long her amorous descant sung ;
Silence was pleased : now glowed the firmament
With living sapphires ; Hesperus that led
The starry host rode brightest, till the moon,
Rising in clouded majesty, at length

[1] *Resolution and Independence.*

Apparent queen, unveiled her peerless light,
And o'er the dark her silver mantle threw.
                    (Book IV, 598–609.)

In elevation, colour, and suggestion of sounds
of nature at evening, it is interesting to compare these lines from Wordsworth:

                    the broad sun
Is sinking down in its tranquillity ;
The gentleness of heaven broods on the sea ;
Listen ! the mighty Being is awake
And doth with His eternal motion make
A sound like thunder—everlastingly.
                            (Sonnet.)

A song falling upon silence suggests another
comparison. In the *Ancient Mariner* two lines
have the Miltonic uplift.

And now it is an angels' song,
That makes the heavens be mute.

These two lines from Wordsworth have the
same mysterious Miltonic elevation:

Breaking the silence of the seas
Among the farthest Hebrides.
                    (*The Solitary Reaper.*)

In the last part of one of Milton's descriptions of the garden of Eden there is a
reminiscence of the delights of nature found in
accounts of Araby the blest. The last five lines

have a lilt that again suggests a comparison with some more modern lyrics.

> The birds their quire apply ; airs, vernal airs,
> Breathing the smell of field and grove, attune
> The trembling leaves, while universal Pan,
> Knit with the Graces and the Hours in dance,
> Led on th' eternal spring.
> (Book IV, lines 264–268.)

The sound of the rippling of leaves and waters is heard again in these lines:

> . . . th' only sound
> Of leaves and fuming rills, Aurora's fan,
> Lightly dispers'd and the shrill matin song
> Of birds on every bough.
> (Book V, lines 4–7.)

The following lines from Wordsworth lead us where leaves respond to a breeze of the vernal air and add their movement to the vibrating joy of spring; but we notice that the momentum is less than in *Paradise Lost*.

> The budding twigs spread out their fan
> To catch the breezy air.
> (*Lines Written in Early Spring*.)

The sounds of waters in the wood are again the theme of song of another more modern poet, a disciple of Milton. If the melody of the acolyte is lighter and more like the harp than the organ, the sweep of the melody is complete.

> A noise like of a hidden brook
> In the leafy month of June,
> That to the sleeping woods all night
> Singeth a quiet tune.
> (Coleridge, *Ancient Mariner*.)

In a passage more personal than universal, in which the bitterness of grief has passed into pensive sweetness, Milton in an elegiac strain inspired by the reflections upon his blindness again sings of brooks and birds, of the silence of the woods, and of the sweet approach of eve or morn:

> Yet not the more
> Cease I to wander where the Muses haunt
> Clear spring, or shady grove, or sunny hill,
> Smit with the love of sacred song ; but chief
> Thee Sion, and the flowery brooks beneath
> That wash thy hallow'd feet, and warbling flow
> Nightly I visit.
> (Book III, 26–32.)

. . . .

> Then feed on thoughts, that voluntary move
> Harmonious numbers ; as the wakeful bird
> Sings darkling, and in shadiest covert hid
> Tunes her nocturnal note.   Thus with the year
> Seasons return, but not to me returns
> Day, or the sweet approach of even or morn ,
> Or sight of vernal bloom, or summer's rose,
> Or flocks, or herds, or human face divine ;

> But cloud instead, and ever-during dark ;
> Surrounds me, from the cheerful ways of men
> Cut off, and for the book of knowledge fair
> Presented with a universal blank
> Of nature's works to me expung'd and ras'd
> And wisdom at one entrance quite shut out.
>
> (Book III, 37–50.)

All of the best examples of the lyric in *Paradise Lost* are found in brief passages and in every instance joined with a feeling for nature. There may be noticed in these passages quoted from Milton, the lyrical impulse that rises with a lilt toward the end of the selection. It is interesting also to observe how later poets reveal a similar attitude toward nature, without the organ roll of Milton's melody, but with smaller harmonies that are more easily caught and seem nearer to human life, and therefore they are more limited, more personal, and more lovable, perhaps, but less inspiring and therefore less dynamic.

> Flowers laugh before thee on their beds ;
> And fragrance in thy footing treads ;
> Thou dost preserve the stars from wrong ;
> And the most ancient heavens, through thee, are fresh
> And strong.
>
> (Wordsworth, *Ode to Duty*.)

In the selections cited from other poets there is less lyric swing, despite their quicker movement and less stately key; for there is a momentum in Milton's lines that aids the lyric force. The passages that follow more nearly approach the majesty of Milton but have not the lyric freedom of the master's hand.

> Hast thou a charm to stay the morning-star
> In his steep course? So long he seems to pause
> On thy bald, awful head, O sovran Blanc!
> The Arve, an Arveiron at thy base
> Rave ceaselessly; but thou, most awful Form,
> Risest from forth thy silent sea of pines,
> How silently! Around thee and above
> Deep is the air and dark, substantial, black,
> An ebon mass. Methinks thou piercest it,
> As with a wedge! But when I look again,
> It is thy own calm home, thy crystal shrine,
> Thy habitation from eternity!
> O dread and silent Mount! I gazed upon thee,
> Till thou, still present to the bodily sense,
> Didst vanish from my thought: entranced in prayer
> I worshipped the Invisible alone.
> > (Coleridge, *Vale of Chamouni*.)

One may notice also the Miltonic spirit in these lines from Byron; but the expression is not entirely unhampered, and lyric lightness is not attained.

> All heaven and earth are still—though not in sleep,
> But breathless, as we grow when feeling most;
> And silent, as we stand in thoughts too deep:—
> All heaven and earth are still: from the high host

Of stars, to the lull'd lake and mountain-coast,
All is concentred in a life intense
Where not a beam, nor air, nor leaf is lost
But hath a part of being, and a sense
Of that which is of all Creator and defence.
                                        (*Childe Harold*, III, 89.)

Milton's lyrical impulse may be inspired by the light of morning, suggesting the radiance of the throne of God, by the sound of waters which are as the voice of the Almighty, by the lightnings which are his ministers of vengeance, by the songs of birds, vibrating in harmony with celestial music, by the fresh verdure of the new earth, watched over by benignant forces of heaven from above and imperilled by sinister forces of hell from beneath, by sympathy with the solicitude of divine messengers, or of guardian angels rejoicing over earth's beauty or sorrowing over its ruin. His lyric tendency may arise from nature love and human love blending in an inseparable experience and borne upward toward divine love, until all nature, with man and woman, join in triumphant notes of praise to the Creator in a *Gloria in Excelsis*, or in a *Benedicite Omnia Opera*.

In this range of subject, that gives the source of the lyric impulse to Milton, we notice the tendency toward that which is too high for

man to attain unto. In his elevation, there is
severity; he looms like a snow-clad Alp. For
this reason he is more an inspirer of nature
poets than a popular poet of nature and this
is because of his epical cast of genius. This
epical uplift gives his type of lyric power. The
tendency, therefore, is not to remain personal
but to pass toward the universal; not self but
the larger consciousness of humanity is the
theme, and not man but the manifestation of
the divine. In the upward lilt of his lyric
there is always a tendency toward the elevated
style, even when not dominant; it is not sought
but it is inevitable. For this reason, perhaps,
with the noble simplicity of his well regulated
grand style, he may approach the pastoral,
without affectation. This tendency to grasp
universal thought and experience, and his mastery of noble expression, give him his power in
the epic style and cause him to stand in our
minds as the prince of writers of epic, in English, if not in universal literature.

Undoubtedly Milton cannot appeal to the
majority of readers as an interpreter of nature,
for they miss in him the ear to hear the " sad
sweet music of humanity," or the eye to see " in
the meanest flower that blows thoughts that lie

too deep for tears." He sends no Lucia to bear us gently in her arms to the summit of his earthly Paradise. We must climb thither ourselves by the stirring inspiration of his melody.

There always will be those who will turn to Wordsworth and Tennyson, there will be others who will turn to Bryant and Lanier for poetry of nature; so also there will be those who will prefer the gentle prophets of Sargent to those Titanic heroes, the prophets of Michael Angelo; but Milton's *Paradise Lost* despite its severity will always be a Pierian spring for nature poets, because they will read in his lines the "deciphering of the handwriting of God in the wonders of his creation," [1] and if we read the characters aright the message is benignant.

[1] Carlo Dati.

NOTE.—All references to scientists have been made from the standpoint of their mental attitude toward nature as infinite. It has no importance for any bearing that this may have upon either their method or conclusions. It is a question of poetical outlook, not of scientific criticism.

BIBLIOGRAPHY

I

SOME VERSIONS OF MAN'S FALL AND PRESEN-
TATIONS OF SATAN IN DIDACTIC, NARRATIVE,
DRAMATIC, AND EPICAL LITERATURE, BE-
FORE THE END OF THE SEVENTEENTH CEN-
TURY.

St. Augustine, Bishop of Hippo.
> *Opera Omnia, Patrologiæ Cursus Completus.*
> Migné, Paris, 1865.
> *The City of God.* Translated into English
> by J. H. London, 1610. (Part II, Book
> II, 13).

Lactantius.
> *Divinarum Institutionum.* Libri VII.
>> Book I, *De falsa religione.*
>> Book II, *De origine erroris.*
>> Book III, *De vita beata.*
> *Opera Omnia, Patrologiæ Cursus Com-
> pletus.* Migné, Paris, 1862.

Prudentius.
> *Psychomachia.*
> *Hamartigenia.*

Opera Omnia Patrologiæ Cursus Completus. Migné, Paris, 1862.

St. Avitus.

De Spiritalis Historia Gestis.

Liber Primus, *De initio mundi.*

Liber Secundus, *De originale peccato.*

Liber Tertius, *De sententia dei.*

Patrologiæ Cursus Completus. Migné, Paris, 1862.

Cyprianus.

Corpus Scriptorum Ecclesiasticorum Latinorum, Editum consilio et impensis Academiæ Litterarum Cæsareæ Vindobonensis Cypriani Galli, poetæ Heptateuchos, ex recensione Rudolfi Peiper, Volume 23.

Pragæ, Vindobonæ, Lipsiai, Tempsy and Freytag, 1891.

This work also attributed to Juvencus.

Cædmon. *Metrical Paraphrase of Parts of the Holy Scriptures in Anglo-Saxon,* with an English Translation, Notes, and a Verbal Index by Benjamin Thorpe. London, 1832.

Author Unknown. *Story of Genesis and Exodus.* MS. not later than 1250, done from Latin into English. Richard Morris, Early English Text Society. London, 1865.

Author Unknown. *Cursor Mundi.* Northumbrian Poem of the 14th Century. Richard Morris, Early English Text Society, 1874.

Vida, Marco Girolamo. *Christiados.* Libri
Sex. Early edition, 1535. Edidit Eduar-
dus Owen. Oxon., 1725. *Complete Works,*
2 Vols. London, 1732.

Sannazaro, Jacopo. *De partu Virginis.* Dedicated to Clement VII, Pontifex Maximus.
1539.

Du Bartas, Guillaume de Salluste, Sieur du
Bartas.
La Première Sepmaine. 1579.
La Seconde Sepmaine. 1593.
His Divine Weekes and Workes. Translated
by Josiah Sylvester. London, 1633.

Tasso, Torquato. *Setti Giornate del Mondo
Creato.* 1594. Pisa, 1823.
Jerusalem Delivered (Council in Hell).
1574. Wiffen, 1894.

Fletcher, Giles. *Christ's Victory and Triumph*
(1610). In *Complete Works.* A. B. Grosart, London, 1868.

Stafford, Anthony. *Niobe, or Age of Teares*
(1611). (Speech of Satan on banishment
from heaven.)

Peyton, Thomas. *The Glasse of Time.*
1st Volume, London, 1620.
2d Volume, London, 1623.
Reprinted by John Alden. (Undated).

Fletcher, Phineas. *Locustæ Vel Pietas Jesui-
tica* 1627. (Mr. Sterling's Version in

Miscellaneous Poems, Original and Translated, by Several Hands, Dean Swift, Parnel, Delany, Brown, Ward, Sterling, Concawen, and others. Published by Mr. Concawen, 1724.)

Locusts or Appolyonists. 1627. A. B. Grosart, 1869.

CRASHAW, RICHARD. *The Suspicion of Herod,* from Marini's *Strage degli Innocenti,* Book I. (1633.) Translated 1648 by Crashaw. In Fuller Worthies Library, A. B. Grosart, 1872.

QUARLES, FRANCIS. *Book of Emblems,* 1635. See "Serpent and Eve," "Lament over Adam's Fall." Rev. George Gilfillan, London, 1857.

DENHAM, SIR JOHN. *The Sophy.* 1641. In *Poems, Translations with the Sophy.* London, 1703.

BEAUMONT, SIR JOSEPH. *Psyche.* London, 1648. 2d Edition used. Cambridge, 1702.

COWLEY, ABRAHAM. *Davidëis.* 1656. J. Tonson, London, 1710.

FLETCHER, JOSEPH. *Perfect - Cursed - Blessed-Man.* (Before 1657.) A. B. Grosart, London, 1869.

FALL OF MAN IN SEVENTEENTH CENTURY TRAGEDY

GROTIUS, HUGO. *Adamus Exsul.* First edition,

1601. Reprint from fifth edition in *Delectus Auctorum Sacrorum Miltoni facem prælucentium*, etc. W. Lauder, London, 1752.

ANDREINI, GIOVANNI BATTISTA. *L'Adamo*. First edition 1613. *Saccra Rappresentazione*. Milan, 1617. Reprinted in *Saggio di Critica*. Fillippo Scolari, Venezia, 1817.

Analysis of *L'Adamo* by W. M. Hayley in *Poetical Works of John Milton*. London, 1842.

VONDEL, JOOST VAN DEN.

Lucifer. First edition, 1654. *Adam in Ballingschap*. 1664.

Lucifer in Volume VI, *Adam in Ballingschap* in Volume X, *De Werken van Vondel*. J. Van Lennep, Amsterdam, 1859–1869.

Lucifer. Translated from the Dutch into English by Leonard Charles Van Noppen, New York and London, 1898.

II

The following list is not exhaustive. It includes epics, tragedies, historical and critical works, theories of nature, and nature poems, that have aided the author of these essays in forming an estimate of the epic quality of *Paradise Lost*, and of its influence.

ADDISON, J. *Essays on Milton*. *Spectator*, No.

267-, Dec. 31, 1711- May 3, 1712. London, 1869.

ÆSCHYLUS. *Tragedies.* E. H. Plumptre, 1868. E. D. A. Morshead, 1901.

APOLLONIUS OF RHODES. *The Argonautics.* Fawkes, 1780.

ARATUS, *Astronomy and Meteorology.* (278 B.C.) C. Leeson Prince, 1895.

ARIOSTO, LUDOVICO. *Orlando Furioso* (1515). Panizzi, 1833-'41. John Hoole, London, 1799.

ARISTOTLE. *Poetic.*
Metaphysics, Ethics, Rhetoric. Thomas Taylor, London, 1818.
Poetics, S. H. Butcher, London, 1895.

ARNOLD, MATTHEW. *Essays in Criticism.* Second series, 1889.

ARRHENIUS, SVANTE. *Zur Kosmogonie.* Archives Neerlandaises, La Haye, 1906.

AUBREY, JOHN. Work incorporated, 1690, in Athenæ Oxoniensis.

BEAUMONT, FRANCIS. *Works.* Dyce, 1843-6.

BODMER, J. J. *Kritische Abhandlung von dem wunderbaren in der poesie und dessen Verbindung mit dem Wahrsheinlichen in einer Vortheidiegung des Gedichtes Joh. Milton's von dem Vorloren Paradiese.* Zürich, 1740.

BOIARDO, MATTIO MARIA. *Orlando innamorato.*

1486. Le Sage, 1783. Edition of Antonio Panizzi, London, 1830-'31.

BOILEAU, NICHOLAS. *L'art poetique* (1674). A S. Cook, Boston, 1892.

BOSANQUET, BERNARD. *History of Æsthetic,* 1892.

BOSSU, RENE LE. *Traite du poeme épique* (1675). Monsieur René Le Bossu. *Treatise on the epick poem.* Made English from the French with a preface upon the same subject by W. J. Second edition in two volumes. London, 1719.

BRADLEY, A. C. *Shakespearean Tragedy,* 1905.

BROOKE, S. A. *Milton.* London, 1878.

BYRON, GEO. GORDON. *Poetical Works.* Albion Edition, New York and London, 1893.

CAMOENS, LUIS DA. *Lusiad* (1572). W. J. Mickle, 1791, 1810; Richard Burton, 1885–1888.

CANTOR, GEORG. *Grundlegen einer allgemeinen mannichfaltigkeitslehre ein mathematisch-philosophischer versuch in der lehre des unendlichen.* Leipzig, 1883.

CHATEAUBRIAND, F. A. R. DE *Essai sur le littérature Anglaise.* Paris, 1856.

Cheatham Miscellanies. Volume the First. *Papers Connected with Affairs of Milton and His Family,* printed for Cheatham Society, 1851.

CHRESTIEN DE TROYES. *Li roman di la charrete.* Jonckbloet, v. 2, p. 51, 1849.

King Arthur and the Table Round. W. W. Newell, Boston, 1897.

CICERO. *Vision of Scipio.* C. R. Edmunds, 1865.

CLAUDIANUS. *Rufinus.* (Epic, 396 A.D.). (Council in infernal world, irruption in mist into outer world.) In *Omni opera,* 1820.

CLAVIUS. *Christophori Clavii Bambergensis, ex sociate Jesu. In Sphæram Joannis de Sacro Bosco Commentarius nunc quinto ab ipso auctore hoc anno,* 1606; edition, Rome, 1607.

COLERIDGE, SAMUEL TAYLOR. *Notes and Lectures upon Shakespeare and Some of the Old Poets and Dramatists, with Other Literary Remains.* Volume 4. Mrs. H. N. Coleridge, New York, 1853.

Complete Poetical and Dramatic Works. J. D. Campbell, New York and London, 1893.

COLLIER, J. P. *History of English Dramatic Poetry.* London, 1831.

CORNEILLE, PIERRE. *Œuvres.* Paris, 1862–68.

COWPER, WILLIAM. *Latin and Italian Poems of Milton. Translated into English Verse and a Fragment of Commentary on Paradise Lost, with Preface and Notes by Various Authors.* Editor, W. Hayley, London, 1808.

Dante Alighieri. *Il convito*. Katherine Hilliard, London, 1889.
  The Divine Comedy. C. E. Norton, Boston, 1878; H. W. Longfellow, 1887.

Davenant, William. *Gondibert*. See the preface of that work (1650). London, 1673.

Delepierre, Octave. *L'Enfer, Decrit par ceux qui l'ont vie*. Miscellanies of Philobiblon Society, Volume VIII and IX. London, 1863–1864.

Dowden, Edward. *Transcripts and Studies*. 1888.
  Shakespeare, His Mind and Art. 1880.

Dryden, John. *Discourse on Epic Poetry*.
  Essay of Dramatick Poesy.
  Essay of Heroick Plays.
  Dedication of *Translation of Juvenal*. (Estimate of Milton.)
  Complete Prose Works. London, 1800.
  Comedies, Tragedies, Operas. London, 1701.

Ducis, J. F. *Shakespeare*. 1733–1792

English Miracle Plays, Moralties, and Interludes (*Everyman*). Edited by A. W. Pollard, 1890.

Euripides. A. S. Way. 3 volumes. London and New York, 1894.

Faguet, E. *Dix huitième Siècle*, 1898.

Fahie, J. J. *Galileo, his Life and Work*. New York, 1903.

FLAMMARION, CAMILLE. *Astronomy*. J. Ellard Gore. (Book undated.)

FLETCHER, JOHN. *Works*. Dyce, 1843–6.

FORD, JOHN. *Works*. Dyce, London, 1895.

GARDINER, S. R. *The First Two Stuarts and the Puritan Revolution*. London, 1897.

GARNETT, RICHARD. *Life of Milton*. London, 1890.

GOETHE, J. W. VON. *Faust. Werke,* Vol. 14–15. Weimar, 1887–1906. Taylor, New York, 1870.

GOSSE, EDMUND. *Studies in the Literature of Northern Europe*. London, 1879.

GOTTSCHED, JOHANN CHRISTOPHER. *Versuch einer kritischen Dichtkunst*. Leipzig, 1742.

GURTEEN, S. HUMPHREYS. *The Epic of the Fall of Man*. New York and London, 1896.

HAUPTMANN, GERHART. *Versunkene Glocke*. T. S. Baker, New York, 1901.

HOMER. *Odyssey*. George Herbert Palmer, Boston and New York, 1897.

Iliad. Lang and Leaf, London, 1895.

HORACE. *De arte poetica*. A. S. Cook, Boston, 1892.

HORWOOD, A. J. *A Commonplace Book of John Milton, from the Original MSS*. Royal Society of Literature, 1876.

HUME, PATRICK. *Annotation on Milton's Paradise Lost*. Printed for Jacob Tonson, London, 1695.

IBSEN, HENRIK. *Peer Gynt*. William Archer, New York, 1906.

JENNY, C. K. *Milton's verlornes paradies in der deutschen literatur des 18 jahrhunderts*. St. Gallen, 1896.

JOHNSON, S. *Life of John Milton*. British Poets, 1822.

JUSSERAND, J. J. *Shakespeare en France sous l'ancien régime*. Paris, 1898.

KANT, IMMANUEL. *Cosmogony, As in his Essay on the Retardation of the Rotation of the Earth and his Natural History and Theory of the Heavens*. W. Hastie, Glasgow, 1900.

KEATS, JOHN. *Poetical Works*. E. Buxton Forman, London, 1895.

KEIGHTLEY, THOMAS. *An Account of the Life, Opinions, and Writings of John Milton*. London, 1855.

KER, W. P. *Epic and Romance*. London, 1897. *Dryden*. Oxford, 1900.

LACROIX, ALBERT. *Histoire de l'influence de Shakespeare sur le théâtre française*. 1824.

LA HARPE. *Cours de Littérateur*. Paris, 1818.

LAMB, CHARLES. *Miscellaneous Essays*. Lucas, 1903. (*On the Tragedies of Shakespeare*.)

LAPLACE. *Le Théâtre Anglais*. Four parts dedicated to Shakespeare, 1745–1749.

LESSING, GOTTHOLD EPHRAIM. *Ausgewählte Prosa und Briefe*. H. S. White, New York, 1888.

LUCRETIUS. *De rerum natura.* T. Busby, London, 1813.

LUKES, FRANZ. *Die grundbegriffe in dem kosmogonien der alten volker.* Leipzig, 1893.

MACAULAY, T. B. *Essay on Milton. Edinburgh Review,* 1825.

MALORY, SIR THOMAS. *Morte d'Arthur* (1470). Temple Classics, London, 1903.

MAMBRUN, PIERRE. *De poemate epico* (1652), opera poetica, La Fleche, 1661. (Not seen.) In *History of Criticism.* George Saintsbury, New York, 1904.

MARLOWE, CHRISTOPHER. *Dr. Faustus.* (Bond with Satan.)
Tamburlaine. London, 1826.

MASSINGER, PHILIPS. *Works.* Gifford, London, 1859.

MASSON, DAVID. *The Life of John Milton, Narrated in Connexion with the Political, Ecclesiastical, and Literary History of his Time.* London, 1859–1880.

MERCIER, L. SEBASTIAN. *Memoirs of the year 2500.* Tr. by W. Hooper. London, 1772.
Songes et visions philosophiques. Amsterdam, 1788.

MILTON, JOHN.
Facsimile of Paradise Lost. London, 1667. B. M. Pickering. Reproduced, 1873.
Facsimile of the Manuscript of Milton's

Minor Poems preserved in the Library of Trinity College. Cambridge, 1879.

Facsimile of First Edition of Paradise Lost. W. A. Wright, Editor. London, 1877.

Complete Poetical Works of John Milton. Introduction and notes, by Henry John Todd, 4th Edition, London, 1842.

Poetical Works of John Milton. Edited by David Masson, London, 1887.

The Complete Poetical Works of John Milton. W. V. Moody, New York, 1899. (Text of 1667 for *Paradise Lost,* prose translation of Latin poems.)

The Poetical Works of John Milton, with a Life of the Author. By William Hayley, London, 1794.

Le Paradis perdu, traduit de l'Anglais, avec les remarques de Addison, nouvelle edition augumentu du Paradis reconques. La Haye, 1740.

Paradis perdu, traduit par Jaques Delille. V. 13–15, œuvres, 1824.

Milton's Historical, Political, and Miscellaneous Works, with a Life of the Author. By J. Toland. Published in Holland, 3 volumes, folio, 1698.

A complete collection of the Historical, Political, and Miscellaneous Works of John Milton, Correctly Printed from the Original

Editions with an Historical and Critical Account of the Life and Writings of the Author. By Thomas Birch. In 2 volumes, London, 1738. First edition, 1733.

The Prose Works of John Milton. London, 1806. 1st edition, 1804. Charles Symmons, D.D.

Prose Works by John Milton. Robert Fletcher. London, 1834.

Prose Works by John Milton. Rufus Wilmot Griswold, 1847.

Prose Works of John Milton. J. A. St. John and Sumner, London, 1884.

(*Treatise on Christian Doctrine,* translated first by Mr. Sumner, 1825.)

NASHE, THOMAS. *Works.* Huth Library. A. B. Grosart, 1883–84.

PATTISON, MARK. *Milton.* English Men of Letters Series. New York, 1880.

PEELE, GEORGE. *Works.* A. H. Ballen, London, 1888.

PHILLIPS, EDWARD. *Theatrum Poetarum Anglicanorum.* First published 1675, enlarged by Sir Egerton Brydges, Canterbury, 1800.

PLATO. *Timæus.* Pages 523–564, Jowett (theory of origin of evil and nature of free will). 1892.

Ion. Pages 62–65, Jowett and Knight.

Phædrus. Pages 37, 43, Jowett and Knight.

Statesman. Pages 236–40, Jowett and Knight.
*Ueber das Cosmische System des Platon
mit Bezug auf die nevesten auffassungen das-
selben* von Wolfgang Hocheder. Undated.

PTOLEMÆUS, CLAUDIUS. *Opera quæ exstant omnia.*
Leipsiæ, 1898–1903.
Almagist. Georgio Trapezuntio, Venetiis,
1528. *Almagist.* Halma, Paris. 1813.

PULCI, LUIGI. *Il Morgante Maggiore* (1481).
G. A. Lucchesi, Firenze, 1732; Lucca 1739.
(Part translated by Byron, London, 1853.)

RACINE, LOUIS. *Œuvres.* 1865–73.

RALEIGH, WALTER. *Milton.* London, 1900.

RATHERY. *Relations entre la France et L'Angle-
terre. Revue Contemporaine,* 1855.

RICHARDSON, J., Father and Son. *Explanatory
Notes and Remarks on Milton and Paradise
Lost, with the Life of the Author and Discourse on the poem* by J. R. Sen. London,
1734.

RUSKIN, JOHN. *Modern Painters.* New York,
1850–1856.

RYMER, THOMAS. *Reflections on Aristotle's
Treatise of Poesie.* London, 1673.
A Short View of Tragedy. London, 1693.
Tragedies of Last Age. London, 1678.

SAINTSBURY, GEORGE. *Elizabethan Literature.*
Chapter IX.
History of Criticism. New York, 1904.

SCHARF, LUDWIG.   *John Milton and Jean Jacques Rousseau, studien und skizzen.*   1882.

SCHERER, EDMOND.   *Essay on English Literature.*   1891.   George Saintsbury, New York, 1891.

SCHILLER.   *Sämtliche Werke.*   Stuttgart, 1904.

SENECA.   *Tenne Tragedies.*   Collected by Thomas Newton, 1581.
  Three Tragedies.   Sir Edward Sherburne, 1701.
  Medea and Troades.   E. I. Harris, New York, 1899.

SHAKESPEARE.   *Works.*   W. J. Craig, Oxford Press.   Undated.
  Variorum, H. H. Furness, 1871.

SHELLEY, P. B.   *Complete Poetical Works.*   1889.

Song of Roland.   (11th century.)   Leon Gautier, Tours, 1883.   John O'Hagan, London, 1880.

SOPHOCLES.   Robert Whitelaw's translation.   New York, London, and Bombay, 1897.

SPENSER, EDMUND.   *Faery Queen.*   Macmillan, 1884.

STATIUS.   *Achilleidos.*   Libri XII.
  Thebaidos.   Libri X.
  William Lillington Lewis, 1810.

STRADA, FAMIANUS.   *Prolusiones Academicæ* (before 1649).   Oxford, 1745.

TASSO, TORQUATO. *Jerusalem Delivered* (1574).
John Hoole, 1810. Wiffen, 1894. Italian
Edition, Pisa, 1823.

Il Poema Eroica. Pisa, 1823. (1st pub.
1587.)

Discorsi di Torquato Tasso.

Del poema eroica.

*Discorsi dell' arte poetica e in particolare
sopra il poema eroica.*

TELLEEN, J. M. *Milton dans la littérature française.* Paris, 1904.

TENNYSON, ALFRED. *Idylls of the King.* London and New York, 1890.

TEXTE, J. *Jean Jacques Rousseau and the Cos-
mopolitan Spirit in Literature.* 1895.

VERECOUR, RAYMOND DE. *Milton et la poésie
épique. Paris and London,* 1838.

VIDA, MARCO GIROLAMO. *De arte poetica* (1537).
A. S. Cook, Boston, 1892.

VIRGIL. *The Æneid.* J. W. Mackail, London,
1885.

VOLTAIRE, FRANÇOIS MARIE AROUET. *Essai sur
la poésie épique.* Composed in London,
1726.

Candide. 1795.

Adaptations from Shakespeare.

All references to English Literature in 50
volumes of *Voltaire's Complete Works.*
Paris, 1877.

WARD, A. W. *History of English Dramatic Literature*. London, 1899.

WEBSTER, JOHN. *Works*. Dyce. 1866.

WHITMAN, WALT. *Leaves of Grass*. Philadelphia, 1891.

WOOD, ANTHONY A. *Athenæ Oxoniensis and Fasti*. Printed for Thomas Bennet, 1691, 1692.

WOODWARD, R. S. *Observation and Experiment*. New York Academy of Science, No. 4, July, 1901.

Measurement and Calculation. *Science*, No. 390, June 20, 1902.

WORDSWORTH, WILLIAM. *Complete Poetical Works*. Dowden, 1892–3.

INDEX

A

Addison, 2, 306.

Æschylus, 18, 21, 61, 65, 233, 327.

Allegory, in epic and tragedy, 77–80; 116, 118–119, 121.

Andreini, 188, 189, 210; *L'Adamo*, 11, 36, 50, 122, 139, 190, 191; summary, 191–206; temptation, 197–201; Eve, 196–205, 206–208; necessity of epic treatment of theme, 209–210; 215, 263, 268, 280.

Areopagitica, 89; quoted, 93; 100, 310.

Aristotle, 13; quoted, 53–54; 60, 65, 69, 129, 312.

Aubrey, 125, 250.

B

Baudius, 144.

Beaumont, Sir Joseph, 240; *Psyche*, quoted, speech of Satan, 241–242.

Beda, 133.

Beethoven, 122, 320, 334.

Bible, 38, 88, 104, 127, 132, 133, 338.

Bodmer, 306.

Boileau, 54, 76; quoted, 77–78; 306.

Bossú, 13; quoted, 53; 69.

Brahé, 310.

Breitinger, 306.

Browning, 1.

Bryant, 350.

Bunyan, 79.

Byron, 326, 331, 338; quoted, 332, 339, 340, 347–348.

C

Cædmon, *Genesis*, 133–140, 142.

Casaubon, 144.